WHY JANE AUSTEN?

Why Jane Austen?

Rachel M. Brownstein

COLUMBIA UNIVERSITY PRESS   NEW YORK

COLUMBIA UNIVERSITY PRESS
Publishers Since 1893
NEW YORK   CHICHESTER, WEST SUSSEX

Library of Congress Cataloging-in-Publication Data
Brownstein, Rachel M.
Why Jane Austen? /Rachel M. Brownstein.
p. cm.
Includes bibliographical references and index.
ISBN 978-0-231-15390-4 (cloth : alk. paper) — ISBN 978-0-231-52724-8 (ebook)
1. Austen, Jane, 1775–1817—Appreciation. I. Title.
PR4037.B76   2011
823'.7—dc22   2010043421

Columbia University Press books are printed on permanent and durable acid-free paper.
This book is printed on paper with recycled content.
Printed in the United States of America

c 10 9 8 7 6 5 4 3 2

This age of personality, this age of literary and political gossiping, when the meanest insects are worshipped. . . . When the most vapid satires have become the objects of a keen public interest, purely from the number of contemporary characters named in the patch-work notes . . . and because, to increase the stimulus, the author has sagaciously left his own name for whispers and conjectures!

—SAMUEL TAYLOR COLERIDGE

The truth is that every true admirer of the novels cherishes the happy thought that he alone—reading between the lines—has become the secret friend of their author.

—KATHERINE MANSFIELD

CONTENTS

ACKNOWLEDGMENTS

I AM OF AN AGE TO HAVE FORGOTTEN MANY OF MY DEBTS
and to be haunted by a sense of obligation to people whom I can no
longer repay. The influences of my first, best teachers—and generations
of students, colleagues, and friends—are legible to me in nearly every word
that follows, but it's hard to disentangle one from another. The influence on
my thinking of the writers of my time and before it—you decide which—is
incalculable. For my footnotes as well as my memory I ask forbearance.

This book makes much of the importance of perspective, and I will begin
naming names from where I am now, near the end of the project. I thank,
first of all, my brilliant and generous extraordinary friends Ann Peters and
Mary Ann Smart, who (at different stages) kindly volunteered to read the
whole messy manuscript and commented thoughtfully and meticulously and
(mirabile dictu!) encouragingly. Wendy Fairey, Meechal Hoffman, Kristina
Huang, and the unnamed readers from Columbia University Press, who read
parts and versions, also made suggestions that have kept some of the egg off
my face.

For nearly a lifetime of emotional support, intellectual exchange, and everything friends are for, including feedback to my ideas about this book and the
parts of it they patiently read or listened to and helpfully responded to, I am

grateful to Myriam Chapman and Doris Friedensohn. Helpful in a different key and tenor—but also for being there as well as for commenting critically—have been the listeners, interlocutors, and speakers at meetings at Chawton House Library, the Jane Austen Society of North America, the MLA, the Byron Society, ASECS, Brooklyn College, and the Graduate Center. Juliet McMaster and Elsa Solender especially, but many other JASNA people as well, have given me the opportunity and the confidence to think through my Austen-related ideas. I am grateful for the opportunity to be Goucher College's Burke Scholar-in-Residence, and to avail myself of the Julia Rogers Library's extensive Jane Austen collection; thanks to Nancy Magnuson and her staff—as well as to Alberta Hirshheimer Burke, the donor, collector, and passionate Jane Austen fan who assembled the basis of the collection. For financial and other support I am grateful to the CUNY Research Foundation; the Rockefeller Foundation and the staff at Bellagio; the Humanities Institute of the Graduate Center, CUNY, and the members of its Mellon Seminar on biography; to Jean Bowden at Chawton Cottage and Gillian Dow and Clare Hanson at Chawton House Library; and to Paul W. Rose.

Because we have met head-to-head over the subject, the impact on my thinking of what Zelda Boyd, Alice Chandler, Edward Copeland, Margaret Doody, Sandra Gilbert and Susan Gubar, Susan Fraiman, Jocelyn Harris, Claudia Johnson, Deidre Lynch, Juliet McMaster, Marylea Meyersohn, Nora Nachumi, Mary Ann O'Farrell, Ellen Pollak, and John Wiltshire have said and written about novels in general and Jane Austen in particular has been different in kind from the impact of earlier not-at-all similar critics such as Wayne Booth, Mary Lascelles, Q. D. Leavis, Walton Litz, Stuart Tave, and—his name will come up again here—Lionel Trilling. I am indebted to all these people's ideas and to their example.

I am very grateful to all the students with whom I have reread Jane Austen, most recently the participants in my Austen seminar in spring 2010 at the Graduate Center of the City University, whose names must stand here not only for their unique selves but also for generations of students before them—Meredith Benjamin, Colleen Cusick, Elena Delgado, Nicole Fennimore, Claudia Geller, Yulia Greyman, Meechal Hoffman, Anna King, Alison Powell, Emily Raabe, Shang-yu Sheng, Nora Slonimsky, Amanda Springs, Stuart Watson, and Heather Zuber, and especially the very smart, eloquent, and clubbable Bill Goldstein, who at the end of the term helpfully clarified things by telling me what I had been saying.

Geoffrey Nunberg, in his telephone voice from the other side of the continent, has been my basic word man, co-conspirator, consultant, and egger-on
throughout this project: one section in chapter 5 about *Emma* is a version of
a paper for which he did much of the thinking. I have relied on his confidence
in me as well as his wit, intelligence, and know-how. I have also relied, a little
too much, on Katherine Koutsis, who helped me with this book in more
ways than I can remember, and whose smarts, skills, laughter, good sense,
and good judgment have made all aspects of my working life much easier and
more interesting than they would have been without her. I have also relied,
not so diurnally, on the always savvy and reasonable Georges Borchardt. For
their sympathetic responses to aspects of this book (and more) that have been
immeasurably valuable to me in writing it I am grateful to my other long-
term, long-suffering, and inspiring friends and advisers, especially Mirella and
Charles Affron, Jean and Richard Gooder, Elisabeth Jakab, Alice Kaplan, Ed
Koren, my shrewd and indefatigable morning walking partner Alice Kessler-
Harris, and the reliably curious and responsive Linda Young—for over thirty
years my ideal reader. For talking with me and letting me talk, over many
years, about matters related to this project, and/or for sending clippings, I am
grateful as well to Mary Ann Caws, Anne Humpherys, Gerhard Joseph, Patricia Laurence, Rich McCoy, Nancy K. Miller, Honor Moore, Alan Nadel, and
Suzanne Ouellette. And for their invaluable help toward the end of this project, I am indebted to Melina Moore, Kerri Cox Sullivan, and Rhea Wilson.

Special thanks to Ellen Tremper for her good ideas, intelligence, and generosity, and to Ellen as well as to Joe Wittreich, Bill Kelly, Joan Richardson,
and Steve Kruger for enabling me to talk about Jane Austen with students at
Brooklyn College and the Graduate Center. Thanks to Jennifer Crewe, who
had faith, and to my fellow members of the Women Writing Women's Lives
seminar. Questions about the relevance of biography (and celebrity) to literary criticism, the secrets of personality and intersubjectivity, and the compulsion to narrative are central to my thinking.

Finally, for reliable if inevitably spasmodic surges of hope and inspira-
tion and comfort and delight, I am very grateful to my family: to Shale first
of all; to Daniel and Mary Ann, Gabriel and Marcia, and Ezra and Charlotte;
and especially—in order of appearance—to Eliza, Lucy, Clara, Agnes, and
Henry Amos.

Page numbers in parentheses refer to *Jane Austen's Letters*, ed. Deirdre Le Faye (New York, 1995) (i.e., *Letters*); to *The Novels of Jane Austen*, ed. R. W. Chapman (London, 1923) (i.e., *SS, PP, MP, E, NA, P*); or to Chapman's edition of the *Minor Works* (Oxford, 1954; rev. 1969, 1982) (i.e., *MW*).

Chapman's—still the basis for most inexpensive editions—remains more accessible for most readers than the new *Cambridge Edition of the Works of Jane Austen*, ed. Janet Todd et al. (2005–2009). Although I cite Chapman here, *Catharine and Other Writings*, ed. Margaret Anne Doody and Douglas Murray (Oxford, 1993), is preferable to Chapman's edition of the early works.

WHY JANE AUSTEN?

FIGURE 1. Carl Rose, "The Two Camps of Jane Austen Devotees," *New York Times*, October 23, 1949.

S OMETIME IN THE 1980S, SOON AFTER THE PUBLICATION OF my first book, I went to a literary party in Brooklyn at the home of a fashionably gritty playwright: jug wine, cheese and crackers, and brownies laced with cannabis, homemade by his wife. Someone introduced me—rather unsettlingly—as a "feminist critic" to a tall, thin young man whose name I recognized: his first novel, about a boy and his dinghy on the rockbound coast of Maine, had just received rave reviews. The novelist looked way down at me, curled his lip in a mocking smile, and recited derisively, "'Is a pen a metaphorical penis? Gerard Manley Hopkins seems to have thought so.'" It took me a minute to realize that he was neither mad nor high on grass-fed brownies, merely quoting the opening sentences of *The Madwoman in the Attic*, the then-hot work of feminist literary criticism by Sandra M. Gilbert and Susan Gubar published in 1979. He was counting on me to recognize the quotation and to be impressed that he knew it—also to understand that he had no use for it, or for feminist critics, penis substitutes, and certainly that pansy poet-priest Gerard Manley Hopkins. He was condescending to me as a novelist to a critic and a manly man to a woman, and throwing it all—pointed by the shock-word "penis"—in my face. I had no trouble getting his drift: it was a sexual invitation, sort of, and we were to begin in the tradition of Beatrice and Benedick and Elizabeth and Darcy, by jousting with words.

Academic feminist literary criticism is no longer current or sexy: I recount this anecdote partly in order to situate myself and my subject in time and place—as it were, in the long ongoing conversation about and around Jane Austen. To account for the special status of this novelist and her novels in contemporary culture it seems necessary to me—as it might not to another—to begin with the feminist literary critics of the last quarter of the twentieth century. Among so many other things that the women's movement of the 1970s changed were ways of thinking about Jane Austen, inside the academy and outside it. In the mid-1950s, when a woman I know was a graduate student in English at Harvard, her advisor discouraged her from writing a dissertation on Jane Austen, she told me, by arguing that no woman could possibly do justice to so important a subject; a graduate student I knew in the mid-1980s dedicated her Austen dissertation—one of many hundreds—"To Elizabeth Bennet, who taught me to speak up." The following essay about Jane Austen's surprising achievement and sustained tenure as an icon of "high" and "popular" culture ranges beyond those thirty or so years, but those years of change in what "Jane Austen" meant to most people—the revising of her image, the changes rung on her name—is where it is, as we used to say, coming from.

Although it was affiliated with the counterculture that repudiated the literary canon, the women's movement of the seventies paradoxically valued the great women writers in English; that none was more canonical than Austen was part of the problem she posed. From the beginning, feminist efforts to retrieve and revalue "lost" writers who had been overlooked by the patriarchal establishment in scholarship, criticism, and publishing were accompanied by new studies arguing for the importance of the Brontes, Emily Dickinson, George Eliot, and preeminently Virginia Woolf. In college courses in women's studies, undergraduates—many of them not particularly interested in literature—looked to writers from Sappho to Toni Morrison for wisdom about women's issues and women's lives. *A Room of One's Own* (1929), the short, eloquent book based on a series of lectures Virginia Woolf gave at Cambridge, was regularly assigned in such courses. Whether it was read as a liberating manifesto or as an elitist tract, *A Room of One's Own* was immensely influential. Celebrating the rich tradition of English women novelists before herself, Woolf traced it back—as others had done—to Jane Austen, crediting her with inventing the "women's sentence." Austen had seen that the prose written by men was too cumbersome for a woman's hand, Woolf wrote—so she "laughed at it and devised a perfectly natural, shapely sentence proper for her own use and never departed from it."[1] This claim, which was excitedly debated, ensured Jane Austen's place—in spite of what many deplored as her lamentable re-inscriptions of the marriage plot—in the feminist pantheon, and therefore, I will argue, in the course of time in a popular culture inflected by feminism. If many of Austen's sentences failed to make it into the movies, the laughter, the apparent naturalness, and especially the shapeliness did.

As recent scholars have richly shown, there had been earlier popular vogues for Jane Austen; if her anonymously published novels famously did not cause a stir in her lifetime—but in fact *Pride and Prejudice* did!—discriminating critics valued them then and have valued them since then. She has been regularly compared—as a great writer and a quintessentially English one—to Shakespeare. For that reason, hers was among the big names that got trashed in the revolutionary sixties: Katie Trumpener has suggested that someone's boyfriend's burning of a copy of *Mansfield Park*, in a novel by Angela Carter, signaled the student revolution.[2] In the nineteenth century, more than one British or American culture maven pronounced a taste for Jane Austen's novels to be a sign of taste itself: Claire Harman recalls George Saintsbury's claim, in 1894, that "a fondness for Miss Austen" could be considered "itself a patent of exemption from any possible charge of vulgarity." In 1885, as Harman notes, "Jane Austen made it into the *Dictionary of National Biography*, an honor not granted to Elizabeth Inchbald or Charlotte Smith."[3] A volume in the English Men of Letters Series was devoted to her in 1913.[4] And although Charlotte Bronte objected that the characters in Austen's novels were not men and women but ladies and gentlemen through whom the blood failed to throb, those books had an influence on her, as well as on novelists from Walter Scott through Trollope and Thackeray, Angela Thirkell, Angela Carter, and Karen Joy Fowler, who wrote *The Jane Austen Book Club* (2004). The shapes of her sentences—gendered or not—have influenced the way English is written and spoken: their characteristic rhythms and epigrammatism are widely considered ideal. Her aficionados are fabled, and they are legion: for generations, Jane Austen has been the darling of possessive coteries whose ardor exceeds that of merely idolatrous Browning Societies. Many of her "disciples and devotees," because they feel so close to her, confound "dear Jane" or "Aunt Jane" with their own actual or imagined aunts, as Virginia Woolf wrote.[5]

Kathryn Sutherland argues persuasively that personal interest in the novelist began with the publication, in 1870, of the biography by her nephew; as my epigraph from Katherine Mansfield suggests, another source is the novels themselves, which invite the reader's complicity. The interest in Austen the woman provoked by James Edward Austen-Leigh's *Memoir* of his aunt was renewed, sustained, and intensified in 1884, with the publication of the novelist's private letters collected and edited by another collateral descendant, her great-nephew Lord Brabourne, and dedicated to Queen Victoria. Meanwhile the success and the domestic emphasis of prolific Victorian novelists influenced by them helped to create the taste for her novels. Macmillan's publication of an edition of *Pride and Prejudice* charmingly illustrated by Hugh Thomson, in 1894, inspired the vogue for "everyone's 'dear Jane'" that Henry James would deplore, some ten years later, as commercially driven and antithetical to the spirit of the fastidious artist he tremendously admired (and imagined as an artless singing bird). Additional spurts of popular interest have recurred in the wake of later Austen-related efforts in merchandising and publishing, including biography, fan fiction, dramatizations and films, and even literary criticism.

The late-twentieth-century Austen vogue combined obsession with the woman writer with an effective dismissal, or at the least a high-handed under-reading and condescending rewriting, of what she wrote. In the late twentieth century, as reading fiction began to compete with other forms of entertainment, writing about lives was theorized into a metaphor. Carolyn Heilbrun suggested that "writing a woman's life" was every thinking woman's project, or should be—the alternative to living the life others had written ("scripted") for you.[6] To write was to imagine, assert, and "inscribe" your personal identity, originality, and "agency." Feminists influenced by the modernist writers enumerated the patriarchal tendencies of not only traditional plots but closure itself, and language: for *The Madwoman in the Attic*, Gilbert and Gubar borrowed from Emily Dickinson the title of a chapter (about Jane Austen), "Shut Up in Prose." Book reviewers, meanwhile, devoted columns to new work by women writers, and new lives of women writers also got juicy reviews. The idea that old books could help you save your own life changed not only the shape and substance of college courses and the literary-critical conversation but the wider culture as well: on their covers, new paper-backs of classic fiction sported reproductions of paintings of pretty girls in old-fashioned dresses and what looked like modern makeup, and nineteenth-century domestic novels in three volumes were boiled down into scripts for televised adaptations. Enrollment surged in courses in women and fiction (I taught some) and, later on, in book groups.

It was by no means a bad thing that forgotten women writers should be recalled to life, and that the great women writers in English—burning Char-lotte Bronte, large-brained George Eliot, and the feminist prophet Virginia Woolf—should be embraced as heroines and role models. Jane Austen proved to be a little more problematic than the other greats: some feminist critics and scholars deplored her allegiance, as they saw it, to the status quo and to the marriage plot and what seemed to them the undervaluing of women's friendships, in the novels.[7] Aunt Jane, Saint Jane, dear Jane had long been the darling of die-hard conservatives, although shrewd critics since Reginald Far-rer and D. W. Harding had shown that Austen was more satirical and com-plex than those people saw. The new feminist critics labored to trace echoes of Mary Wollstonecraft in the novels, and locate in them a critique of mar-riage and, later, of heterosexuality. The Age of Celebrity, in which the media would replace both politics and ideas with personalities, was beginning in earnest: writing heroines were in demand; Jane Austen, a writer universally acknowledged, was a politically shrewd choice of emblem for the women's party. One chapter about Austen in Gilbert and Gubar's study lingered over the metaphor—Woolf had made it unforgettable—of her hiding her writing under the blotter when a creaking door alerted her that someone was com-ing into the room. A substantial section of my first book, *Becoming a Heroine* (1982), was about the ambiguous treatment of the marriage plot in Austen's novels: the women's movement had enabled me to notice, belatedly, that all the novels were about the social imperative to get married, and it had given me permission to acknowledge that.

I simplify and exaggerate in retrospect, as people tend to do. Since the 1980s I have spent many hours wondering whether I was in fact a feminist critic, and a good deal of time in college classrooms where students with heads full of pop social science described the Bennets (distressing me) as a "dysfunctional family." Having also, over many years, watched generations of children learn to read, I have become more and more convinced that some people read to find out what happens in the story while others, almost from infancy, also read for the way that story is told. My personal penchant for the second approach was exacerbated by a turn for Jamesian subtlety that was nourished by reading James the way mid-twentieth-century critics read him, as an analyst of the moral life, and extending that practice (as they did) to reading Jane Austen. In the mid-1950s, the required course for first-year students like me at Barnard, the women's college of Columbia University, was called "Man and His World": my section was taught by a retired magazine editor with great legs who addressed us as if we were in a fashionable prep school, and sought to bring scholarship girls up to speed by calling us by our surnames, which was startling, since there was a real "Roosevelt" in the classroom. She bewildered me further by assigning *The Brothers Karamazov* to be read in weekly chunks, each part to be discussed at a different class meeting: I had never read a novel in separated sections, like an orange, but dutifully tried, and could make nothing of it. Twenty years later, facing students who assumed that *Pride and Prejudice*, their very first "classic," had the same purpose as articles they read in a women's studies course, I was dramatically reminded again that there are different styles and habits of reading.

As the following pages aim to show, many and complex factors contributed to what I call, here, Jane-o-mania—deliberately following "Byromania," the term Lady Byron coined to characterize the first commercially driven, erotically charged mass passion for a high-end English writer. Half-consciously, the belated vogue for Jane Austen, Lord Byron's contemporary, perversely mirrors the earlier fashion: that the little lady in the muffin cap should have glamorous Byronic associations accounts for some of the jokey, self-congratulatory flavor of the current fashion. Over the years Jane's has become an increasingly familiar and finally a bold-face name.[8] The Austen craze of the late twentieth century, which has spilled over into the second decade of the twenty-first, has been fed by multiple complicated forces of history and social change, the ambitions of entrepreneurs and the fluctuations of business, new technologies, the new media, the information revolution, and ways of apprehending a world being reshaped by all those phenomena.[9] The "AGE OF PERSONALITY" that Coleridge deplored in Jane Austen's own era has developed into an Age of Celebrity. Gossip and prurience about the private lives of well-known people are pervasive; it seems to be a given that dark secrets are the flip side of fame; that little is known about Jane Austen although she has been long remembered has ceased to be an ordinary problem in biography and become a promising, even titillating paradox. Apropos of Jane Austen, readers who prided themselves on belonging to a little band of the elusive author's secret friends have been crowded out by hordes of the in-the-know and knowing.

Obsessed by both personal identity and celebrated persons, our "age" is characteristically self-reflexive. "England's Jane," as Kipling called her, presents a likely subject for cultural critics—and indeed she has been read as a cultural critic herself. In "Three Around Farnham," Raymond Williams had discussed Jane Austen's novels as records and analytic studies of a society moving toward modernity, comparing them to the works of her neighbors and near-contemporaries, the journalist William Cobbett and the naturalist Gilbert White of Selborne.[10] The author of novels about social status and personal life appeals to us on other grounds as well—as a delightful novelist of manners or a stern moralist, a realist or a satirist or even a writer of pastoral— or an exquisite brand of highly refined romance. Jane Austen has been praised now for her pure style and then for her didactic value, esteemed for being above her sex and above sex, and for making too much or too little of sex. She has had her critics too, who called the love stories cold and the narrative voice judgmental and even coercive: early on, Madame de Stael, the banker's daughter, had pronounced this confident arbitress of "real elegance" *vulgaire*.

A woman who wrote novels about falling in love, Jane Austen has figured for years in the oddly erotic conversation about texts and sex, words and meaning, and men and women exemplified by my anecdote about the novelist I met at the party in Brooklyn. The popular vogue of the 1990s changed the emphasis by narrowing the focus to that. It imagined all the protagonists of all the Austen novels as aiming to realize the undervalued female self by marrying up, marrying money, and marrying the best and sexiest guy, and celebrated the author herself as a tantalizing conundrum, an independent woman who managed to express herself and get published and achieve lasting fame (if not fortune) and—which was very interesting—never married herself. Austen's critique of selfishness and greed and a society that measured human worth and human relationships in terms of land and money somehow got lost in the course of all this.[11] Reduced to the lowest commonplace denominator, these were the kinds of questions people asked about her: Did she choose not to marry in order to keep her freedom? Was she afraid of bearing children, at a time when that was dangerous? Was she a victim of the bad old times for women or—in her intellectual freedom and unparalleled gaiety and her good hard sense about money and social pretensions and especially in her ironic take on people as they are—a smart, savvy woman ahead of her time, and made for ours?

In retrospect I have hardly any trouble acknowledging that I did write, in the eighties, as a feminist critic. At the time I believed I was responding to critics like Gilbert and Gubar, who generalized magisterially about the nineteenth-century literary imagination as I refused (except ironically) to do. In the wake of the culture wars and the gender wars, it is clearer now than it was to me then that those wars—and with them, the question of which side Austen was on—have taken up too much energy, as wars do. I write now (I echo heavy Mr. Collins) partly in order to atone for joining the chorus that has ended by imagining Jane Austen as first of all and most of all a woman, the paradigmatic prisoner of sex and gender, and a paragon of proto-feminist romance—in other words, by misreading her, and not reading her as she meant to be read, and finally by reading her weaker sisters in her stead. If Austen's class and gender position informed her perspective as a writer—and it did—her genius made that perspective singular. The unique specificity of that genius—its distinctiveness and distinction—is what the novels most importantly convey. To read them for truths about the author's personal life and times, or wisdom about the reader's own, is to read through or around or past them: the project is, finally, beside her point, and mine.

Jane Austen's subject is, as she wrote, human nature—the play between the sameness and differences of people and groups, and between the conventional, general, theoretical, and inevitable, on the one hand—the plot of romance and the related, different, quite as inexorable biological plot—and on the other hand the minute and various particulars. She writes about the ways people and places—fathers, mothers, brothers, clergymen, nubile young women; cottages, villages, dances, and great houses—are knowable because they resemble others like them and wonderful because they are different. Precision was her strong suit, ambiguity and paradox her stock-in-trade. She continues to interest us because her pellucid novels seem so accessible and transparent, and prove to be so rich and strange; because their moral clarity is a pleasure to share; and because the positions the novels develop on what constitutes "right" and "wrong" conduct and feeling, and on such matters as class, gender, and nation—her themes and ours, partly because her novels have informed our culture—remain elusive. She seems at once to insist on and to undercut such mutually constitutive oppositions as rich and poor, parent and child, self and other, duty and desire, fact and fiction. She illuminates the unlikely marriage of the idiosyncratic and the ordinary, the clashes between real elegance and hard facts, human sympathy and harsh judgment. Exuberantly—for all her small output—she elaborated, explored, and riffed on the play of opposites, generating variations.

She was gifted and burdened with self-consciousness, about being a woman—a genteel unmarried lady—and a novelist; she was preternaturally attuned to the ways language simultaneously expresses and suppresses and either way informs meaning and feeling. Constrained by the absurd limits of her personal situation, she was perfectly made (by it) for her subject and style. While it is probably not true that (as her brother Henry put it) everything came finished from her pen, she never questioned what she meant and had to write: the evidence is her whole body of work, as well as the often-quoted letter she wrote to James Stanier Clarke, the Prince Regent's librarian, who had suggested that she follow up *Emma* with another kind of book:

> I am fully sensible that an historical romance, founded on the House of Saxe Cobourg, might be much more to the purpose of profit or popularity than such pictures of domestic life in country villages as I deal in. But I could no more write a romance than an epic poem. I could not sit seriously down to write a serious romance under any other motive than to save my life; and if it were indispensable for me to keep it up and never relax into laughing at myself or other people, I am sure I should be hung before I had finished the first chapter. No, I must keep to my own style and go on in my own way; and though I may never succeed again in that, I am convinced that I should totally fail in any other.   (*Letters*, 312)

In other words—I owe this formulation to my friend Ann Peters—she was unable to write the kind of novel that too many readers today believe she wrote.

Jane Austen is a daunting subject to write about because she was so smart and because so many clever and intelligent people have already risen to the challenge. As Juliet McMaster wisely observes, "We all want to write about Jane Austen, but we each of us want to be the only one doing it. We want everyone to admire Jane Austen, but we each suspect the others do it the wrong way. We want her to be our particular Jane, and to share her with a multitude too."[12] Hers was a specifically comic genius, and while that truth is insufficiently acknowledged, the often too-solemn discourse around her is rich in comic possibilities. In the course of writing the following pages, in defense of Jane Austen and in self-defense as well, I have been laughing a little at myself as well as at other people. Seriously but also for the fun of it, I engage with Jane Austen yet again.

"It is possible to say of Jane Austen, as perhaps we can say of no other writer, that the opinions which are held of her work are almost as interesting, and almost as important to think about, as the work itself," Lionel Trilling wrote in 1957.[13] I have been thinking about her work and those opinions at least since my first year of college, when my young instructor, a graduate student of Trilling's, responded to my jejune reference to "Jane Austen's silly young men," by writing in my margin, in a firm round hand, "Mr. Bingley may be weak, and Mr. Wickham is wicked, but Mr. Darcy is *never* silly." Cowed by the force of her syntax, which I accurately recognized as the sign and substance of her superior knowledge and knowingness, I took her point: that I had a lot to learn from Jane Austen about choosing both men and words. (I was beginning to suspect that those difficult matters were related.) I have continued to absorb her message over the years, learning what I could, in dialogue with myself and others about Jane Austen, discovering along the way that it is almost as much fun to develop and dispute opinions of her work (and her characters, and her) as it is to read it.

Wonderfully, the fun continues: the cover of the *London Review of Books*—which memorably, in the 1990s, had posed the daring question, "Was Jane Austen Gay?"—teased readers with a further question in April 2009: "Could Darcy Swim?"[14] How extraordinary is it that, almost fifteen years after Colin Firth as Darcy, in the BBC miniseries, plunged into a lake to cool his ardor, it should be remembered—and that readers of a literary paper could be counted on to recognize the provenance of the question, and to wonder how Byronic Darcy really was, before Colin Firth swam, as it were, in his wake. Inside, in his review of a couple of new books, the venerable critic Frank Kermode disparaged the pedantry and nitpicking of contemporary academic Austen studies on the one hand, and the giddiness of pop-cultural Janeism on the other, as well as the tireless exploitation on all sides of the continuing vogue. I am with him there. Nevertheless the phenomenon engages me.

The following pages reflect some of what I have learned from the opinions of Austen and her work, opinions of academics and amateurs, of my colleagues and students. Trying to account for the continuing appeal of the novelist and her novels—different matters—I have been informed by the thinking of generations of Austen critics: the early astute critiques by Richard Simpson, Richard Whateley, and Walter Scott, the brilliant assessments of Margaret Oliphant and Reginald Farrer, later on, and later yet of Mary Lascelles; the insights of D. W. Harding, Marvin Mudrick, A. Walton Litz, Stuart Tave, and Wayne Booth; the extraordinarily rich late-twentieth-century criticism that situates Jane Austen in political and social and literary history, of which more later; and the important recent work on Austen in cultural history by Marilyn Butler, Claudia Johnson, Deidre Lynch, Roger Sales, John Wiltshire, and others. Lionel Trilling's subtle essays about Jane Austen, which tease the reader into thought—as her novels teased him—about her relation to modernity, have been on my mind nearly as long as Austen's novels have been. I have been influenced as well by the new work on Jane Austen and the theatre, which has helped persuade me to be even more skeptical about claims of her "realism."[15] In what follows I combine literary and cultural analysis with personal anecdotes and recollections of a lifetime of reading, teaching, and talking and thinking about Jane Austen. Going back and forth—between opinions of the work and readings of the novels, incidents from my life and hers, textual analysis and intertextual association, one writer and another one—seems the appropriate approach to my subject, central to which is the troubling, interesting sense that in this peculiar case the author, her characters, and the generations of her readers are connected, even entangled, with one another.

For the most part, partly for those reasons and in defiance of feminist orthodoxy and, by now, convention, I usually refer to her as "Jane Austen." "Austen," which would have startled her, makes me wince a little; furthermore I am haunted by Lionel Trilling's unforgettable parsing of "the homely quaintness of the Christian name, the cool elegance of the surname, [that] seem inevitably to force upon us the awareness of her sex, her celibacy, and her social class."[16] (By "sex" and "celibacy" he meant what we now call gender; by "social class" he meant that she was not a wannabe Englishman like him, an American English professor, but upper-class English in fact, the authentic thing.) The plainness of "Jane" and the hint of austerity in "Austen" make more meaning; and the value as a brand that the common currency of the full name now possesses—see, e.g., "Calvin Klein" or "Prada"—has made it a less-than-usually-arbitrary sign.[17] The instructive overfamiliarity of the brand-name "Jane Austen" insists on the socially constructed self. Lionel Trilling's sensitivity to the aesthetics of proper names was deeply felt: one recalls the spiteful whispers that were current in his time about his having invented his own fancy moniker: the "real" (more identifiably Jewish) name a colleague once told me he had originally borne was the one that had in fact been made up. As his high school friend Clifton Fadiman, who also had quite a name, wittily observed, "Lionel Trilling bears, doubtless with fortitude, the most aggressively euphonious name of any writer since Edna St. Vincent Millay."[18] It is, in my view, one neatly nominal basis for his bond with Jane Austen. I stand on Trilling's tweedy shoulders here with trembling knees. Shortened, the title of the last essay he wrote—"Why We Read Jane Austen," without the question mark—provides my title: he left the essay unfinished when he died in 1975.

The punctuation in my title is a clue to my own position. This book boasts no bright new take on Jane Austen. Neither am I concerned to show that she herself had an agenda, a position about marriage or sex or Romanticism or property, as many academic critics continue to argue she had. It does not seem important to me that her novels succeed one another in a narrative line that demonstrates the coherence of her oeuvre and presumably therefore of its creator. I do not argue here that "she" figures in a line of English satirists or a line of novel-reading English novelists descended from Richardson, ironically a line of mostly ladies, that culminates amusingly in Henry James. The claim I make about Jane Austen here is that she is a great writer, delightful to read. In the following pages I explore the tensions between reading "Jane Austen" and returning to a delightful known world where everything is pleasant and polished, old-fashioned, familiar, safe, and cozy—and taking in the meanings of the words on those pages that put the reader in a not unpleasant state of uncertainty about where Jane Austen stands, and indeed who and where in the text "she" is. The pages that follow are experiments and explorations in what might be called—if the term is very broadly defined— biographical criticism. I am interested in why Jane Austen is on our minds now, and in her relationship to her characters and her readers—how she runs in and out of the minds of the people she imagined (like blood in their veins, Virginia Woolf thought), and—most broadly—in the ways that imaginary others, historical and fictitious, inhabit and inform minds and lives.

My first chapter is in three parts. The first, "Questions of Truth," begins as a teaching memoir; in the second part, "Questions of Interpretation," I situate the recent two-faced sexing up and sending up of Jane Austen in cultural history, and in my own. The third part, "Jane Austen in Contexts," discusses some academic approaches to Jane Austen that have informed the contemporary Austen vogue. In this chapter I have more to say about *Pride and Prejudice* than any other Austen novel: it is the book of hers that is most often and effectively identified with the author, as the vogue continues to insist. The early advertisements for Amazon's "Kindle" conveyed the literary credentials of the new device by showing the familiar engraving of the novelist on the screen; advertisements for its rival, the Barnes & Noble "Nook," showed the first paragraphs of *Pride and Prejudice*.

Chapter 2, "Looking for Jane," also begins autobiographically. It considers the changing, clashing accepted ideas about Jane Austen herself from the time I came to consciousness in the mid-1950s, when students were enjoined to keep an author at arm's length, until just before the beginning of this century, when "Jane" (a.k.a. "Austen") became a symbol of her sex and close to a sex symbol, a "name" and a star and in the common phrase an icon. Obsession with the novelist personally has expressed itself most absurdly in the little dolls in frilled caps (made for grown-ups in fabric and paper and plastic) that quite literally belittle her. I argue that the increasingly giddy competing interpretations of the novels (and the life) have lowered the level of the conversation around her, but I have been amused by much that has emerged from the vogue. Like all dead writers, she has become her admirers, as Auden wrote about Yeats—but this does not always constitute a clash. If the annoyingly self-congratulatory and self-conscious tone of the Jane Austen vogue is characteristic of the postmodern condition and endemic to it, it is also one anticipated by Mary Crawford, the intelligent and witty well-read anti-heroine of *Mansfield Park*, who is less interested in scenery than in people, and coolly responds to Fanny's rhapsody about the beauties of nature, "To say the truth, . . . I am something like the famous Doge at the court of Lewis XIV; and may declare that I see no wonder in this shrubbery equal to seeing myself in it" (*MP*, 204). We see ourselves in Jane Austen's novels partly because we remain preoccupied with the interesting questions that interested her, partly because her take on them has trickled down and informed ours even if we have not read her, and partly because we admire (and need) her still-fresh critical take on the world and its inhabitants and their words, and her interest in characteristic ways of seeing.

In chapters 3 and 4 I consider Austen's actual and more metaphorical neighbors, beginning with the views of the people she knew that are expressed outright, in her letters, and implicitly, in her novels. In the "Biographical Notice" her brother Henry wrote soon after her death, he piously insisted that his sainted sister drew from nature but not from individuals. The distinction, if it ever was one, no longer makes sense. Gossip about the neighbors or the "news" that is the solace of Mrs. Bennet's life is the substance of the domestic lives the novels chronicle: what the people in Austen's books most often do is talk about one another and about themselves. What the neighbors say to and about one another is her theme. She was a writer with an eye on the market: her often-quoted statement in a letter that her family "are great Novel-readers & not ashamed of being so" (*Letters*, 26) shows, among other things, that she always had half an eye, as well, on what the neighbors thought, in this case of novels. She wrote down their opinions of *Mansfield Park* and *Emma*. And it is with a sense of the neighbors just in view, over her shoulder, that she writes, for instance, that from "the tell-tale compression of the pages" we know that "we are all hastening to perfect felicity," characters and readers and author—neighbors, all—together (*NA*, 250). Jane Austen's novels, I suggest, explore the ways that self-consciousness and even meta-fiction are related to awareness of the neighbors, eagerly looking on at our good fortune and bad, shaking their heads—reading other people's lives, like novel-readers.

In chapter 4 I extend Austen's physical neighborhood to include other writers, some of whom she was aware of and others she could not have known about, and the accepted ideas of what it meant then (and means now) for a person to read and write and publish stories about personal relationships. It explores the questions her novels raise about character and language, and the ways the figure of the author participates in Romantic texts. I argue that Austen's notorious personal reticence is less importantly a function of her decorum and her society's than a deliberate aesthetic choice, a refusal of the autobiographical-biographical imperative, the fashion of self-writing that was in vogue in what Coleridge called the AGE OF PERSONALITY[19]—and still is in an Age of Celebrity descended from it. Meanwhile it tries to account for her continuing very personal appeal, which persists. My final chapter attempts to answer the question of what's to be gained from reading and rereading the novels by estranging the text of *Emma*, and looking hard at a few words in that novel. Austen concludes her famous defense of the novel in *Northanger Abbey* by insisting on "the best chosen language," putting that phrase last, for emphasis. Her choices of words are considered: we are obliged to consider them. Doing that in this chapter, I insist—from a different angle and to a different end, but as Trilling also insisted—on the strangeness and importance of the imaginary world the novels create. In the "Afterwords," I come back from several different angles to the question of Jane Austen's pleasantness and seriousness, comedy, and truth.

FIGURE 2. Jennifer Ehle as Elizabeth Bennet in *Pride and Prejudice*, directed by Simon Langton (BBC, 1995).

CHAPTER I

Why We Read Jane Austen

Questions of Truth

> We remember that Jane Austen wrote novels. It might be worthwhile for her
> critics to read them.
> —*Virginia Woolf, "Jane Austen and the Geese" (1920)*

> Nowadays the teaching of literature inclines to a considerable technical-
> ity, but when the teacher has said all that can be said about formal matters,
> about verse-patterns, metrics, prose conventions, irony, tension, etc., he must
> confront the necessity of bearing personal testimony. He must use whatever
> authority he may possess to say whether or not a work is true; and if not, why
> not; and if so, why so. He can do this only at considerable cost to his privacy.
> —*Lionel Trilling, "On the Teaching of Modern Literature" (1955)*

"A single man in possession of a good fortune must be in want of a wife": I
would be happy to read a novel that starts like that. Charmed by the sound of
the sentence, I would settle for a second one that backed up the generalization, for example like this: "As Sir Eustace Beauregard [or Sir Solomon Gold-
berg] approached the Bennet establishment, his cousin Francis Peake was galloping across the adjacent fields toward Longbourn." But I'd be just as pleased

to find it going in a different direction, e.g., "Rich Mr. Bingley blushed as he recalled his sister's voice mockingly repeating the maxim," which underscores the ambiguity of Jane Austen's modal "must" (well, if he must, he must).[1] The tantalizing tautology of Austen's opening statement—the hint that what most people say or acknowledge is not worth saying—remains intact in the part of the sentence I've severed from the one she actually wrote.

But the "real" sentence offers many more delights than the abbreviated knock-off I've fabricated. How pleasantly and perversely disorienting of Jane Austen to begin a novel—which by definition presumes a reader prepared to suspend disbelief—with a declaration about the truth: "It is a truth universally acknowledged, that a single man in possession," etc. How provocative is it for a writer to begin a work of fiction by stipulating what *is*—or perhaps *is not*—true, being merely, if universally, acknowledged to be true, which is to say only said or taken to be true? And what is the point, what the effect, of specifying "a truth," that is, a single one, as opposed to "the truth"? (Reviewing a recent book about memoir, Daniel Mendelsohn reflects that "novels, you might say, represent 'a truth' about life, whereas memoirs and nonfiction accounts represent 'the truth' about specific things that have happened."[2]) Can a "universally acknowledged" truth—as opposed to a truth that most people don't or can't see or talk about, a truth more subtle and hard to come by—in fact be true? Whatever else it may do, for openers this sentence raises the question of truth and fiction's relation to it. As Katherine Mansfield's comment regarding "the truth" about "every true admirer of the novels" also suggests, it is the right place to begin thinking about Jane Austen.[3]

When the word "truth" occurs in *Pride and Prejudice*—twenty-four times after "a truth" is introduced (twice) on the first page—the definite article usually precedes it, sometimes modified ("the real truth," "the unhappy truth"). When it stands alone ("too much truth," "civility and truth," "truth in his looks," "in truth," "some truth") there is the same implication that truth is absolute and more-or-less unitary, and that we know what it is or might be. To specify *a* truth is to suggest it is one truth among several, while to characterize it as "universally acknowledged" (very different from "universally recognized") is to begin to suggest it is no truth at all. That "this truth" (as the word is immediately repeated) is that "a single man . . . must be in want of a wife"—that is, that a single man is obliged to be or must be a single man, i.e., a man who lacks a wife—is not worth saying, being as they say too true. Is the meaning of the sentence merely that most people tend to talk nonsense?

What exactly is the universe in question—who is "everybody," here? Is this work of fiction mocking or pretending to be like a philosophical treatise or argument, the kind of book that pursues the matter of truth? Arguably, that first sentence is meant to draw attention to the fictiveness of fiction and the differences among discourses (e.g., what most people have to say). What is this novel's relation to the pursuit and the telling of truth(s)? Is fiction to fact as lies are to truth, or is the equation different? Broaching these questions at the beginning of the book sets the reader up to see the single man in question, and the people talking about him, in a particular way. Does the sentence prepare us to sympathize with his plight—in want of a wife, he will be pursued by women—or to see him as a familiar figure in gossip and fiction, or even as a trope? The reader begins to decide whether this will be an old story or a new one, a comedy or a satire—and if the latter, on what and whom.

Much of the discussion of truth in and around fiction has focused on the relation of the novel to news, facts, and history, on the one hand, and on the other hand to the fantasies and formulas and tropes of romance (often, "mere romance"). *Don Quixote* and *Northanger Abbey* are stories about overly credulous readers who believe fictions are true. Defining the "formal realism" of the novel that "rose," as he saw it, along with the middle classes in England in the eighteenth century, Ian Watt emphasized the plausibility and credibility of this new form of story, which reflected (and inflected) ordinary people's actual domestic lives. In contrast to earlier stories, the novel, according to Watt, describes actions middle-class readers could imagine performing themselves (galloping across fields toward houses, not descending into the underworld) undertaken by characters with first names and surnames like modern people's names (Robinson Crusoe or Sir Eustace Beauregard, not Aeneas) whose motives and relationships are believable. The conventions of mimetic realism that the realistic novelists developed, according to Watt, convey time and space as ordinary people apprehend them; novels are about issues in ordinary (if slightly exaggerated or elevated) domestic lives concerned with the making of families, communities, profit, and love. At the center of such stories are credible characters like Pamela Andrews the virtuous servant, Tom Jones the raffish foundling, and Clarissa Harlowe the daughter of a scheming middle-class family that seeks to rise into the gentry. In his chapter on Richardson, Watt praised that novelist (as Diderot had done before him) for truth to his characters' inner lives and to motives of which they themselves are unaware—psychological truth.[4]

There are different kinds of truths, and reasonable novelists and readers disagree about whether the "truths" that different novels tell are acknowledged or universal, or plausible or too pleasant, and/or about whether they are worth telling. Matthew Arnold deplored Charlotte Bronte's novels for expressing the "hunger, rebellion, and rage" he took to be the writer's own, and Virginia Woolf agreed with him to some extent, writing that one passionate feminist speech by the ideologically driven rebellious heroine spoiled *Jane Eyre*. Charlotte Bronte, for her part, had criticized Jane Austen's novels for being about "ladies and gentlemen, in their elegant but confined houses," instead of the throbbing men and women who peopled her own more natural and authentic fictions.[5] Reading Austen critically contributed to Bronte's view—and her representations—of the truths about people that are worth writing about. There's no accounting for tastes, which vary and change; and writers inflect, and readers interpret, the tropes of fiction very differently.

Both historical novels and novels of manners promise or pretend to some kind of truth to life. In the first group, imaginary characters sometimes encounter "real" ones, as the protagonists of *Waverley* and *War and Peace* and Norman Mailer's *An American Dream* do. In the second, motives and customs, ceremonies, and domestic details we recognize make imagined and sometimes fantastic worlds seem plausible: being convinced of a fiction's truth involves comparing and contrasting it to the lives we know. The appetite for narrative fiction is related to the appetite for gossip. As Patricia Spacks has argued, the domestic novel is related to gossip (consider the last sentence of the first chapter of *Pride and Prejudice*, about Mrs. Bennet: "The business of her life was to get her daughters married; its solace was visiting and news").[6] Stories about imaginary people, like stories about our neighbors or news of local weddings in the papers, satisfy the hunger to consider our lives in relation to other people's, and the related desire to plug new and different names and details into the narratives we know and expect. News about the neighbors or people like them is intrinsically interesting. Gossip is familiar and predictable and also full of coincidences, as novels are: some you're prepared to marvel at, others are hard to swallow, and some you don't even notice are coincidences. Reading *Pride and Prejudice*, comfortably suspending disbelief, we don't bother to wonder how plausible it is that Darcy and Wickham, who grew up on the same estate in the north of England, should find themselves—annoyingly, embarrassingly—interested in the same girl in a country village in the south. At their first encounter, when one of the men turns white and the other turns red, this dramatic sudden contrast between their countenances—otherwise not described—pleasingly persuades us that these rivals are moral opposites. They (and other characters: Darcy and Elizabeth, but also Elizabeth and Jane, Elizabeth and Charlotte, and Elizabeth's different aunts Phillips and Gardiner) are paired to please us with the promises of balance, coherence, and some kind of truth.

In the famous first paragraphs of Austen's most-read and best-loved novel, which raise questions of truth and universality and what kind of truth gets acknowledged and what kind remains unsaid, her irony is palpable, thick. But it is not clear what it is directed at. Are we meant to read the first sentence of *Pride and Prejudice* as calling attention to the opposite of what it seems to be saying, that society is concerned about the fate of unmarried women, not men? Critics have suggested that the tautological statement that a single man with a good fortune (i.e., money and/or luck) is "in want of" a wife (i.e., that he doesn't have one) implies that a single woman without a fortune is on the other hand obliged to find a husband to support her—and that most novels (but possibly not this ironic one) are about that predicament. Can anyone but a habitual reader of romantic novels—and critical articles about such novels—be relied on to get this point? What about a habitual reader of wedding notices in the newspapers? Or is the irony also directed more generally—more universally—at the relation between what respectable people profess to believe (acknowledge) and what they really think and do and even sometimes say? The tone of this magisterial, mocking narrative voice enchants and challenges.

The narrator's initial philosophical generalization is immediately undercut by the first scene of the story, in which an ill-matched long-married couple banters at cross purposes about the new man in town, who might be a good catch for one of their grown daughters. The curtain falls on this scene of dialogue—and on the chapter—with a summation of Mr. and Mrs. Bennet's characters that matches the curtain-raising first paragraphs in its authority, but takes a slightly different tack and tone. The narrative voice at the end of the chapter is as direct and to the point in dispatching the Bennets (as if for good) as it was philosophical and ironic at the beginning. "Mr. Bennet was so odd a mixture of quick parts, sarcastic humour, reserve, and caprice, that the experience of three and twenty years had been insufficient to make his wife understand his character. *Her* mind was less difficult to develop. She was a woman of mean understanding, little information, and uncertain temper"

(*PP*, 5). (Dickens observes by the way, in *Barnaby Rudge*, that what's called an uncertain temper is certain to be a bad one.) In other words, the narrator points out to us what the couple's conversation has already demonstrated — and also that understanding character or human nature will be the project and the subject of a book that will devote itself to these home truths. To finish the first chapter is to know what it expects of its reader.

There is a sly echo, in the famous first sentence of *Pride and Prejudice* (1813), of a rhetorical question Edmund Burke asks in *Reflections on the Revolution in France* (1790): "*Is it then a truth so universally acknowledged*, that a pure democracy is the only tolerable form in which human society can be thrown, that a man is not permitted to hesitate about its merits, without the suspicion of being a friend to tyranny, that is, of being a foe to mankind?" Arguing against what he sees as an undiscriminating fashion for democracy that doesn't allow for finer distinctions, Burke seems to be glancing back at Thomas Jefferson ("We hold *these truths to be self-evident*, that all men are created equal" (Declaration of Independence, 1776; my italics). Where Jefferson argued for putting into effect (i.e., making true) "truths" that are not yet universally accepted and acknowledged, Burke and Austen are criticizing what most people think of as truths — and, it would seem, criticizing most people. Although he is no friend to tyranny, Burke has reservations about the pure democracy being cried up by people in favor of the French Revolution: did Jane Austen, who drafted her novel during the revolutionary 1790s, have similar reservations about the rights and freedoms of individuals? She certainly seems to have had reservations about the courtship plot, although it turns out she's writing a novel based on it; since (as everyone knows) she herself never married, and since most of the marriages she portrays are less than good, she perhaps had reservations about the universally acknowledged obligation to marry. Was she, then, a social conservative — a Tory, if, as Marilyn Butler has argued, a Tory feminist?[7] From a conservative point of view, on the other hand, marriage is central to the social fabric, which requires that a single man of good fortune marry, so that the race (and the class) will continue and the nation remain in the same — the right — hands. (But in this case the single man at issue has merely rented Netherfield Park: he does not own real property, and his fortune derives from trade, that is, speculation and luck.) Is this narrator's tongue so firmly in her cheek that we cannot know her meaning? Does she mean to communicate or to conceal what she thinks is true?

Class discussions of the first chapter of Austen's most oft-assigned novel tend to be lively. American college students are struck first of all by the oddity of Mrs. Bennet's calling her husband "Mr. Bennet": it puts them off. Did husbands and wives really talk to one another that way in England at that time, they ask, even at home—even (mischievously) in bed? Or did only the rich ones take this peculiar formal little distance from one another? Someone notices that in the first scene Mr. Bennet calls his wife "my dear," not "Mrs. Bennet": does that mean she is looking up to him, while he is condescending to her? Is that Jane Austen's feminist satire? Or is the novelist taking an equal distance from both characters? Is the book a satire on middle-class people who are pretentious and stuffy and polite instead of casual and intimate the way people are today? If someone remarks that this married couple is just like the married couples in sitcoms today—the distant husband, the ditzy wife—we remain on the subject: what's true to life—and what kind of people's life—and what's merely conventional. Talking about how sitcoms reflect the influence of Austen's novels can be as fruitful as talking about the novels that influenced hers—more fruitful in a beginning class, when the students have read very little. The question on the table is how this book is different from the usual run of domestic comedies and love stories, why it is considered a classic, why they should have to read it in school. As they argue about whether Mr. or Mrs. Bennet is the better parent—she's too involved in managing the girls' lives, he's too aloof and detached—I try to get them to notice and take pleasure in the play of differences and similarities among the characters, the subtle distinctions in the way they express themselves—the words they use. To compare and contrast first this husband and wife and then the Bennet and the Lucas families, and Mr. Bennet and his brothers-in-law, and Mrs. Bennet and the much grander but quite as gauche and manipulative matron, Lady Catherine de Bourgh. To teach them to read.

Was everyone really so witty back then, they ask, and did they all have such large vocabularies? Or is the book trying to make them sound better than people actually sounded, even then? We talk a little about different kinds (I might even say, tentatively and as if casually, "classes") of people, and I tell them a few facts about the landed gentry and the land-based economy, and how things were beginning to change, economically and socially, at the time Jane Austen wrote. Perversely hungry for facts in this course in fiction, the students are especially interested in the entail on Mr. Bennet's estate, which makes it impossible for him to pass it on to his daughters, enjoining him instead to leave it, in defiance of feeling and reason, to Mr. Collins, the distant relative who according to law is the male heir. They see this as a sign of how undemocratic things were then. I observe that the documents that entitle people to property are still operative in our world, and that just like novels they are made up of mere words, and that civil society continues to depend on what we sometimes call legal fictions.

In other words, to begin to talk about the novel is inevitably to engage with the question the narrative points toward from the start, the question of language and its power to tell truths of one kind or another. What truth does this or any novel actually tell? And (this is school, after all) what can and should you learn from the work of reading and studying this book? In what sense might this story about chaste and virtuous English virgins and their suitors, none of whom have to work, be of serious interest today? As they read they prove to be full of notions about what Elizabeth or Jane Bennet should or should not have done in order to get her man: is Charlotte Lucas right when she says that Jane smiles too much? (An older student in one class recalled the 1970s feminist injunction to women to stop smiling.) They are prepared—over-prepared, I try to show them—for the book to have an instructive moral, probably in this case about the evils of pride and prejudice. I quote Gilbert Ryle's profound remark that Jane Austen is a moralist, but she does not moralize: they might remember it later.[8] Now, in school (as they think of it), they expect a book to teach them a lesson that will be useful in their lives—to teach them something about themselves, as some of them put it. (I manage to slip them the fact that Jane Austen herself left school before she was ten.) The students familiar with group therapy and twelve-step programs are impressed when I point out that Elizabeth, after reading Darcy's letter about himself, thinks, "Till this moment, I never knew myself" (*PP*, 208). They notice and savor the reversal and I am encouraged by this: I hope to get them to see themselves mirrored in a text that is by and about someone very different from them, the way Elizabeth does. This is a formidable task: unlike Darcy's letter, these people's stories do not seem to impinge on these readers' lives, and they are not already a little in love with the writer, as Elizabeth is, and I am.

On the contrary, many of them are suspicious of Jane Austen, as a bogey representing high culture and sexual repression and also as required reading for the course. Even the ones familiar with the name of the author of love stories assume that like all parents and teachers and clergymen everywhere, she aimed to instruct. A student whose style is cynical might point out that like all writers she was really only trying to sell books; she wrote to please people, and give them what they wanted; real life and falling in love were never in fact like this in anyone's family, ever, anywhere. (I inform them that although she dearly hoped for profits from her novels she made precious little money—"pewter," she called it, jauntily borrowing a brother's slangy idiom.) Someone might go back to the dialogue in the first chapter, and point out that not only are the Bennets unhappily married ("dysfunctional") but their whole conversation is based on a lie, Mr. Bennet's implicit lie that he does not intend to visit Mr. Bingley. (Someone else might point out that Mr. Bennet's actually doing so proves that Mrs. Bennet really does communicate with him, and that he listens to her—that in fact the marriage is not all that bad.) I am gratified that language is still the subject, but avoid pointing that out. Someone is bound to suggest that for Jane Austen to write about Mr. and Mrs. Bennet in their old-fashioned genteel English politesse is to set them up as role models for the rest of us, even though all the while it seems to satirize them—to get us to admire hypocrites who talk in a roundabout way and cover up their true emotions and try to act genteel. Doesn't canonical English literature, don't the novels of Jane Austen especially, coercively instill ruling-class attitudes in her readers—the view that the West is best?

They have not read Edward Said, but they do watch television, and ideology trickles down. In a heterogeneous group of mostly young people in a college classroom at the beginning of the twenty-first century, there is—in spite of her name's familiarity, or because of it—a fair amount of automatic distrust of Jane Austen, her foreign formality and stiff politeness, her evident elitism, her distance, hardness, and coldness. ("Human nature is so well disposed towards those who are in interesting situations that a young person who marries or dies is sure of being kindly spoken of" (*E*, 181): the young person who actually reads and takes in this smooth sentence from *Emma* will find it disturbing.) Many of them won't have seen the movies that were made of the novels in the 1990s; a few will have seen one or two, or later adaptations, and found them pretty but inaccurate, unreliable as substitutes for the required reading. If you let them know that Jane Austen was about Elizabeth Bennet's age (and theirs, "not one and twenty") when she drafted the first version of this novel, curiosity briefly deflects them from combative high-mindedness. They always already believe that fiction is veiled autobiography, on some level true to the writer's life (as well as an effort to conceal the real truth). Isn't *Pride and Prejudice*, aren't all her novels about girls who want and need to marry, fantasies based on her own sexual frustration? And don't the books have no sex in them because back then that was how you had to write in order to get published? Or was it because she herself was pathetically ignorant of sexual life? Some of them may have seen the movie *Becoming Jane* (2007), which projects Jane Austen's life story through the scrim of *Pride and Prejudice*, and imagines her having once dated Mr. Darcy (in real life, a boy named Tom Lefroy, who reminded her of another boy named Tom in a novel [Fielding's *Tom Jones*]). In this version, Jane comes to know herself—and therefore comes to be a great writer—because of this love affair, in other words, because of a guy. I encourage them to speculate that taking this view might be a way of denying the existence of female genius. Privately I reflect that, especially since the 1990s, it may be harder to "teach" *Pride and Prejudice* than *Moby Dick*, a novel that is easier to recognize as serious and important and about serious, important matters.

We talk more about romantic fantasies and fantasies about romance, and how people still expect life to be like a novel. I tell them about the poet and critic Anna Laetitia Barbauld, who made an important point about this in Jane Austen's lifetime. At the height of the debate (it went on for years) about whether it was harmful for girls to read novels, when the standard argument was that romantic fictions misled them to seek romantic heroes (and reject potential good husbands), Barbauld identified the real evil that novels encourage. It is, she argued perceptively, the expectation that the reader's actual life would have a pattern and a purpose and a meaning, as characters' lives do in fiction.[9] The conversation moves to the general subject of whether fiction reaffirms the kinds of truths universally acknowledged, as opposed to the truth that is actually true. Is *Pride and Prejudice* an extended critique of the romantic platitude (see Shakespeare), "Whoever loved, that loved not at first sight?" They look alert and some of them nod when I observe that as soon as he enters the ballroom in Meryton, they all know that Mr. Darcy will marry Elizabeth. Do readers come away from this novel with the false expectation—as false as any romantic notion, when you come to think of it—that the guy (or girl) who makes a bad first impression on them will turn out to be The One? (In its first draft, this novel was called "First Impressions.") If novels do not shape specific expectations, they prepare one to see and expect some kind of pattern, I repeat, quite as Mrs. Barbauld argued. On the brink, as they see it, of their own real lives, young people are easy to interest in the subject of the shaping force of narrative.

Is fiction true to human nature, as Jane Austen, following Fielding, said it was? And exactly what might human nature be? Is it different in different times and places—and classes, and classrooms too? Do novels—in spite of being constrained by literary patterns and tropes, or perhaps because of that—teach us useful things about motives, meanings, and the kinds of social and psychological truths that are concealed by appearances, secrets, lies, posturing, teasing, and even (still) discretion? Is human nature here and now the same or different from the way it is in Austen's novels? Does it vary in different families and societies, and among the more and less affluent? How to account for the different views of what's most true and important in human life that Jane Austen and, say, Charlotte Bronte had? As we talk about truthfulness to life, someone might remark that the movie versions of Austen's novels are of course not true, meaning faithful to the novels. The students are less certain about whether—foregrounding the flesh as the movies do—they are faithful to life as Jane Austen herself experienced it. Someone who has seen it in reruns observes that in the 1995 BBC/A&E version of *Pride and Prejudice*, you can see how hot for Elizabeth Mr. Darcy was, which is not so clear in the book, but must have been true. If they had read *Mansfield Park*, I would talk about "feeling," as Austen called what we call passion or desire, and how Maria Bertram, who marries out of sexual pique and vanity, seems to her father not to have it, while gentle Fanny emphatically does.

I lecture a little about social conventions and distinctions, and vulgarity and taste, and how money and class aren't always in the same hands; someone brings up the rich and famous real estate developer Donald Trump. I admit that Jane Austen appeals to snobs, indeed gives readers the language in which to distinguish vulgar people from elegant ones. I tell them what they already know, that there are all kinds of snobs, and I add that the world-class expert on "snob" as a category was an English novelist of manners, a writer in Jane Austen's tradition, William Makepeace Thackeray. They are not surprised to learn that a novelist who learned from Austen was a connoisseur of snobs and probably a snob himself. They are patriotically tickled when I tell them about Mark Twain's animal repugnance for Jane Austen— his expressed desire, "every time" he read *Pride and Prejudice*, "to dig her up and beat her over the skull with her own shin-bone."[10] We discuss the unsettling specificity of the idea, and how many times he might have read the infuriating novel. I tell them about the coteries of so-called Janeites, a term coined by the English literary critic George Saintsbury, and the gallant gentlemen Virginia Woolf wrote about who felt about criticism of their darling as they would feel about an insult to one of their aunts (these were gay guys, they guess). I tell them about the well-born English man of letters Lord David Cecil, who flattered himself to think he was Jane Austen's spiritual nephew, and about the working-class English writer Fay Weldon, who had a different version of the same fantasy, and wrote a lively, novelistic introduction to reading Austen in the form of a letter from an aunt like herself to a modern, hippie, novel-writing niece. I talk about the complicit and peculiarly personal relationship many different people have claimed to have with this writer, and write on the blackboard what Katherine Mansfield wrote about her, that "every true admirer of the novels cherishes the happy thought that he alone, reading between the lines, has become the secret friend of their author." (Someone objects to the masculine pronoun; I write Katherine Mansfield's dates on the board, say she was a friend of the feminist heroine Virginia Woolf—and seize the opportunity to point out that these books are not just for girls.) I bring up D. W. Harding's argument that many of Austen's most ardently devoted fans, the ones who aspire to be her most intimate friends, are precisely the sort of people she most loathed, and made fun of.[11] "Does she mock snobs or make them?" is the big question, my students decide.

Finally I tell them—taking that tone myself—that the sleek, sly, confiding tone of *Pride and Prejudice*, the assumption that the reader will look for and see beyond truths universally acknowledged, is still flattering readers, including them. It invites them into an exclusive, exclusionary in-group of the knowing; in more than one sense of the phrase, it works to take them in. I try to show them how the novelist includes them. Reading this novel, I say (with perhaps too much faith in my class and in readers generally), you register on your pulses how excruciatingly humiliating it is to be embarrassed in public, as Elizabeth is by Mr. Darcy, when he calls her "tolerable, but not handsome enough to tempt *me*" (*PP*, 12), and later on by her parents and her younger sisters. I show them how the novelist lets them in on things—that, for instance, they know before Elizabeth does that Mr. Darcy is stalking the shrubbery near Rosings in order to meet her, that he is not turning up there (as she thinks) by accident. I persuade them that they are aware as Darcy is not, quite, that he's a character in a courtship plot, free to see (as he cannot) that his self-involved proposal is analogous to that of the odious Mr. Collins.

They are privy to the truth, they are "in the know," I insist, working to make a coterie of a college class. I give an example that only the best of them will understand: how is it that they know that Mr. Bennet ranks higher on the moral scale—that he is smarter and more sensitive, more refined and complex—than Sir William Lucas, even though the latter has a title? And what might that mean about Jane Austen's standards and values, translated into our terms? I try to persuade them that although she doesn't tell them the truth outright, she manages to let them in on it, through the meanings she has encrypted in her chosen language. My own tone is confidential as I try to persuade them that she persuades us that all of us are in it, and in on it, together. God knows what they make of it, and of me. In his essay on the teaching of modern literature, Lionel Trilling observes that "to stand up in one's own person and speak" of such personal matters "in one's own voice to an audience which each year grows younger as one grows older—that is not easy, and probably it is not decent."[12]

I'm not suggesting that all my students get engaged in these discussions all of the time, or that I always pursue them with equal energy. Neither do I mean to imply that class discussions of Hardy and Dickens, indeed of Shakespeare and Milton, don't similarly engage good students. Character and motive, the relations between parents and children and potential lovers, always interest undergraduates, and while talking about those matters in English class may not have a measurable effect on their lives, it is good for them to have this time to do it. (Many of them don't have the time or place to talk or the habit of talking seriously about moral issues or personal problems.) And to me it is gratifying, indeed wonderful, that this serious talk should still be happening around Jane Austen. Lionel Trilling, who pronounced the opinions that are held of her work to be almost as interesting, and almost as important to think about, as that work itself, might not have been interested in what gets said in my classroom, but it never fails to interest me. This term, the shabbily dressed girl who asserts that Elizabeth should have married Mr. Collins and saved her whole family, instead of holding out for being "happy" (her sardonic air quotes), takes me by surprise: are we in for a revolution against romance? As I watch them break into different groups—the parties of Charlotte Bronte, Mark Twain, D. W. Harding, Fay Weldon, and even Lord David Cecil, of Freudian, Marxist, queer, and postcolonialist critics—I wonder why we are still talking about Jane Austen, and whether she would have agreed that in fact we were.

Questions of Interpretation

> We do not go into society for the pleasure of conversation, but for the pleasure of sex, direct or indirect. Everything is arranged for this end: the dresses, the dances, the food, the wine, the music! Of this truth we are all conscious now, but should we have discovered it without Miss Austen's help?
> —George Moore, 1919[13]

> I would hate to see Darcy and Elizabeth, smoking a cigarette afterwards. That would be unnatural and wrong and I would quickly lose interest.
> —Bridget Jones, 1996

> "And after all, Marianne, after all that is bewitching in the idea of a single and constant attachment, and all that can be said of one's happiness depending entirely on any particular person, it is not meant—it is not fit—it is not possible that it should be so."
> —Elinor Dashwood, in *Sense and Sensibility*

About thirty years ago, I was standing in front of a classroom trying to prepare a group of Brooklyn College students to read *Emma* and to like Emma—no easy task, partly (and paradoxically) because Emma Woodhouse, introduced as "handsome, clever, and rich," is less strange than familiar to them. The richest young woman in a country village in England in the early nineteenth century, she is, just like them, engaged in a struggle for social superiority—and unlike them, she has already won hands down. This is one good reason for "teaching" *Emma:* if Charlotte Bronte is remarkable for her insight into the erotic aspects of the schoolroom, Austen is the expert on its competitive dimension. But Emma's excessive concern with social status also stands in the way of caring about this heroine. While some readers, mostly elderly men, have boasted of feeling tender indulgence toward Emma, recalling that the author supposedly said that no one but herself would like this heroine, it has become increasingly difficult for young people in a place like Brooklyn to see Emma as anything but a smug little snob. My job, I think, is to get them to try. With an implicit nod to their general attitude toward life, I begin my plea for sympathy by explaining how boring it must have been for her at Hartfield.

"Imagine you're stuck in this big drafty old house in the country, just you and your father, no brothers or sisters, no mother, no neighbor upstairs or next door," I begin. The plot (such as it is) takes off after a wedding, I point out—the marriage of Emma's governess Miss Taylor—which sounds the keynote for the courtship narrative to follow but also sounds a sour note, leaving Emma (who thinks she's made the match) with nobody to talk to. "Your only friend just left for good; you don't have any friends your own age," I tell my class. "Your sister is married and lives hours away; you don't have school or a job to go to; the servants do all the housework, and you have nothing to do but try to amuse your selfish invalid father every evening." Some students are mildly interested by the suggestion that the father will be criticized in the book, but most of them are ready to agree it would be boring, and couldn't care less. I continue, determined to engage them and set them up for understanding why snobbish Emma should take up with Harriet Smith, a pretty but otherwise unremarkable younger girl of unknown parentage, a mere parlor boarder at Mrs. Goddard's undistinguished local school. Ten years later, an instructor in this same classroom would probably try to grab a similar group's attention by asking whether anyone thought Harriet's soft blue eyes were alluring to bossy, "handsome," less than feminine Emma; my tamer point back then was that Emma plays with Harriet's feelings and arrogantly tries to shape her life as if she were a novelist and Harriet her creature. (*Frankenstein* was published three years after *Emma*.) The narrator actually calls Emma "an Imaginist" (with a capital "I," which might have been the printer's choice but might have been Austen's own).[14]

I go on: "So you're in this big old house in the country without a car or even a bicycle, and nowhere to go, anyway. It's not as if there's a local bar or café where people go to hang out. There's no radio, no television, no"—I pause for dramatic effect and ominously elongate the vowels—"no phone." (Text messaging was in the distant future.) And then—Bingo!—from the back of the room a young woman's voice whines peevishly, "I'd go out of my mind!" I must have leaped off the desk I would have been sitting on. "Exactly," I exclaim, but of course it's not exactly right: Emma Woodhouse is nowhere near going mad (although one critic has compared her to the bored Emma Bovary), nor does the student mean that she herself would actually become deranged in Emma's situation.[15] But she does see a connection between herself and the girl in the book, and although my larger project will be to convince my class that every word counts, in this novel and beyond it, and that in this and other respects the world of the novel is altogether unlike the world they live and talk in, I also want them to be personally engaged in their reading—which is why this remains a "Eureka" moment, a high point in my teaching career that I still, more or less, remember.

You get the picture: I am not unique among American college teachers of my time and place in doing what I can to make a book seem "relevant." So it won't surprise you that I loved Amy Heckerling's *Clueless* when I saw the film in 1995. A handsome, clever, and richly inventive morph that transposed the characters and situation to a Beverly Hills high school, it translated Austen into the idiom of Hollywood, acknowledging the conventions of both fiction and film like no adaptation since Robert Z. Leonard's *Pride and Prejudice* (1940). Leaning hard and pivoting gracefully on the key word "rich," *Clueless* views contemporary life through the lens of an Austen novel and (I thought) a sensibility informed by reading Jane Austen. (That *Emma* is not named or even gestured toward is an aspect of that sensibility.) Fifteen years later, in *The Three Weissmanns of Westport* (2010), the novelist Cathleen Schine would riff in a similar way on *Sense and Sensibility*, in a satirical comedy, more homage than adaptation, about a small group of privileged, parochial, pleasant-seeming people. (By the time Schine's novel was written, some reference to Jane Austen was almost obligatory in a novel about contemporary women in America.[16]) But Heckerling's film was too early and way too cool to mention *Emma*, or draw attention to the remarkable thing it was doing: forcibly marrying high and popular culture by transplanting the character and smarts of an Austen heroine into the body of the lovely young actress Alicia Silverstone, in the role of a heroine of a teen movie. Cher Horowitz is a long-legged, long-haired California girl, a Jewish American princess with the concerns and unconcern of her self-indulgent moment. Like Emma's, her mother is long dead (here as a result of a "routine liposuction"); like Emma, she has her socially impossible father (here, an unmannerly litigator) on her hands. Just as nearly twenty-one-year-old Emma imagines she reigns over the lesser families of Highbury, Cher (who is younger) assumes she is above the rules that govern high school, sexuality, and traffic. High school is a perfect analogue to the hierarchical society of a country village; Cher's glossy pastoral Hollywood cleverly updates Austen's tidy Highbury; and her fashion statements are as studied as Regency costumes.

Unlike Emma, Cher has a co-conspirator, her best friend Dionne; possibly to signal the increment of implausibility—that is to say, of fiction—Dionne happens to be black. (Like Cher, it's explained, she was named after the star of an infomercial.) A more than usually literary film that exploits voice-over for narrative irony,[17] *Clueless* winks at Austen's novel by updating some names and retaining others: a druggy classmate is—with a glance at the pop star Elton John—Elton, and the Mr. Knightley figure, Cher's step-brother, is joshingly named Josh. (Name-play would also figure in *The Three Weissmanns of Westport*: the eponymous three are not wise men but *un*wise *wo*men, and the name of Joseph, the husband and father who throws them out of the lavish New York City apartment they call home, is diminished and feminized, by his step-daughters, to "Josie." The Jewish names are among the Jewish jokes that put a wry spin, as *Clueless* also does, on the impish analogy with Austen's old-moneyed English society.) Where Emma tries to teach homeless, parentless Harriet the manners of a lady who can marry a gentleman and move up in the world, Heckerling's Beverly Hills High School glamour girls, frankly superficial, team up to change Tai's crude look so she can fit in with their dressy crowd. In a brilliantly edited sequence, the girlfriends joyously redo her makeup, wardrobe, and hair. The analogy is as mischievous as the girls: like them, Amy Heckerling—in the irreverent, knowing, teasing high spirit of postmodern pastiche—was giving Jane Austen a makeover.

When I praised *Clueless* to her, my friend in the country, a recent convert to political, cultural, and sartorial correctness, was not amused. She deplored the triviality of this high school movie (was I aware it was a genre?) and its overly indulgent take on the narcissism and materialism of American teenagers. The mother of a teenage girl, she especially disapproved of the sequence in which Cher, dressing for school, coordinates the elements of her costumes on her personal computer, which seemed to her to suggest—it was 1995—that every girl had such an expensive toy, or should have. What values were being condoned by this film, my friend asked sternly; surely Austen didn't share them. Formed by the countercultures of the 1970s, she associated the novelist's name with required courses and presexual life before the pill. Wasn't Jane Austen a byword for, well, Victorian morality? Surely *she* didn't think appearances were important, the way the movie does. Dubiously, my friend examined my pop-cultural credentials: had I seen Amy Heckerling's earlier film, *Fast Times at Ridgemont High*? Wasn't this new teen movie a hostile send-up of everything Jane Austen stood for? Holding my peace about manners and morals, pastoral and pastiche, realism and romance, and especially comedy and satire, I murmured that I'd found the film funny—usually a conciliatory thing to say, as comedy tends not to be taken seriously. As Emma Woodhouse remarks to her father, one half the world does not understand the pleasures of the other.

No question, *Clueless* was too clever by half, as *Emma* also is. But soon I discovered that many people were taking pleasure in it. I found myself rather uncomfortably in the majority—indeed, borne aloft on an astonishingly big pop-cultural wave. Implausibly, suddenly, "Jane" was everywhere, her name in charming pink calligraphy or one or another inadequate version of the familiar homely image of her. This Jane was not the author of classics that every cultivated person should have read, and not the starchy old maid who was the essence (in spite of her dates) of things "Victorian," and not the idol of adoring Janeites, but Jane Austen as remade in the image of her onscreen heroines, fey, fetching, funny, and flirtatious, if you understood her in the ironic postmodern mode. More and more people seemed to be getting the pervasive joke, which seemed to be (I couldn't tell) either about Jane Austen or on her. *Clueless* was followed up by a television serial featuring the same characters and actors; it must have influenced Delia and Nora Ephron's movie about the book business, *You've Got Mail* (1998), which nods at *Pride and Prejudice*, updating it as well as the classic Ernst Lubitsch film, *The Shop Around the Corner* (1940). Jokes about the difference—and similarity— between Jane Austen's world and the modern world are not new: in 1979, for example, a little magazine had published "I Dated Jane Austen," a story by T. Coraghessan Boyle in which the prim lady is escorted out of her genteel parlor into a car and then to a sexy Italian movie.[18] What was new about the Jane Austen jokes of the 1990s was that they changed what "Jane Austen" meant.

Two odd small films were harbingers of the blockbusters, and the mainstream vogue to come. One, *Jane Austen in Manhattan* (1980), was inspired by the discovery of a manuscript of an adaptation by Jane Austen (and a niece) of Richardson's *Sir Charles Grandison*: it is about a team of Method actors rehearsing a production of an artificial but violent old play. Made by Merchant Ivory Productions, which included the novelist Ruth Prawer Jhabvala, it is notably unlike the lavish and loving literary adaptations the company was known for—films based on novels by Austen's most distinguished progeny, Henry James and E. M. Forster, *The Europeans* (1979), *The Bostonians* (1984), *A Room with a View* (1985), and *Howards End* (1992). (Merchant Ivory never did adapt a novel by Jane Austen.) Ten years afterwards came a second curtain-raiser to the Jane Austen extravaganza, also set in New York,

Whit Stillman's *Metropolitan* (1990), which developed analogies between performances of gender, social class, and sex among contemporary young people and the characters in *Mansfield Park*. (The virtuous heroine reads Lionel Trilling's essay on that novel.) Unlike these films—and unlike *Clueless*—the Jane Austen movies that took off in the mid-1990s were costume dramas, historical romances elaborately true (as in Colonial Williamsburg) to another time. The Ang Lee–Emma Thompson *Sense and Sensibility*, Roger Michell's *Persuasion*, and the English and American versions of *Emma* were, like Emma herself, handsome and rich—indeed, opulent—and very clever, too. They sought and found visual equivalents of Austen's language in delicious images of people, things, and vistas. All about romance and matchmaking, they were egregiously chaste, in the spirit of past times, not modern movies; and they boasted big stars and high production values. Intelligent and artful in the Merchant Ivory mode, they had a savvy, cocky approach to the classic novels—more knowing, and much less reverent. Instead of finding visual pleasure in burnished surfaces recalling candlelight on fine calf bindings, the moviegoer was given more fleshly delights, the play of beautiful young bodies and glances; the characters danced and ran and flirted in beautiful settings. The new films approached Jane Austen with a sense of mischief: look at her now, they crow in chorus, liberated from the library, shooed out of the parlor and into the fresh air!

Literary adaptation was all the rage, in the mid-1990s, and sophisticated moviegoers were talking about why. Jane Campion's *The Portrait of a Lady* (1996) was another stylish film of the period, as was John Madden's enormously successful *Shakespeare in Love* (1998), which was co-authored by Tom Stoppard, who had borrowed Shakespeare's Rosencrantz and Guildenstern for a play of his own a few years before. Postmodern, postliterary, and terminally ironic, the decade was haunted by ghosts of the past, often in drag. In 2002 Spike Jonze's film *Adaptation* would explore the Darwinian resonances of the idea, as well as the trend. "Traduttore, traditore"—and whatever else it may be, adaptation is translation. To make movies of Jane Austen's novels was by definition to alter them. The modern actors dressed up in period costume seemed to inhabit the fashionable Regency society that Byron had called "the world in masquerade," a more exalted milieu than the world of Austen's characters, the great world of Sir Walter Elliot's distant grand relations and Mary Crawford's offstage friend, Lady Stornaway. And while the implicit analogy the movies made between theatrical performance and polite manners did derive from Austen, the cameras lingered adoringly on eyes and hair, dancing and eating and swimming, landscape and glittering expensive tableware as if these were what mattered most, in life. Austen's novels provide few details of what objects and people look like: in *Sense and Sensibility*, Elinor is free to guess that the hair in Edmund Ferrars's ring is either her sister's or his sister's, and then to discover that it is Lucy Steele's, because nobody's hair color is mentioned. In the modern movies, by contrast, hair is all-important: it does much of the work of characterization, but not only because the medium is visual. Increasingly, we are what we brush. In the recent British television series *Lost in Austen* (2008), the modern heroine yearns to trade her life and her clothes for Elizabeth Bennet's—but not the signature blow-dried bangs and bob that are integral to her identity. In a novel by Cathleen Schine that riffs on Jane Austen's *Sense and Sensibility*, the Lady Middleton character is neatly characterized by a rust-colored helmet of hair that resembles a Richard Serra sculpture.

The Jane Austen films of the mid-1990s were smart and sophisticated and gaily irreverent, knowledgeable about the novels and literary theory, too; they read against the texts in a poststructuralist spirit, offering new, crowd-pleasing interpretations. Feminism was one emphasis: in *Sense and Sensibility* (1995), the role of Margaret, the third Dashwood sister, is expanded: she becomes a charming tomboy in the service of a feminist point. The double wedding of the older sisters at the film's happy end is celebrated with a giddy postfeminist cascade of cash. What academics were calling new-historicist theory also inflected the films. Brilliantly pointing up Austen's satire, and by the way locating *Persuasion* in history, as the critics were doing, Roger Michell's adaptation opens with a slow, panoramic long shot of the glittering sea, lets us in on the hearty fellowship of gallant sailors with bad teeth coming home from the Napoleonic Wars, then moves to a contrast with the bustle of greedy business on land, as Mr. Shepherd's carriage wheels rush toward Kellynch Hall, watched by the wretched tenants and servants of Sir Walter Elliot. Noticing the shrewdness of the readings, the casting, and the acting, furthermore, we keep what feels like a proper Jane Austenish distance from the action—which from time to time, much as in the novels, startlingly and mysteriously moves us.

Released around the same time and aware of one another, the movies were mostly good. Celebrating the woman writer Jane Austen, they oh-so-lightly implied that all the pretty heroines were versions of her. Two contemporaneous adaptations of *Emma*, one made for television in England and the other in America for the big screen, pressed the point differently. In Diarmuid Lewis's version, brown-haired Kate Beckinsale is a country girl whose romantic fantasies about Frank Churchill are portrayed in conventional, over-the-top dream sequences; in the Hollywood version written and directed by Douglas McGrath (who had written for *Saturday Night Live*), gleaming Gwyneth Paltrow plays Emma as a manipulative sly vixen. Singly and together, mindful of *Clueless* and one another, these films suggested, as Austen's novel does, that Emma has much too good an opinion of herself but also that this scheming, matchmaking heroine, whether yearning and imaginative or arch and artful, is something like a novelist—and a filmmaker. Like Jane Austen the novelist before them, the filmmakers were teasing people to identify the heroine with the lady who invented her; like her they were devising clever variations on the theme of a bright young woman's desire—chapters of a single novel, even.

The films winked broadly at old-fashioned decorum and chastity; and specific complicit broad winks were directed at readers of the novels, movie buffs, and also at the filmmakers themselves—the very idea of making a fun movie of a novel by stuffy old Jane Austen! From the start, mixing up the novels and confounding their conventions with conventions of popular romantic and comic films was part of the Jane game; so was insisting on Austen's comparative littleness in the greater scheme of things. McGrath's *Emma* begins by panning across the starry sky—the universe—then descending to the spinning globe and then to the little bauble of Highbury, and finally to old-fashioned framed miniatures on ivory of the town's major inhabitants, an allusion to Austen's "bits . . . of ivory," and, as well, to the beginning of *Pride and Prejudice*, which moves from the *universally* acknowledged to a single family. The British *Emma* also engages and challenges the cosmos, here with an opening shot of the moon; in a more startling move, it defies expectations of yet another sweet, nonviolent Jane Austen movie by beginning with a gunshot—a reference to the *rumor* of poultry thieves in the neighborhood that allows Mr. Knightley to marry Emma and move to Hartfield so as to protect her father, at the novel's *end*. Janeites were tickled by the in-joke. Movie buffs appreciated other signals of complicity: the anachronistic archery match in McGrath's *Emma* refers back to the same anachronism in the 1940 *Pride and Prejudice;* Ms. Geist, the old-maid teacher in *Clueless*, is revealed as a desirable bride for Mr. Hall as women like her in the movies always are, when her glasses come off. On the level of gossip, there were further entertaining connections: were you aware that Phyllida Law, Mrs. Bates in the McGrath *Emma*, is in real life the mother of Sophie Thompson (who plays Miss Bates, and is Emma Thompson's sister)? That Ciaran Hinds, who's said to look Irish, in *Persuasion*, is Irish in fact? That Emma Thompson and Kenneth Branagh had divorced, which was probably why Thompson took on writing the script of *Sense and Sensibility* and—at thirty-seven!—the role of dour nineteen-year-old Elinor Dashwood, a far cry from the merry Beatrice she had played in Branagh's film version of *Much Ado About Nothing* (1993)? And do you recall that critics and biographers have described Elizabeth Bennet, a very different Austen heroine, as a version of Beatrice? The cozy tangle of connections made people new kinds of experts on, inhabitants of, Austen-land.

In conversation with one another, the films produced further conversation, with more than a little help from the reviewers, journalists, and romance writers, women, and occasionally misogynists, who set themselves up as their critics. Once the province of an elite coterie, as people kept repeating, Jane Austen was now—no question—everyone's. Democratic revolution or crass, commercial vulgarization? Commentators competed to account for the phenomenon and pronounce on whether or not it was a healthy sign. New academic disciplines—film studies, media studies, cultural studies—complicated the hierarchy of critics, scholars, and brilliant amateurs; as always in Austen circles, people jostled competitively (as in Austen's novels) for the upper hand. Your Austen expert, during and since the nineties, still had to be sharp and witty; eccentricity remained more than acceptable, as it had been ever since Reginald Farrer botanized in the Himalayas, traveling in a palanquin on an elephant, with *Northanger Abbey* open on his lap. A good memory was still a help, and the capacity to threaten disapproval in Jane's name. But increasingly, an advanced degree, a classy accent, and traditional social credentials were no longer mandatory. There was a new inclusiveness, an eagerness to accept the new and even to revise older notions of tone and taste.

Increasing Jane's fame, if not her traditional cachet, were cannily marketed and targeted spin-offs and tie-ins, books and things: delicious-looking new paperback editions of the novels and new biographies, as well as Austen-branded chairs, wallpapers, tea towels, nightgowns, note cards, and of course shopping bags. Fan fiction, previously written for a coterie, attracted new and different readers and writers: "Fifty-Six and Counting!" crowed a headline in the summer 1998 issue of *JASNA News*, published by the Jane Austen Society of North America, over a long list of titles dating from 1850 (*The Younger Sister*, by the Austen family member Mrs. Catherine Hubback). Among these were a plethora published in the 1990s, including six books by Joan Aiken, eight by Jane Gillespie, and four by Emma Tennant.[19] There were sequels and prequels and parallel narratives, versions that told a minor character's neglected story, versions that took the main story in another direction, and, increasingly, books about contemporary Jane-Austen-heroine-wannabe readers, sexually active young women looking seriously for true love and/or semi-serious Janeites who played at pretending that they and their best girlfriends were just like Marianne or Elinor or Elizabeth or Anne.

The jacket copy for Emma Tennant's novels boasted of the author's connection with the Austen family; a pair of American women devised an Austenish name ("Julia Barrett") for their two sequels; another pseudonymous writer produced a series of archly titled Jane Austen mysteries—*Jane and the Unpleasantness at Scargrave Manor* (1996), *Jane and the Man of the Cloth* (1997), *Jane and the Wandering Eye* (1998), through *Jane and the Barque of Frailty* (2006), and more to come—featuring the sharp-eyed novelist as sleuth. Also for sale in the Jane Austen marketplace were chaste "modern" versions of Austen novels by the Internet Christian minister Debra White Smith, whose Web site promoted abstinence before marriage ("The Silver Ring Thing") but sold, as well, "body chocolate" for married couples—and of course also sold her. And there were—there continue to be—many spicy volumes of "chick lit" (of which Jane Austen had been pronounced the great-great-grandmother) in which "Jane Austen" meets "Sex and the City." Amazon.com was selling *Jane Austen's Guide to Dating* and *Dating Mr. Darcy: The Smart Girl's Guide to Sensible Romance*. The afterlife of Mr. Darcy especially continues to be ingeniously imagined: sometimes he is a beleaguered but benign father of too many daughters, but more often a glowering enigma with a secret—homosexuality, perhaps, or vampirism.[20] *Jane Austen in Style*, by Susan Watkins, a prescient piece of publishing that appeared in 1990, included, in the back of the book, a directory of Georgian design, with the names and addresses of merchants.[21] New and trendy and something of an in-joke, Jane Austen was for everyone. A lot of people made a lot of money.

Popular and profitable, trans-Atlantic and international, corporate-sponsored and media-made, the Austen vogue that took off in the mid-1990s was choral and collaborative. It mischievously diverged from earlier, starchier notions of Jane, and it was giddily productive of differences. On the other hand, its distinctive keynote was clear. Just as *Pride and Prejudice* was Austen's signature novel, the film that set the tone for a decade and more of re-versionings was the jaunty six-part miniseries of *Pride and Prejudice* that was aired in Britain in the fall of 1995 and in North America in January 1996. Produced by Sue Birtwistle for the BBC, with additional funding from the A&E network, it starred Jennifer Ehle as Elizabeth and Colin Firth as a Byronic Mr. Darcy. Definitively—as it seems now, once for all—it altered the image of Jane Austen from a thin-lipped old maid adored by an elitist coterie into a glamorous popular celebrity. The trick was turned by eliding her image into the still famous image of the first high-end, high-class, high-culture English writer to become a popular celebrity, the Romantic poet Lord Byron, her contemporary. His poems were no longer much read by the end of the twentieth century, but his famous name and face—much reproduced, in his own time, on manufactured commodities—remained identifiable, if not familiar. Colin Firth as smoldering Mr. Darcy brought Byron back. The Austen–Byron connection was deliciously perverse and piquant; for anyone who knew anything about the virgin and the rake, its wit was irresistible. And there was something in it for the literary historian as well: like Jane Austen's fans, Lord Byron's admirers had imagined themselves his intimates, or special friends, or (in their dreams) the man himself.

Long before Colin Firth jumped in the lake, in the miniseries, readers had adored *Pride and Prejudice*. The early draft that Jane Austen called "First Impressions" was so much in demand among the friends she read it to that she pretended to fear that Martha Lloyd meant to memorize and publish it. *Pride and Prejudice*, the final version, is a much smoother text, a more polished and perfect work of art than *Sense and Sensibility*, the first novel Austen published: like most of her readers, the author seems to have preferred it ("my own darling Child" [*Letters*, 201]) to the earlier work ("a sucking child" [*Letters*, 182]). On receipt of the printed book she wrote complacently to her sister:

> Upon the whole however I am quite vain enough & well satisfied enough.—The work is rather too light & bright & sparkling;—it wants shade;—it wants to be stretched out here & there with a long Chapter—of sense if it could be had, if not of solemn specious nonsense—about something unconnected with the story; an Essay on Writing, a critique on Walter Scott, or the history of Buonaparte—or anything that

would form a contrast & bring the reader with increased delight to the playfulness & Epigrammatism of the general stile.—I doubt your quite agreeing with me here—I know your starched Notions.—The caution observed at Steventon with regard to the possession of the Book is an agreeable surprise to me, & I heartily wish it may be the means of saving you from everything unpleasant;—but you must be prepared for the Neighbourhood being perhaps already informed of there being such a Work in the World, & in the Chawton World!   (*Letters*, 203)

News of the novel (and the author—whose identity her brother Henry soon was whispering about to friends) quickly went beyond the neighborhood of Chawton. *Pride and Prejudice* was the book of the London season in 1813 (Lord Byron's poem in two cantos of Spenserian stanzas, *Childe Harold's Pilgrimage*, had been the literary rage the year before). Annabella Milbanke, the correct and literary young woman who was soon, to her grief, to marry Byron, expressed her eagerness to meet the author of the new novel, "or –*ess* I have been told," she wrote, and in a letter to her mother she praised it as the "most *probable*" fiction she had ever read.[22] It continues to be considered proper reading for the young and innocent—as Jane Austen herself wryly remarked of some ornamental naked cupids shown to her when she visited a niece's school, "a fine study for girls" (*Letters*, 211). It was the first work by a woman to be placed on the "Great Books" curriculum of St. John's University in Maryland (in 1949), and in 1985, some twenty years after the trashing of the Western literary canon and two years after the admission of women to the college, to be included in the Humanities curriculum at Columbia College in New York. It was the template for the Regency romances featuring pert virtuous heroines who marry up that Georgette Heyer started writing in the 1920s.

"The best romance novel ever written," one writer pronounces it; the feminist scholar Claudia Johnson has called it "almost shamelessly wish-fulfilling." You can read it as erotic romance or as the paradigmatic "family romance"—the common fantasy Freud described in which the protagonist manages to extricate herself from an unworthy family to become part of a grander one in a big house in the happy end. "Dearest, loveliest Elizabeth," Darcy's final, fulsome endearment, in the novel, is echoed in James Strachey's translation of Freud's essay describing the fantasy based on a child's memories of infancy, "the happy, vanished days when his father seemed to him the noblest and strongest of men and his mother the dearest and loveliest of women"—an accident, surely, but a happy accident. In another vein, but also emphasizing its dreamy dimension, Franco Moretti has described *Pride and Prejudice*—along with Goethe's *Wilhelm Meister*—as one of the two formative myths of modernity. Tweaked and transformed by recent adapters, Elizabeth Bennet's story has come to seem more and more like Cinderella's. But in its time the critic William Gifford read the novel as a welcome corrective to cliché-ridden romances written, as he put it scornfully, for ladies' maids and washerwomen; and Walter Scott, for his part, criticized Elizabeth for making a prudential marriage, judging her story not romantic enough ("But where is Cupid?," he lamented). Recently the Austen scholar Richard Jenkyns has gone against the romantic flow by matter-of-factly making Miss Milbanke's point that this is an unusually plausible fiction: "It is not a fairy-story ending when a pretty and amusing girl marries well," Jenkyns pronounces; "it is life."[23] It all depends, of course, on how you live. Interpretation is always a function of context; and this novel brilliantly holds in solution visions of romance and skeptical views of them.

Reprinted by Bentley along with the other Austen novels in 1832, *Pride and Prejudice* has stayed in print ever since. Success is part of its story. When the elegant edition illustrated with line drawings by Hugh Thomson was published at the end of the nineteenth century, over 11,600 copies were sold in Britain within a single year, "totaling more than the lifetime sales of all Austen's novels put together," writes Kathryn Sutherland. It was for the preface to that book that George Saintsbury "coined the term 'Janeites' to describe the quality of 'personal love' as opposed to mere conventional admiration . . . which now characterized the growing band of Jane Austen devotees,"[24] and it was the enlargement of that band that provoked Henry James to deplore the commercial forces that had made Jane Austen—a great artist, in his view, if an artless one—into that vulgar thing a familiar commodity, "everyone's 'dear Jane.'" Moralists might scold, but personal charm, as Mr. Darcy learns, can prove irresistible. And personal love requires a person as its object: the disappointing dearth of biographical data about Jane Austen and the sparkle of the novel itself have led people—long before the movies—to read Elizabeth Bennet, who scorns conventional admiration and (pace Scott) refuses prudential marriage as a self-portrait of the author. Elizabeth is commonly identified with both the novelist and the novel: the first American edition, published in Philadelphia in 1832, was entitled *Miss Elizabeth Bennet*, and A. A. Milne used that title for a 1936 dramatization.[25]

When she first speaks up in the story, the heroine emerges from her text as a figure does from marble; so finely blended is her voice with the narrator's that it's unclear which one of them caustically describes the Bingley sisters' maids as "the two elegant ladies who waited on" them (*PP*, 41). Free indirect speech is only one technique that identifies the narrator with the protagonist. After she hears him read aloud the letter in which Mr. Collins introduces himself, Elizabeth asks her father, "Can he be a sensible man, sir?" and Mr. Bennet responds that he has "great hopes of finding him quite the reverse"; the next chapter, which brings Mr. Collins to Longbourn, begins by repeating Elizabeth's question as a statement: "Mr. Collins was not a sensible man" (*PP*, 64, 70). We watch Elizabeth assess her own love story as if from a little distance when we are told by the narrator that, on first seeing it, she "felt, that to be mistress of Pemberley might be something!" (245), taking an arch tone even in the recesses of her mind, even on tender subjects. (Her irony is legible in the word *mistress*, the modal *might*, and especially in *something*.) When she tells her sister, later, that she fell in love with Darcy on seeing his beautiful grounds, Jane begs her to be serious, for even Jane knows that Elizabeth, like a novelist, finds "great enjoyment in occasionally professing opinions which in fact are not [her] own" (174), as Darcy has observed somewhat earlier. And toward the end of the story, we are made privy to the way she jokingly formulates opinions not her own even in the privacy of her mind and bed: anticipating Mr. Bingley's proposal to Jane, she entertains the notion that Darcy will once again get between him and her sister, but quickly follows that up with another, more "serious" thought: "Elizabeth went to bed in the happy belief that all must speedily be concluded, unless Mr. Darcy returned within the stated time. Seriously, however, she felt tolerably persuaded that all this must have taken place with that gentleman's concurrence" (346).

If the blending of heroine and narrator offers special pleasures to a close reader, *Pride and Prejudice* meanwhile fairly cries out for dramatization, with its lively dialogue and intricately linked romantic plots, its comic characters and elegant structure—three books analogous to acts of a play, with the crisis of Darcy's first proposal at the center. In the scenes at Netherfield Park and Rosings, we watch Darcy watch Elizabeth as she watches him doing so—as we would do, watching a film. Although Austen would treat the theme of theatricality more elaborately and profoundly in *Mansfield Park*, performance is one of this novel's themes: Elizabeth presumes to pronounce on Darcy's social performance and discusses her own performance at the piano, and the performances of her family, musical and other, embarrass her. To bring the story to life by having actors embody its characters is to elaborate the play within the novel of the natural and plausible with the conventional and artificial—to play it out in another dimension.

The comedian Harpo Marx saw *Pride and Prejudice, A Sentimental Comedy in Three Acts*, written by an Australian, Helen Jerome, in Philadelphia in 1935—and immediately wrote to Hollywood, suggesting a movie version. When the film was finally made and released in 1940 there was a war going on. The MGM film, directed by Robert Z. Leonard, aimed to entertain and educate American audiences, but also to persuade them to pitch in and join the war to save embattled "Olde England," the mother country that was being threatened by Germany. Stressing the familial relationship, it suggests that democracy began in the land of the Magna Carta: Darcy the disdainful aristocrat falls against his will for "middle-class" Elizabeth Bennet—as, in the end, his snooty aunt Lady Catherine also does, here. "What you need is a woman who will stand up to you," she tells her nephew; "I think you've found her." Greer Garson's gallant, high-minded Elizabeth, in bloomers and petticoats, was an implausibly costumed version of Hollywood's brisk and articulate, strong modern working women, Katherine Hepburn and Rosalind Russell. (Shopping for her girls, Mrs. Bennet chooses pink for Jane, and blue for boyish Elizabeth, who later in the story gets to sport a mannish cravat.) Forty-five years later, as the second wave of feminism began its melancholy, long, withdrawing roar, the dynamic between perky, savvy Elizabeth and the painfully aroused Darcy would look very different.

As the films of the 1990s would do, the 1940 film inspired a surge of popular interest in Jane: a new Regency romance by Georgette Heyer, *Beau Wyndham*, and numerous lavish editions—presentation volumes and matched sets—of the six novels. In England and America, dramatizations were aired on radio and television; toward the end of the decade book reviewers were reminded of the restrained biography by Elizabeth Jenkins (1938) by Helen Ashton's middlebrow novelization, *Parson Austen's Daughter* (1949). A "sequel" to *Pride and Prejudice* by an elderly first novelist, D. A. Bonavia-Hunt, came out in England in 1949: *Pemberley Shades* does not acknowledge the Hollywood film but nevertheless it pointedly corrects it, insisting on the importance of the eponymous estate and restoring Lady Catherine to her unregenerate self. One American publisher produced a *Pride and*

FIGURE 3. Greer Garson and Laurence Olivier as Elizabeth and Darcy in *Pride and Prejudice,* directed by Robert Z. Leonard (MGM, 1940).

Prejudice illustrated with stills from the movie, and on both sides of the Atlantic women bought Regency-themed frocks with, for instance, "Jane Austen sleeves."

But the mid-century vogue the movie set off was romantic rather than irreverent, and it was not comparable in scale to the much more profitable crazes of the 1890s and 1990s. Film versions of the other novels were not made. The first six-part miniseries of *Pride and Prejudice* was not aired on British television until 1952; it was remade with the same script in 1958. In the same solemn decade, in a rare spirit of fun, Abe Burrows, in 1959, adapted and staged on Broadway *First Impressions*, a musical comedy based on Helen Jerome's play, but it was plagued by painful complications and closed after eighty-four performances. Another six-part miniseries of *Pride and Prejudice*, this time in color, was telecast in Britain in 1967. In 1980, at the height of the women's liberation movement, BBC-2 aired a miniseries in five parts with a script by Fay Weldon, who had been a writer for *Upstairs, Downstairs* (1971–1975), the award-winning ITV television serial about the contrasting, connected, parallel, and intersecting lives of masters (upstairs) and servants (downstairs) in a well-appointed London townhouse in the giddy years before World War I. Weldon interprets *Pride and Prejudice* as a precursor of her own feminist, satirical novels: the Bennet girls, by no means a bevy of beauties and badly dressed, are stifled and bored and cranky in the family's cramped quarters, and Mr. Bennet is a bitter philosopher. The adaptation was too serious and sour to catch on with either traditional Janeites or the broader anti-establishment or apolitical publics.

In contrast, the films of the mid-1990s would appeal to all kinds of audiences by reveling in the glamour of mannered upper-class life in years gone by—a theme derived from *Upstairs, Downstairs*. Viewers watched Elizabeth captivate Darcy against his will with envy and admiration and also with a sense of superiority to a simpler past or fiction, as if at once from above and below. Wittily accounting for the Austen craze, Edward Rothstein wrote in the *New York Times* that "we gaze upon Austen's world with a form of manners envy, much the way filmgoers gaze upon the lost worlds of social privilege in Merchant Ivory films."[26] (But Merchant Ivory's *Jane Austen in Manhattan* suggests that the team imagined Jane Austen's world more traditionally, as closer to the rowdy eighteenth century, and nothing like the lazily erotic and lavishly appointed Romantic world that moviegoers since the 1930s had associated with the glamorous, amorous Lord Byron.) The 1995 miniseries celebrated rich and beautiful people and things, and classy classic literature, too. Translating Jane Austen's liveliest novel into light, and bright, and sparkling visual form, it was true to the novelist's own metaphor and arguably truer to the text than earlier adaptations. It was certainly true to the pleasure of reading and dreaming about the love story of pert, arch Elizabeth Bennet and stormy, steamy Mr. Darcy, Jane Austen's version, or put-down, of that notorious sexual athlete, Lord Byron.

Advance reports of epidemic Darcymania that made grown women swoon preceded the airing of the first long episode in America: in Britain, they said, ten million viewers had put their lives on hold for six successive Sunday evenings to sit rapt before their tellies, enchanted by the dialogue and dancing, the comic turns and cozy returns (as in *Upstairs, Downstairs*) to a familiar gracious home. The makers and marketers of the film promised an improved version of what we already knew and liked, with sex superadded. In London, a journalist named Helen Fielding had devoted a witty series of columns to the obsessive fantasies the miniseries stirred in a fictitious fan, Bridget Jones, an overweight working "singleton" living in London who falls in love with the love story of Darcy and Elizabeth on television. *Bridget Jones's Diary* quickly became a trans-Atlantic best-seller, augmenting the hype. In its December 1995–January 1996 double issue, *People* magazine, welcoming the miniseries to America, acclaimed Jane Austen, along with Bill Clinton and Princess Diana, as one of the most intriguing people of the year. At the time, the bedfellows seemed strange.

Opulent and cozy, the miniseries caught the mood of the more and more gay nineteen-nineties. As the titles roll at the beginning of each episode, a woman's hand stitches to the tinkle of piano music, sweetly signaling a domestic female artificer. The narrative begins with winsome, pensive Elizabeth strolling alone in the family garden; cut to her noisy mother and sisters in the house, squabbling over clothes, then back to her looking through the window at her father in his ground-floor study, exchanging an affectionate, knowing roll of the eyes. Soon, the Bennet family troops home from church (Jane Austen's novel does not take the characters to church, but Trollope's Barsetshire had been on the BBC in the 1980s). As the family walks together, Mrs. Bennet informs her husband that Netherfield Park is let at last—prompting Elizabeth to smile smugly and smoothly pronounce, "It is a truth universally acknowledged, that a single man in possession of a good fortune must be in want of a wife." In a short piece in the *New Yorker*, the English novelist

Martin Amis described Elizabeth as "Jane Austen with looks."[27] For people familiar with the book and the author the idea was not new—and it was very much to the point of this production.

Andrew Davies, a former English teacher, had skillfully pillaged Austen's dialogue; Jennifer Ehle (the actress Rosemary Harris's daughter) looked merry and knowing as Elizabeth, and very fetching in a low-cut white dress, a cross bouncing above her high plump breasts. The minor characters were creditably hilarious. But it was Colin Firth's Mr. Darcy that made the "erotic magic" (as the proud script writer called it) of the drama. The role had baffled earlier interpreters. Byronically beautiful Laurence Oliver had been a hit as Darcy, but he himself described Austen's hero as a stick he could do nothing with (Olivier had been more relaxed as a Hollywood Heathcliff, the year before). David Rintoul, forty years later, was stiff and fairly expressionless. Tall, dark, handsome, and grave, Colin Firth, in tight Regency trousers and briefly in the buff, gave Darcy a credibly throbbing inner life. A fleshier type of the Byronic than the earlier screen Darcies, Firth was the kind of sensitive guy valued in the nineties; and the script gave Darcy equal time. In this version, we see him—as Jane Austen never depicts him—alone with his thoughts or his dogs and his friend, swimming in that lake or striding through the mean streets of London in search of Wickham and Lydia, always darkly brooding on his guilty passion. In his second, successful, proposal scene, as the camera searches his face for twitches of heat, Darcy's high-flown diction and inverted syntax—"The turn of your countenance I shall never forget . . ." "Such I might have been were it not for you . . ."—seem to betray his painful distance from his feelings and from Elizabeth (who knows this and coyly, smilingly turns away from the camera). Darcy is a fascinating mystery. In his rigor and formal awkwardness, he is at a distance from us—as he is, in the novel, from bewildered Charlotte Collins, who studies his stare because she "would have liked to believe" he is in love with her friend:

> She watched him whenever they were at Rosings, and whenever he came to Hunsford; but without much success. He certainly looked at her friend a great deal, but the expression of that look was disputable. It was an earnest, steadfast gaze, but she often doubted whether there were much admiration in it, and sometimes it seemed nothing but absence of mind.   (*PP*, 181)

FIGURE 4. Jennifer Ehle and Colin Firth as Elizabeth and Darcy in *Pride and Prejudice*, directed by Simon Langton (BBC, 1995).

If Darcy's baffled stare remains hard to interpret, in the film as in the novel, the camera's steady gaze at Colin Firth, staring, provides more evidence of his helpless passion than Charlotte has. We are closer to him than Charlotte—or for that matter Elizabeth—gets to be, in the book. Most of the fan fiction published since 1995 has been about Darcy, and Austen's romantic admirers routinely praise her rewriting of the gothic, Richardsonian, and Byronic hero as her happiest and best invention.

The novelist wrote of her heroine that Elizabeth was "as delightful a creature as ever appeared in print" (*Letters*, 201). She was also aware that Elizabeth and Darcy were delightful as a couple: "Her liking Darcy & Elizabeth is enough," she wrote to Cassandra about their niece Fanny's response to her novel (*Letters*, 205). Responding to the miniseries in 1995, Bridget Jones falls in love with the couple. (Viewers, as opposed to readers, may find it easier to identify with the couple than with the heroine. In a review of the 1980 miniseries, Nora Ephron criticized the actress who played Elizabeth, protesting that "Elizabeth Bennet looks like me!") By the time *Bridget Jones's Diary* was followed up by a sequel and the stars of the movie version (including Colin Firth as Bridget's sometime suitor Mark Darcy) repeated their star turns in another film, *Bridget Jones, the Edge of Reason* (2004), everyone was in love with Jane Austen's charming lovers—and with Jane Austen as well. The passion for Colin Firth that the British had been calling Darcymania morphed, with a sly, suggestive postmodern gender bend, into something else: Jane-o-mania. By the beginning of the twenty-first century, Jane Austen was an adjective and a brand.

The cultural impact of the miniseries is most clearly legible in the re-versionings that it inspired. The most notable and dramatic one was the Canadian filmmaker Patricia Rozema's *Mansfield Park* (1999), an adaptation of the novel Austen published a year after *Pride and Prejudice. Mansfield Park* (1814) is regularly read as the author's own reaction against the novel that preceded it. Fanny Price is an anti-Elizabeth, meek and passive and depressed: "I cannot act," she insists, when her cousins decide to perform private theatricals. In Rozema's version, the novel is radically revised: the dark, defiant film is an anti-Jane-Austen movie, a reaction against all its girly chaste predecessors. (It even includes an explicit sex scene of Maria Bertram Rushworth and Henry Crawford repellently "doing it.") Only the names of the characters have not been changed: Tom Bertram, here, is a drunken artist, his mother is a nodding drug addict, and Sir Thomas Bertram is played by Harold Pinter as a sinister tyrant deep in the slave trade. (Miramax's publicity for the film quoted both Edward Said and the British feminist critic Margaret Kirkham.) Rozema's most radical move is revising Fanny Price into a version of Elizabeth Bennet—that is, of Jane Austen the budding novelist, extrapolated from her early stories. Frances O'Connor, who resembles Jennifer Ehle, plays Fanny as a young woman writer who is already a feminist and a satirist, a brilliant wit, and potentially a dangerous enemy of the patriarchy. Kingsley Amis, Martin's father, had memorably lamented Austen's turn away from delightful Elizabeth to dull Fanny;[28] Patricia Rozema corrected the source text (and as if by the way, the BBC *Pride and Prejudice*) by rewriting Fanny's story as Elizabeth's—and Jane Austen's. It was a high-handed, muddling move.

Rozema's controversial film was not a huge success, but the greater commercial success of Jane-o-mania encouraged further efforts at re-versioning, of the novels and of the miniseries. In *Bride and Prejudice* (2004), the Anglo-Indian director Gurinder Chadha genially transposed Austen's most famous novel—now even more famous—to the present day and another culture. The action is set on three continents instead of in three English counties; the much-admired music and dancing of the 1995 miniseries is one-upped by extravagant Bollywood song-and-dance routines. There are hilarious analogies to Jane Austen's novel: smarmy Mr. Kohli is an amusing transposition of Mr. Collins not only in name, and the cobra dance reminds us of that other desperate girl who, much earlier, had delighted the company long enough. The miniseries is explicitly recalled when Darcy (here, an American hotel magnate) beats the streets of greater modern London for Lydia and Wickham, passing the Eye before finding his prey among the other hippies around the canals. Jane Austen had come to India a little earlier: a Tamil version of *Sense and Sensibility* by Rajiv Menon, *Kondukondain Kandukondain*, or *I Have Found It* (2000), had starred beautiful green-eyed Aishwarya Ray—the heroine of *Bride*—as the Marianne figure. That film mixed recollections of the Ang Lee–Emma Thompson film with scenes of modern warfare, financial meltdown, and the chaos of market-driven filmmaking. You can read these cross-cultural adaptations as showing the relevance of Jane Austen to a postcolonial world in which traditional courtship and marriage customs are still in force, or as celebrating the freedom of modern Indian women, or perhaps more simply as evidence of the universally acknowledged truth that Austen's novels, out of copyright and free to be exploited by the film industry, are as accessible and available for updating as the Mahabharata.[29]

The Andrew Davies miniseries had encouraged audiences to identify Jane Austen with Elizabeth Bennet; the early-twenty-first-century biopics *Becoming Jane* (2007), starring the American actress Anne Hathaway, and *Miss Austen Regrets* (2008), with the British Olivia Williams as Jane—she had played Jane Fairfax in *Emma*—portrayed the novelist's life as a version or inversion of Elizabeth's, suggesting that failure to marry her true love thwarted and pinched Jane's soul, but fueled her imagination and her achievement. Since Kipling, at least, most romantic biographers had given Jane a handsome sailor like her most emotional heroine's lover, Frederick Wentworth (but Constance Pilgrim had imagined that her lost literary love had in fact been none other than the drowned brother of the poet William Wordsworth).[30] The elderly American novelist Howard Fast wrote a play, *The Novelist* (1990), in which Jane, on her deathbed, marries a sailor as Anne Elliot managed to do. (A giddy high point in the ongoing collaborative construction of meta-Jane is attained in a piece of chick lit, *By a Lady* [2006], written by an actress, Amanda Elyot, about an actress rehearsing the Howard Fast play in contemporary New York City who time-travels between the acts and lands in the London of Jane Austen's time, where she enjoys ecstatic Tantric sex with a well-endowed lord and also runs into the novelist.) But since 1995, *Pride and Prejudice* has colored all things Austen: versions of Tom Lefroy, the boy she flirted with at the time she drafted that novel, have replaced the sailor as her lost love. And it is, after all, only ordinary to imagine this novelist as young and in love. Perhaps the most audaciously telling sign of the cultural impact of the Simon Langton film is the Guy Andrews four-part ITV miniseries, *Lost in Austen* (2008), in which a contemporary young woman comes home from the office, pours herself a glass of wine, and nods off (!) over *Pride and Prejudice*, the novel—and in her dreams replaces Elizabeth Bennet, becomes herself-as-Elizabeth, in a past or fictitious or filmic world.

Even before the vampires and zombies (separately) invaded Meryton, the postmodern aesthetic of the mash-up has blended variations on the legend of Jane Austen—and cynical revisions of it—with altered states of her works. Joe Wright's misty, gritty *Pride and Prejudice* (2005), starring gaunt, photogenic Keira Knightley, is, as one critic wrote, a "Brontification" of the novel. It took pains to naturalize the 1995 version, housing the Bennets in a cottage close to the earth: at one point a large sow, postpartum, swings through the parlor. The cross-class romance of poor Elizabeth and rich Darcy is steamier, and both lovers are stunningly inarticulate; in the final scene of

FIGURE 5. Keira Knightley and Matthew Macfadyen as Elizabeth and Darcy in *Pride and Prejudice*, directed by Joe Wright (Working Title Films, 2005).

the film (cut from the English version after preview audiences laughed), the pair, evidently postcoital, lounge in dishabille before Pemberley (played by palatial Chatsworth), where a pair of swans floats on the lake. He murmurs, "Mrs. Darcy, Mrs. Darcy, Mrs. Darcy." (Austen's novel concludes by mentioning Elizabeth's gratitude to her aunt and uncle the Gardiners, who were responsible for "uniting them.") Wright went on to adapt Ian McEwan's 2001 novel, *Atonement* (2007; also starring Keira Knightley—the star of an earlier film by Gurinder Chadha), which riffs on a variation on a legend of or by Jane Austen in the story of a child writer in an isolated English country house, who mixes up desires and fantasies, truths and fiction. Visions of Jane Austen continue to vie for shock value: in a scene set in Bath in the ITV *Northanger Abbey* (2007), made in Britain for a celebratory "Jane Austen Season," Catherine Morland's false friend Isabella Thorpe informs her that the wicked Lord Byron is in town—then whispers in her ear some scandal, almost certainly (this being a story about pairs of brothers and sisters) gossip about him and his sister. Revisionists have also changed the stories for no particular reason: in the happy end of the ITV *Persuasion* (2007), Captain Wentworth brings his bride Anne—unaccountably blindfolded—to the new house he has built for her, clearly a version of Pemberley.

Jane Austen called her literary work "composition," and emphasized the importance of "the best chosen language." The latter has gone by the way; the former has been turned on its head. Adaptation as homage has become adaptation as decomposition. But being in the know and knowing about "Jane Austen"—a clutter of associations, an emptied signifier—remains cool. In five or so years my graduate students may find themselves facing undergraduates who were first introduced to *Pride and Prejudice* by the retro Marvel Comics version—as I myself was introduced, years earlier, to *The Three Musketeers* by Classic Comics. Or they might encounter a group astonished to read the Ur-text of a story they first encountered on YouTube as a mash-up of five movie versions of Lizzie and Darcy dancing. For those who have heard of her at all, Jane Austen the famous woman novelist will have supplanted Lord Byron as a byword for romantic love, and English Romantic literature.

In his own time, Lord Byron seemed larger than life, more and less and even other than human, a product of his own imagination and language and in effect something of a fiction. When he burst on the literary and social scene in 1812, people compared him to a hero of gothic romance; and he continued to confound himself with his heroes in his narrative poems. His poignant lyrics meanwhile invited readers to share his personal pain. Hazlitt wrote shrewdly of Byron that to be Noble and a Poet was "too much for humanity." He seemed deliberately to be making himself up, making himself a legend. In his comic epic *Don Juan*, he sent up but nevertheless still sustained his identification with his Byronic Hero; his short full life and early death in Greece were the stuff of story. For years after he died, he was still remembered—his beautiful pale face, his stormy scandalous life—as the paradigm of the poet. Decades before the 1990s, gossip about the Noble Poet had come to seem tired and stale: Virginia Woolf had concluded the last essay in *The Common Reader* (1925), "How It Strikes a Contemporary," by calling for an end to discussions of whether or not Byron had "married his sister." In the Hollywood film *The Ghost and Mrs. Muir* (1947), George Sanders, playing an editor, cynically looks a lady author up and down, over her manuscript, and wearily asks, "Not another biography of Byron?" But in 1985 Louis Crompton's *Byron and Greek Love* aroused new interest in Byron's homosexuality or bisexuality (which Leslie Marchand had matter-of-factly presented in his three-volume 1957 biography). The last decade of the twentieth century and the first decade of the next one saw the publication of three new biographies of Byron, all by women, each convicting him of a different sexual crime; later, the Irish novelist Edna O'Brien would limit the subject of her swift, sympathetic retelling of the Byron story to the subject of "Byron in love."[31]

During the first half of the twentieth century, the *New York Times* mentioned "Lord Byron" twice as often as "Jane Austen"; her name did not catch up with his until the late 1980s; in the 1990s, it appeared more than five times more frequently than his.[32] The images of these long-dead writers would change in the last two decades of the century, in response to one another as well as to changes in sexual and literary fashion. Enlarging the spinster novelist with a famously narrow scope to the world-historical scale of the Noble Poet, pitting a lady without a title against a hereditary lord, looked like a feminist or at least a feministic move, to begin with, and a democratic—even an American—one. Some years after Byron's death, Harriet Beecher Stowe, a partisan of the injured Lady Byron, had argued that the idealized version of Byron was the self-serving construct of a ruling-class male literary cabal (which gives Stowe some claim to being the first feminist literary critic). It was almost as if in Stowe's spirit, certainly in a spirit of competition, that Jane Austen was reconstructed in the 1990s as something like the anti-Byron—having been confounded with him, and turned into a celebrity and an icon, a name brand and a household word.

The perverse and the paradoxical were in style in the increasingly gay nineties: that Jane Austen had never written about herself, let alone performed herself in print and on the stage of the great world, lent credence to the queer connection. Her novels having been transformed into scripts, she herself was reconceived as (like Byron) a consummate role-player. In the films—distributed worldwide—actors playing her characters aped the artificial manners of her society. And didn't people say that she herself had played a role, masking herself as "A Lady," and barely concealing her female fury with barbed civilized wit? In the protracted wake of Colin Firth's performance as Mr. Darcy, on a "reality" television show, *Regency House Party*, "in a country house restored to its Regency splendour," you could watch "five aspiring Mr. Darcys and five Miss Bennets attempt to live and find love by the rules of the great age of romance." Jane-o-mania altered Jane Austen into a symbol of that costumed and amorous age. It was amusing to imagine her and Lord Byron as unlikely partners; at the end of reading as we used to know it, the celebrated writers were paired, in effect as bookends.

On the other hand, the startling connection between Austen and Byron—good girl and bad boy, novelist and poet, homebody and cosmopolitan—has been made by many readers and noted by critics and scholars and in rhyme royal by W. H. Auden, in his "Letter to Lord Byron," in *Letters from Iceland* (1937).[33] Auden writes as neither a scholar nor a critic, but an admirer and friend: significantly, he writes *to* Lord Byron, in effect writing back—like all writers of fan letters and fan fiction, in response to having been addressed personally. He begins by explaining that he chose this particular long-dead writer to write to from a desolate place because he had been reading him: he had looked "for something light and easy" and "pounced on you as warm and civilisé." He goes on:

> There is one other author in my pack:
>   For some time I debated which to write to.
> Which would least likely send my letter back?
>   But I decided that I'd give a fright to
>   Jane Austen if I wrote when I'd no right to,
> And share in her contempt the dreadful fates
> Of Crawford, Musgrave, and of Mr. Yates.

Auden—who must mean Musgrove—claims to be less comfortable with Austen than he is with Byron, another man, after all, and working in the same genre ("I like your muse because she's gay and witty"): in the thirties some readers would have heard the pun in "gay," and recognized "pack" as another pun, referring not only to a traveler's bag but also to the pack of playing cards used in the game of "Authors." And they would have been amused by the idea that the timid, disapproving, and proper Jane Austen was shockingly proto-Marxist and proto-modernist:

> You could not shock her more than she shocks me
>   Beside her Joyce seems innocent as grass.
> It makes me most uncomfortable to see
>   An English spinster of the middle class
>   Describe the amorous effects of 'brass',
> Reveal so frankly and with such sobriety
> The economic basis of society.

As Rudyard Kipling did in "The Janeites" (1924), as more mindless generations would do much later, Auden rises to the imaginary challenge that her
shrewd but decorous novels seem to demand: to shock Jane Austen back. But
only briefly, here. Having linked her name with Byron's (largely for shock
value), he says he will write to the poet instead: it is him he aims to imitate. Praising Byron enthusiastically as "a poet, swimmer, peer, and man of
action," who offers "every possible attraction," Auden is as disdainful as a lord
of Byron's academic admirers:

> By looking into your poetic style,
> And love-life on the chance that both were vile,
> Several have earned a decent livelihood,
> Whose lives were uncreative but were good.

He claims to be less interested in the man than in his Muse: the blur or
blend of genders is part of the fun here. But for Auden, at least on the page,
he claims, genre is more important than gender or certainly sex: scornful
of the biographical emphasis, he admires most of all the earlier writer's
literary style and mastery of form. Deferentially, he says he does not dare
to imitate the ottava rima of *Don Juan;* rhyme royal, he maintains, is "difficult enough." Auden's chosen verse form, like Byron's, is tight, strict, and
demanding: it insists on rhythm and comic rhymes, and it plays on words
and plays with them, drawing attention to the fact that—as the older poet
put it, in *Don Juan*—"words are things." Form informs meaning, Auden
insists: in "Letter to Lord Byron" he praises Jane Austen for what she did
with the novel, "the most prodigious of the forms." Respect for their literary artistry is hardly the emphasis of the late-twentieth-century Austen–
Byron connection; nevertheless, their language is what these people
who wrote about love continue to live through. And for years, Regency
style, elegant, formal, and witty, has been the default setting for style
tout court.

Let other pens theorize adaptation. Artists and art depend on intertex-
tuality, which ranges from allusion and reference to imitation, translation,
transposition, and appropriation through parody and now—assisted by
word processors—to mash ups. Can we distinguish among these? Is appropriation different from homage? Does making a film of a novel require
a more radical transformation than making an opera of a play? As Linda

Hutcheon observes, Shakespeare adapted old stories into plays, and Verdi adapted Shakespeare to make operas. In the Spike Jonze film *Adaptation* and in the book (originally a *New Yorker* article) by Susan Orlean of which it is a "screen treatment," theory precedes mimesis, as in many other works of contemporary visual art. Multicultural influences on adaptation include that of scientific theory, like Darwin's: Hutcheon quotes the physicist Richard Dawkins, who proposes that memes are elements like genes that get altered in the process of adaptation.[34] Constructing categories and kinds, worrying and shuffling them, has occupied many recent writers of and about adaptation, who ask, for instance, whether mid-twentieth-century directors of Shakespeare set the stage for Baz Luhrmann's *Romeo + Juliet* (1998). Does the medium alter the message? Does changing the genre change the substance of the story? Does Julie Taymor do with *The Magic Flute* what William Christie does with the seventeenth-century "semi-opera" that Henry Purcell based on *A Midsummer Night's Dream*, and is that work more or less distant and therefore different from the source text than Shostakovich's opera *The Nose*, based on the story by Gogol, staged in 2010 at the Metropolitan Opera by the South African visual artist William Kentridge? Should a film be classified as an adaptation when it borrows only the premise of the plot of a novel, and renders the theft untraceable? Surely it is to the credit of *Clueless* that you don't have to know *Emma* to enjoy it: but does that mean it is a good adaptation? And if biography—certainly of a famous writer—is always something of a fiction, is it fair to conflate one writer's image with another one's, or a work of fiction with the story of a life?

The film versions and re-versions of her novels and the fan fiction that mostly lamely echoes them remind us that Jane Austen herself began by writing imitations, parodies, and send-ups of the stories and plays she herself liked to read. Her entire oeuvre—including the "Plan of a Novel" she drafted as late as 1815—may be described as a series of variations on a single theme, versions of the courtship plot, rearrangements of the structural elements of the heroine-centered novel about a young lady entering the world, with the parents, the hero, the place, the obstacles, etc., altered and recomposed. Her achievement might be described as transforming a popular genre into an art form accepted as an expression of high culture. Concerned with social and aesthetic hierarchies, Jane Austen tempts one to rethink and also to recreate them.

FIGURE 6. Newspaper advertisement for *Pride and Prejudice*, 1940.

Jane Austen in Contexts

"I sent Chapman to her."
—Lady Bertram, in *Mansfield Park*

Pride and Prejudice and Zombies transforms a masterpiece of world literature into something you'd actually want to read.
—Back cover copy, 2009

The old opposition between stern academic and goofy popular Janeites, reflecting notions of Jane Austen and her novels as classic and romantic, serious and silly, high and low, is neatly illustrated by a Carl Rose cartoon of 1949, which appears at the beginning of the Introduction to this book. The popular Jane-o-mania of the 1990s invited one to mind the gap between the opposing parties, but also had a hand in closing it. A quotation from Austen's youthful story "Love and Freindship," "Run mad as often as you chuse; but do not faint—," was used as an epigraph to the chapter on the juvenilia in Gilbert and Gubar's critical study, *The Madwoman in the Attic* (1979); it became the feminist leitmotif of Patricia Rozema's *Mansfield Park* (1999), and was popular as an "Austen quote" on Jane-o-maniac commodities such as pot-holders and note cards. The vogue inspired the writing and publication of serious biographies and critical reconsiderations, insightful new introductions to paperback editions designed for students, a thoroughgoing critique of Chapman's "classic" edition, and an ambitious new scholarly project, the eleven-volume *Cambridge Edition of the Works of Jane Austen* from Cambridge University Press (2005–2009). Georgette Heyer's romances were newly marketed in England as historical novels. An American English professor, Paula Marantz Cohen, riffed on *Pride and Prejudice* in a comic novel about husband-hunting widows entitled *Jane Austen in Boca* (2003). One thing leads to, one hand washes, the other: Jillian Heydt-Stevenson's academic study of Austen's "comedies of the flesh," *Austen's Unbecoming Conjunctions*, aims to prove "Austen's interest in the body, popular culture, material history, and subversive linguistic play"— in other words, in the themes of the latest vogue.[35] In *Jane Bites Back* (2010), the publicity guy who arranges undead Jane's appearances on television to puff her new novel—her first in two hundred years—is delightfully named Nick Trilling.

The major development in late-twentieth-century Austen studies, without which Jane-o-mania could not have been, was the turn to history by Austen scholars in 1975. Before then, most readers imagined the novelist in only literary history: E. M. Forster, in *Aspects of the Novel*, pictured Jane Austen in one of the "moister" [sic] regions of literature, "on a tump of grass beside Emma," for all the world as if the author and the character shared an ontological dimension.[36] Before the last quarter of the twentieth century, people tended not to notice that Austen, Scott, and Byron had been shaped by some of the same historical and cultural forces. The two-hundredth anniversary of Jane Austen's birth was celebrated at conferences across the English-speaking world; in Britain there was a government issue of a set of Austen postage stamps (Park Honan observes slyly that the stamp portraying that louche pair Henry and Mary Crawford would get a letter to Paris.[37]) By far the most important and influential publication of the watershed year was Marilyn Butler's ground-breaking study, *Jane Austen and the War of Ideas*. A briefer piece written that same year, Lionel Trilling's unfinished essay "Why We Read Jane Austen," would prove prophetic of the later phase of the conversation about and around Jane Austen, which continues.

Butler's book was one of the first in a line of "Jane Austen and" titles calculated to shock by pairing the lady novelist's pretty, plain, personal, austere name with not only "ideas" but "war" as well. (Later titles include two provocative essays and two scholarly studies, Edward Said's "Jane Austen and Empire" [1990] and Eve Kosofsky Sedgwick's "Jane Austen and the Masturbating Girl" [1991], and Warren Roberts's *Jane Austen and the French Revolution* [1995] and Brian Southam's *Jane Austen and the Navy* [2000].[38]) F. R. Leavis, Ian Watt, and Wayne Booth had argued for Austen's importance and centrality to the development of the English novel, therefore in social and intellectual history as well. But it was generally acknowledged that her domestic novels about mostly pleasant people sequestered in domestic life were remote from the political and intellectual conflicts of her time, and the novels and their author were imagined as denizens of an unchanging Platonic realm of art. In *The Improvement of the Estate* (1971), Alistair Duckworth began to consider the themes of the novels in the context of the social and economic changes of her time, and Raymond Williams, in "Three Around Farnham," a chapter in *The Country and the City* (1973), had placed Austen alongside William Cobbett and Gilbert White. But *Jane Austen and the War of Ideas* opened the door to further work on the influence on Austen of historical changes and ideas and of her awareness of them—the change from a land-based economy, shifts in social class, and the repercussions of the revolution in France. Austen began to be read in the context of the discourse of her time; and the novels themselves were read as agents of change or reaction. Underpinning the shift in emphasis were new views of historiography and politics, Romanticism and publishing, and political and social controversy, as well as of women and the novel.

Claudia Johnson's *Jane Austen: Women, Politics, and the Novel* (1988) was the most significant response to Butler: it took issue with the description of Austen as a "Tory feminist," and Butler herself acknowledged its force. As other scholars followed the threads of the various arguments, and went beyond them, the emphasis remained on history. Eighteenth-century novels were being reprinted and studied; soon the texts and contemporary reviews of them would be available online. Jocelyn Harris examined Austen's relation to Richardson's novels; others traced echoes of Shakespeare and Cowper (and the Book of Common Prayer) in the texts, altering traditional views of the novelist as an untutored natural genius. Interest in women and in feminist theory—in the relationship of romance-reading to women's lives, and in connections between home, nation, and nationalism—nourished further scholarship. In *Jane Austen and the Enlightenment* (2005), Peter Knox-Shaw studied Austen's relation to philosophy and religion and eighteenth-century concepts like the picturesque; in *The Historical Austen* (2003), William Galperin usefully located the composition (and revision) of the novels in Austen's personal history and the history of the world; Clara Tuite, in *Romantic Austen* (2002), analyzed late-twentieth/early-twenty-first-century romantic imaginings of Austen; William Deresiewicz, in *Jane Austen and the Romantic Poets* (2004), argued for the influence on her novels of the poetry of her time; and scholars working on her "sister" novelists affected the production and the placement in bookstores of her books and theirs.

Popular culture responded to the work of academic scholars and theorists: Roger Michell's meticulous, moving adaptation of *Persuasion* made a point of those Napoleonic Wars that Jane Austen used to be criticized for ignoring, and Edward Said's postcolonial views informed Patricia Rozema's *Mansfield Park*. Unsurprisingly, the vogue of the nineties also inspired writers of literary fiction—Ian McEwan, for one,—to invite Austen's influential ghost rather more explicitly and pointedly than earlier novelists had done. New interpretations of her life engaged with the themes of the vogue: very good, readable accounts by the accomplished biographers David Nokes and Claire Tomalin were published in 1997, the year Valerie Grosvenor Myer's biography also appeared. Earlier in the decade, George Holbert Tucker's *Jane Austen the Woman* (1994) had been published; Jan S. Fergus's hard-headed "literary life," a study of Austen as a professional writer based on her publishers' records and letters, had appeared in 1991. Most important of all, as both a source and a provocation, was the new authoritative version of *Jane Austen: A Family Record* edited, revised, and enlarged by Deirdre Le Faye and published by the British Library in 1989, which consolidated the novelist's life story as told by her family—from James Edward Austen-Leigh's *Memoir* (1870) to *Life and Letters* by W. and R. A. Austen-Leigh, first published in 1913—with additional material from newly discovered letters and papers.

As the Jane Austen world turned definitively and dramatically toward history in 1975, one important voice sounded a different note. At the end of a career marked by several brilliant essays that pondered the question of whether Jane Austen was divided, alienated, and modern like himself or enviably serene in her more comfortable, stable, mannerly, God-fearing culture, the eminent Columbia University professor Lionel Trilling—notable for an interest in history that was not shared by the so-called New Critics of the mid-century—drafted what would be his final essay, "Why We Read Jane Austen," for a celebratory birthday conference in Canada. (In retrospect, it is interesting that the invitation was tendered him by the young professor Juliet McMaster, later to be the invigorating spirit of the remarkably energetic Jane Austen Society of North America.) Trilling's titular question, if indeed it is a question, is on the one hand idiotic—why do we read Shakespeare?—and on the other hand oddly compelling. It seems to me even more compelling today than thirty years ago.[39] Trilling died before he could deliver his talk or even finish writing it; his uncompleted draft was published in the *TLS* in the spring of 1976, with an unhelpful note by his wife, Diana Trilling, saying that he meant to wrap up his argument in the end.

Trilling's title was characteristic: as Cynthia Ozick has shrewdly observed, "we" (even more than "culture") might have been Trilling's favorite word.[40] The argument was tortured, the tone oracular but also—beginning with "we"—poignantly, paradoxically personal. In retrospect it occurs to me that the tense of the verb in the title is ambiguous: is Trilling's question why we *still* read Jane Austen, or why we used to, in the past? But what remains most striking is the "we." Putting the magisterial (editorial?) first-person-plural pronoun up front, in 1975, was mischievous: choosing to flaunt it had to be deliberate. Trilling's essay was written on the cusp of academic feminist literary criticism, which he could clearly see coming in his own university. Kate Millett's influential book, *Sexual Politics* (1970), had begun as a Columbia dissertation; and in 1970 Nina Auerbach had deposited, at Columbia, a dissertation on Jane Austen and George Eliot, a revised version of which would be published as *Communities of Women* (1978). In his final essay, Trilling made a last grasp at securing Jane Austen for his masculinist party: his magisterial "we" separates (as that pronoun always does) "us" from "them."

Questions about communities of readers, canons, and women writers were in the academic air at the time Trilling wrote: one has to wonder whether his choice of pronoun, here, was more defiant or self-conscious than before, or even partly ironic. The paper was written for Austen specialists and devotees:

was he presuming to speak for *them*? Did the pronoun nod toward the continuing existence of what Claudia Johnson would call "Austen cults," thus wryly acknowledge the cozy intimacy of the little band of Janeites with their heads screwed on right, a community of the chosen, the happy few?[41] Jane Austen herself wrote smugly to her sister, "I do not write for such dull Elves / As have not a great deal of ingenuity themselves" (*Letters*, 202), revising a couplet by Scott that she could count on Cassandra to recognize.[42] Was Trilling counting on "our" noticing that to pair the name "Jane Austen" with the first-person-plural pronoun is implicitly to raise the question of what she—so distant and discreet, so disembodied and dead, so very distinguished in the art of making fine distinctions—has to do with the divided and heterogeneous likes of us?

The pronoun intimates the subject of the essay, Trilling's long-time conviction of the social and intellectual importance of Jane Austen, his sense of her as "not only a writer but an issue." Dramatically, on his deathbed, the critic who had weighed in on the big issues—politics and culture, Freud and Marx, Wordsworth and the Rabbis, sincerity and authenticity—faced up to a simple question about the (reputedly) most accessible, lucid, and pleasant of famous writers. His final, unfinished essay argues that the surprising renewal of interest in Jane Austen on the part of Columbia students—their crowding to take a recent course he offered—validated his politics. He took it to mean that the students were nostalgic for a lost civility: it seems not to have occurred to him that they sought to take his course because of his own eminence and interpretive gifts. (The lack of personal arrogance still charms.) Trilling crows over the interest in Jane Austen that seems to him to prove that she is a great and sustaining writer and, in spite of her difference from us, an importantly modern one, as well as to prove that the campus revolutionaries of the previous decade had been all wrong. Not to mention—he doesn't—the feminists. Trilling fastidiously does not inquire into the reasons why the students want to read Jane Austen; he thinks he knows. His essay aims to show that—unaware of how significantly different she was from them—they fail to read her right. His concern is to correct their way of reading; his subject (in spite of his title) is why we *should* read Jane Austen, why reading her is good for us.

The reason "we" crave what Jane Austen offers, Trilling argues, is that human nature requires the restraint, civility, decorum, and organized beauty of art. Apropos of *Emma* he had movingly reflected, in 1957, that the answer to the question of why Jane Austen has been so much loved is perhaps "to be found in the work itself, in some unusual promise that it seems to make, in some hope that it holds out."[43] (He defines that as "intelligent love," presumably love for an intelligent person, or a love object intelligently chosen, or love suffused with intelligence, or all three.) In his final essay he seems to locate hope in the elusive figure of the novelist that haunts her texts—not the biographer's Jane Austen but the metaphor the novelist made of herself, which her admirers have sustained. For Trilling "Jane Austen" seems to promise that civility and civilization are possible; in her continuing appeal, in "our" continuing interest in her, there is the hope of understanding others, therefore of understanding ourselves. The glimpses that Trilling's last essay gives us of his classroom practice, and his populist move of gathering his students with him under the umbrella of his pronoun, underscore the emphasis on the personal relation that mattered so much to the famously distant and inaccessible mandarin professor. (He had written a book on E. M. Forster: "only connect," Forster advised.) Trilling effectively suggests that the personal relation is intrinsic to our interest in Jane Austen, our still reading and rereading her books, and to his own "reading" or interpretation of her sustained and sustaining cultural importance.

Years earlier, he had been witty in a lively essay on the Kinsey Report; but in his last illness Trilling wrote with more than usual ponderousness and moroseness, adumbrating the hard truth that we are all half in love with mournful death: there are some paragraphs about Keats's cold pastoral. The peculiar morbid argument for the value of debility that marks his famous 1955 essay on *Mansfield Park* is here again. But then, in a burst of intellectual energy, he moves out of his own discipline, away from "high" nineteenth-century literature, to borrow an anecdote he had recently heard at a lecture by the young anthropologist Clifford Geertz. He repeats a story Geertz told about a grieving young Balinese man whose beloved wife has just died, who receives his sympathetic callers with courteous, smiling composure. In our society, Trilling observes, such behavior would be considered erratic or mad (he does not mention that the mourning practices of his Jewish faith include the symbolic rending of garments, an outward show of despair). The point— a debatable and much-debated one—is that manners, social norms and expectations and practices, inform the inner and the moral life, that people in the predicament of the Balinese widower, in our society, feel as well as behave very differently. His analogy is between people in Bali and people in Austen's novels; a better one might be between Jane Austen's eye and the (pre-post-modern) anthropologist's. Following Trilling following Geertz, *Jane Austen and the Fiction of Culture* (1992), by the anthropologists Richard Handler and Daniel Segal, would argue persuasively that the culture of the society she writes about, which is to say its manners and habits, is presented in the novels as a kind of fiction and a metaphor for fiction.

Trilling suggests that the difference between us and the Balinese is analogous to the difference between us and Jane Austen's characters—that the relations of the inner and the outer life are ordered much differently in the novels from the way they are in our world. He argues further that "we"—he, that is, and his Columbia students, who don't know what it is like to live with servants—want to read Jane Austen because although they fail to understand it they crave the models of self-restraint she offers. (His point about living with servants doesn't quite get made.) His examples reveal the underlying issues that concern him, mixed questions about reading and feminine decorum. His students lament that they cannot "identify with" Elinor Dashwood's and Anne Elliot's submissiveness, of which Jane Austen seems to approve; the professor advises that they should not try, pointing out by the way the virtues of feminine submission to duty, which in Austen's words is "no bad part of a woman's portion" (*P*, 246). Five years earlier, in the Charles Eliot Norton Lectures he gave at Harvard that were later published as *Sincerity and Authenticity*, Trilling had attacked the laxness of sixties radicals and their sympathetic sloppy-minded teachers who preached "relevance" and urged readers to put themselves in fictional characters' shoes. This final essay was transparently, self-contradictorily personal: a last-ditch effort to persuade readers to see Jane Austen as he did. Like Mr. Casaubon on his deathbed in *Middlemarch*, trying to keep Dorothea from marrying Will Ladislaw, he was hoping to keep her for himself.

That is, for genteel cultivated people like him, the first Jew to be granted tenure in the English Department at Columbia. Although they mock false hierarchies and snobs, and map the shifting distinctions of a society in transition, Austen's novels make class distinctions as finely and implacably as Emma Woodhouse deliberating on exactly how much attention is due the farmer Robert Martin and the newly rich Coles. Snobs, famously, are fans of Jane Austen: a typical Austen admirer is the casually anti-Semitic English dowager in Philip Roth's novel *The Counterlife*, who boasts that she rereads all the novels every year because "the characters are so very good." She burbles:

> "I'm very fond of Fanny Price, in *Mansfield Park*. When she goes back to Portsmouth after living down with the Bertrams in great style

and grandeur, and she finds her own family and is so shocked by the squalor—people are very critical of her for that and say she's a snob, and maybe it's because I'm a snob myself—I suppose I am—but I find it very sympathetic. I think that's how one would behave, if one went back to a much lower standard of living."[44]

Mrs. Freshfield's confusion of standards *for* living with standards *of* living is something Jane Austen tempts one toward: is the novelist herself a snob, and accountable for attracting and encouraging and creating snobs? While the allure of the classy English upper classes continues to enchant both the "Jane" and the "Austen" fans, it has become increasingly tempting to notice that the darling of elitist coteries as well as heterogeneous masses has been, for years, especially attractive to people at the margins of the dominant culture. Recent scholars have argued that the admiration of Jane Austen by people like, for instance, Trilling is related to her own marginal position as a dower-less genteel woman, an impoverished member of the "pseudo-gentry" whose social position placed them just outside the charmed circles of power.[45] Ironically, her brothers' descendants exploited her name and fame in order to rise in society themselves (and distanced themselves from her comparative lack of gentility).

The serious promise her novels hold out, to my mind, is of a meritocracy—by suggesting persuasively that true distinction inheres first of all and most importantly in command of language, where the making of distinctions has no end. Elizabeth Bennet triumphs as a lover but also as a literary woman; her ascendancy to real power in the world reflects the rise of a literate elite—what Coleridge called a "clerisy." Tic-ridden Samuel Johnson of Litchfield became the Great Cham by writing and publishing, in London. Jane Austen the country parson's daughter, no bluestocking, who admired Sam Johnson's sentences, became a great novelist by reading popular novels critically, and learning to complicate the form. Her own novels invite the reader—"us"—to desire and to emulate their intelligence and wit and distinction, to want in on it. Therefore Lionel Trilling the New York Jew, the Australian playwright Helen Jerome, the lesbian Canadian filmmaker Patricia Rozema, and the Anglo-Indian filmmaker Gurinder Chadha are attracted to Jane Austen and make their variously playful claims to be "in" rather than "out" of her charmed circle, reading and interpreting and claiming her from their points of view.[46] The boundaries of the imaginary world that gets called "Austen-land" or "The

Republic of Pemberley" are peculiarly permeable; the impossibly green and pleasant place is shot through with desire and instability.

Although someone has called *Pride and Prejudice* the first Austen sequel— like *Sense and Sensibility*, a courtship narrative about contrasting sisters—and although the six novels get blurred and deliberately mashed together now, they are not of course a series. Nevertheless, it is partly the serial quality that claims the Austen connection in Patrick O'Brian's twenty-one-volume saga about the yellow-haired tar Jack Aubrey, whose initials are Jane Austen's. In reading the novels of O'Brian (not his real name), who advertised his admiration of Jane Austen, we also enjoy the Austenian pleasure of returning to what Raymond Williams called a knowable community. Jack Aubrey's is the flip side of Jane Austen's world—a version of the world of her sailor brothers, which must have impinged on and informed her own the way her sailor brother William Price's world informed Fanny's. The O'Brian sea stories that began to appear in the 1970s are furnished in elegant Regency style with Regency manners and locutions, but the naval battles are violent, and dashing Diana Villiers is confidently promiscuous. But in Jack Aubrey's world— "Jane Austen *sur mer*," one wit has called it—as in Austen's, good people struggle toward the clarity of vision and truthfulness in personal relationships that Austen has persuaded us once prevailed. Immersing oneself in the world she creates and getting to feel like an insider there, we imagine we share the values of personal integrity and loyalty—as we do, while reading. Jane Austen remains on the collective mind partly because her novels have shaped our culture, and ideals, and our feelings, creating an accessible alternative world—because of what Trilling called the hope she holds out, that we can be different, intelligent and loving, and learn to know and value distinction, and have it, as well. Also because we remain interested in the constitution of "we" in couples, families, and communities, those abstract social bodies which depend on the difference between being "in" or "out."

Dying in 1975, Trilling narrowly missed not only the decisive historical, political, feminist turn in Jane Austen studies but also the lush Austen films of the 1990s. Intimations of both were already in the air: a static BBC drama punctiliously faithful to *Emma* was aired in America in 1972. Trilling did live long enough to enjoy the imported television programs that made British actors, nineteenth-century costumes, elegant interiors and diction, and repressed or outright class conflict familiar in American living rooms. Among the typescripts of "Why We Read Jane Austen" stored in the Columbia

University Library are some yellow foolscap pages, in longhand, that indicate he enjoyed *Upstairs, Downstairs*, which was popular from 1971 until the year Trilling died. Presumably, the pages were at one point meant to be included in his final essay on Austen, probably in the service of adumbrating the point he never quite makes about his students' ignorance of life lived with servants. It makes one wonder. Would the professor's bedazzlement by a nostalgic pastoral version of Edwardian England and manners have led him down the garden path into the green and pleasant lands of the BBC's Jane Austen? Would Trilling have moved on to interdisciplinary studies—or embarked on the analysis of popular culture that soon became an academic discipline? "Follies and nonsense, whims and inconsistencies, *do* divert me, I own, and I laugh at them whenever I can," declares Elizabeth Bennet (*PP*, 57), speaking for herself and (we assume) for her creator as well. I have a mug in my kitchen cupboard with a version of the epigram printed on it. Jane Austen would have been diverted by the spectacle of Lionel Trilling being reminded of her by *Upstairs, Downstairs*.

FIGURE 7. Colin Firth as Darcy in *Pride and Prejudice*, directed by Simon Langton (BBC, 1995).

CHAPTER 2

Looking for Jane

Jane Austen, with all her light felicity, leaves us hardly more curious of her process, or of the experience in her that fed it, than the brown thrush who tells his story from the garden bough.
—Henry James, "The Lesson of Balzac"

No writer presumably wishes to impose his own miserable character, his own private secrets upon the reader. But has any writer . . . succeeded in being wholly impersonal? Always, inevitably, we know them as well as their books.
—Virginia Woolf, "Craftsmanship"

Jane Austen herself must often have felt almost more homeless when she was restricted to home than when she was banished from it.
—Carol Shields, *Jane Austen*

Chawton, 1997

When I was in college in the 1950s, Jane Austen was the author of great works that were by the way delicious, six peaks of pink icing on the cake of English literature (or perhaps its rich center). As Deidre Lynch recalls, "R. W. Chapman's 1923 edition of the novels for Clarendon Press was the first to bestow on a novelist the sort of editorial care previously reserved for the English canon's dramatists and poets."[1] Lynch (like Kathryn Sutherland after her) insists on the importance of Chapman's being a classical scholar: his approach to the texts informed our reading of Austen. There were other influences, as well. To American students untrained in Greek and Latin studies, the narrow focus of the Austen novels and their linguistic precision clearly invited the kind of analysis that mid-twentieth-century academic critics were giving the lyrics of Donne (also valued then for their strong repressed sexual content). Their self-conscious artistry invited reading them with the high seriousness that modernist critics brought to—having taken it from—Henry James, whose prefaces to the collected New York Edition of his works had set the standard for modernist analysis of fiction. Although F. R. Leavis left it to his wife, Q. D. Leavis, to write (too fancifully) about Austen's novels, he influentially identified them at mid-century as the source of the Great Tradition (1950). What we talked about in class in the late fifties was the beauty and the lucidity, the poise and the balance, of Jane Austen's sentences and scenes, and the charged constellations of characters and motives that composed her moral calculus.

That we knew so little about her own life seemed proof, in those years, that she was a great artist. The lack of documentation, even the story of Cassandra's selective destruction of some of the letters, seemed almost an aspect of her art and its elusiveness, that style so fine no substance could violate it, that refined narrative persona you can barely glimpse. In the nineteenth century Macaulay had compared her to Shakespeare: as Kathryn Sutherland suggests, the Austen family and other Victorians constructed "England's Jane," a prose writer and a woman, to match England's Bard.[2] In the middle of the twentieth century, in the heyday of the New Criticism, it seemed fitting and telling that the mists of time—so much less time!—should have obscured Jane Austen's life as they had obscured Shakespeare's. At Barnard College, for my generation, it did not seem remarkable that she had been too fastidious to write directly, even to her sister, in the intimate tone that we ourselves took in our journals. Not that one could imagine her writing thus. A great artist, surely she had been too rational, self-controlled, and superior—too little like most women—to experience the embarrassing debilitating feelings that we tried to keep secret from each other and from ourselves. Of course she was not a woman like us (we were girls); but she was the kind of writer we wanted to be. She inspired us to be oblique and literary, ironic and satirical: reading her made us feel smart. She herself had been very smart, which was why she was so slippery. That you could not really tell from what she wrote to Cassandra about flirting with Tom Lefroy whether she really liked him or only thought she was expected to seemed exactly right: we didn't know what we thought about boys either. She was playing with the idea of Tom as a suitor, as she would play with the idea of suitors generally by setting up pairs for the heroine (and the reader) to choose between—Willoughby and Brandon, Edward and Willoughby; Collins and Darcy, Darcy and Wickham, Wentworth and Mr. Elliot (not always, as romance writers insist, contrasting the sensible choice with the personal favorite).

You had to respect her reticence, much as you didn't inquire into the nature of the "obscure hurt" that kept Henry James out of the Civil War, or ask exactly what small vulgar object it was that rich Mrs. Newsome's dead husband's factory had so profitably manufactured, before *The Ambassadors* begins. Reticence and fastidiousness were among the qualities literary young women aspired to, back then; upper-class refinement and wit and understatement were elements and signs of the culture and distinction we aimed to acquire along with a higher education. If we brought a sense of irony to this climbing project, as some of us did, Jane Austen's irony cheered us on. Her novels had, still have, a special appeal to young women in the process of being formed and (as she would have put it) informed, clear-eyed girls like Elizabeth Bennet who like to read and mean to improve themselves by extensive reading. "We were always encouraged to read," Elizabeth proudly tells Lady Catherine (*PP*, 165) — but she protests against Miss Bingley's charge that there is nothing she likes better than a book, and her bookish sister Mary is platitudinous and no fun. Jane Austen's tone appeals to girls who club together to giggle at self-interested and self-important people who take themselves too seriously (e.g., Lady Catherine, Miss Bingley). "Girls of fifteen are always laughing," Virginia Woolf observed about the stories Austen wrote as a teenager.[3] Girls who read *Pride and Prejudice* love to hate Miss Bingley—and Mr. Darcy too, for putting Elizabeth down. (It's a pleasure to change your mind, when he changes his.) Girlish laughter ripples even through *Sanditon*, which Jane Austen left unfinished when she died at forty-one.

In the middle of the twentieth century, many of the dead great writers and some of the living ones seemed to partake of the nature of literature, and have legends instead of mere life stories. Many of the most engaging people in English departments then had been driven there for solace and sanctuary from the cruel facts of history, and preferred to turn their backs on it. They smoked pipes, devised epigrams, made lists of Great Books, and hankered after a science and/or a religion of literature. On my first trip to Europe, in my early twenties, I made a pilgrimage to Hampstead to see the house where Keats had lived next door to Fanny Brawne, and the tree under which he had heard the nightingale; I even traveled to the Protestant Cemetery outside Rome to put a flower on his grave. But although I spent time abroad in subsequent years, it did not occur to me to visit Chawton Cottage until 1997, at the height of Anglo-American Jane-o-mania. Everyone was doing it, then: the Jane Austen Society of North America was sponsoring tours on which people brought their husbands, and roadside signs had been posted in Hampshire so you could see from the bus that you were in "Jane Austen Country." Winchester, Southampton, and Bath being part of the Austen package, the tour was more attractively extensive and worldly than a mere visit to an isolated shrine. Chawton and its environs felt rather like a stage set when I got there, which was shortly after one of several on-site BBC interviews with a *Pride and Prejudice* personality who had chosen to chat for the camera while being driven in a donkey cart just like Jane's.

As early as 1902, in *Jane Austen, Her Homes, and Her Friends*, Constance Hill had detailed the joys of looking for Jane (she looked alongside her sister, an artist like Jane Austen's sister) in what she called "Austen-land," pleasantly confounding places and people, living and dead, historical and fictitious. Nearly a hundred years later, at a moment when the names of the characters in Austen's novels evoked the lineaments of actors who played their roles, it seemed important to see Steventon and Chawton for oneself. Visiting the small rooms at Dove Cottage had utterly changed the way I thought about the relations between the Wordsworths: how could I miss the (larger) rooms the novelist had lived and worked in? For a reader of Austen's letters for whom maps and numbers are not evocative, it turned out to be useful to know on one's pulses the distance from Steventon to Basingstoke. The pump, I was informed, is all that remains of the long-gone parsonage: although I knew it could not possibly be the same pump still, I have not forgotten the look of it in the long grass.

Before setting out for Hampshire, I went to look at Cassandra Austen's little pencil-and-watercolor unsigned sketch of her sister, in the National Portrait Gallery in Trafalgar Square. In 1997 it was still as it had been when I'd last been in London, in a small glass case at the side of a room among miniatures of Austen's contemporaries, under a protective leather cover you had to push back. (When I entered the room, the museum guard identified my objective after one glance at me, and waved me toward "that little one there.") On a later visit to London, in 2003, I would find Cassandra's sketch impressively aggrandized, framed and sandwiched within a hunk of presumably protective light-resistant Plexiglas: Jane-o-mania had raised Jane Austen up to a place of honor opposite a gorgeous oil portrait of Lord Byron, dividing pride of place with the Noble Poet. (The sketch was subsequently moved again.)

Jane Austen lived in Chawton Cottage with her mother and sister and their friend Martha Lloyd, whose sister had married James, the oldest of the Austen brothers—Martha herself would marry Francis Austen late in life—from 1809 until close to her death in 1817. It was there that she composed her last three novels and rewrote the early drafts of her first three for publication. (In a doggerel poem she included in a letter, she praised the cottage for its "rooms concise and rooms distended" (*Letters*, 176), quite as if she saw them as sentences or chapters in a Jamesian House of Fiction.) Maybe because we know she was not born in this house but in nearby Steventon Parsonage, torn down long ago, or because we know of those original drafts written elsewhere—as "Elinor and Marianne," "First Impressions," and "Susan" (later, *Northanger Abbey*)—Chawton Cottage does not manage to be evocative of the origins of genius. Spacious and solid and right on the road, it does not have the powerful effect on the literary-touristical imagination of the birthplace at Stratford-on-Avon, the subject of a shrewd story by Henry James about literary pilgrimage, or the spooky Bronte Parsonage and Museum at Haworth. I traveled from Haworth to Chawton, in 1997: doing that reinforces the contrast—itself Romantic—between the legend of placid Jane Austen, who shut herself up to write novels, and the equally compelling Bronte myth of the wild children of the heath and their roiling female passion and genius.

The Jane Austen's House Museum at Chawton Cottage was conceived on the model of the Bronte Parsonage Museum, which opened in 1857, soon after the publication of Elizabeth Gaskell's *Life of Charlotte Bronte*. The Jane Austen Society was founded in May 1940, "with the object of getting possession of the house in Hampshire formerly known as Chawton Cottage," as the organizers wrote in their appeal for Anglo-American funds. They included the then-Duke of Wellington, who would arrive at meetings in a car with the Union Jack fluttering from the fender, and members of the Austen family, as well as such literary luminaries as Elizabeth Bowen, David Cecil, G. L. Keynes, Mary Lascelles, C. S. Lewis, C. B. Tinker, and R. W. Chapman. The lives of its writers are integral to the history of the nation, as George III had observed when he asked Dr. Johnson to write the Lives of the English Poets. In the eighteenth century, when Britain ruled the waves, the king had been interested in composing a glorious history; in 1940, the motive was more defensive. Concerned to maintain its pride and self-respect, the beleaguered nation was a little inclined to retreat, via Jane Austen, to a preferable past, a safer and more organized and powerful position—and a much prettier and cozier one. Regarding the appeal for funds, the London *Times* explained to readers who would recognize elements of the Austen legend—the pond that used to be just outside the cottage, the coach to London that ran right past it, and the creaking parlor door that warned the author to hide her paper beneath a blotter—that:

> The historical imagination can do much. The pensive pilgrim has but to close his eyes and open his mind, and water will rise in the pond, the coaches will rattle by, the door will creak, and "syringa, ivory pure" will scent the air. But the historical imagination needs at least a vestige on which it may build. The promoters of the appeal hope, and their hopes will be echoed, to preserve for posterity more than a vestige: a solid monument of Georgian comfort and Georgian elegance.[4]

Vestiges of comfort and elegance, a monument to the past, would nourish—in one of the garden spots of England—the pilgrim's imagination of that flower of domestic novelists, England's Jane. The cultural historian Alison Light has argued that military defeat and retreat was what turned the English into a nation of gardeners.[5] The loss of national glory had a solemn personal dimension for many people: T. Edward Carpenter, who bought the cottage and created the Jane Austen Memorial Trust to administer it, did so in memory of his soldier son, who had been killed in a battle in Trasimene, in Italy, in July of 1944. Chawton Cottage is a reminder that—as either Anne Elliot or the narrator reflects at the end of *Persuasion*—domestic virtues and national importance may be mutually constitutive. The project of the shrine at Chawton suggests there's no distinguishing between them.

Since the cottage was finally opened to the public in 1949, there has been an Annual General Meeting of the Society there every year. Speakers have included novelists and critics, Elizabeth Bowen (1950) and Sir Harold Nicolson (1956), and more recently John Bayley, Margaret Drabble, and P. D. James. In 1961 Andrew Wright, an American professor of English, presented a talk about Jane Austen from an American viewpoint. By then Americans had become deeply involved in things Austen. Notable among them was the wealthy fan and collector Alberta Hirshheimer Burke of Baltimore, who accumulated—among other things—ten fat scrapbooks stuffed with heterogeneous clippings and correspondence painstakingly entitled "*Pride and Prejudice* and other Material Relating to Jane Austen," which she faithfully kept up to date over the forty years between the time she saw Helen

Jerome's play (the same year Harpo Marx saw it) and her death in 1975. It
was Alberta's husband Henry G. Burke, together with Joan Austen-Leigh
and J. David Grey, the assistant principal of a New York City public school,
who founded the Jane Austen Society of North America in 1979. (The Jane
Austen Society of Australia was founded in 1984.) During the war the British Society had encouraged the transportation of memorabilia from Britain
to America for safekeeping, but the general consensus, at the 1949 meeting,
was that the Burkes were morally obliged to return the precious lock of
Jane Austen's hair that was in their collection in Maryland. Having whispered, more-or-less sotto voce, "I will give them the damned hair," at the
meeting, Mrs. Burke grandly rose and majestically offered to do so: the
moment has become a part of the legend.[6] Nearly half a century later, in
1993, Sandy Lerner, another rich American Jewish Janeite in a very different
style, purchased Chawton House, the big place near the cottage that had
remained—and deteriorated—in the family of Edward Austen Knight, and
helped establish the library there.

The bits and pieces displayed in the cases at the museum—the topaz
crosses brought back by the sailor brothers that recall Fanny's amber cross
in *Mansfield Park*, some lace and a patchwork quilt made by the novelist's own hands—don't manage to evoke a spectral body the way Charlotte Bronte's astonishingly small gloves still do. Just across the street from
"Cassandra's Cup," where the tourist can take tea, the house memorializes
Jane as the symbol of cozy, floral, gossipy low-end domesticity. (Nevertheless, incorrigibly, the great house dominates the Janeite imagination:
glossy photographs of the grounds and furnishings at Stoneleigh Abbey
and Godmersham, grand houses belonging to grand members of the Austen family, are for sale in the Cottage bookshop.) When he was stationed
in Macedonia during the Great War, in 1916, the classicist R. W. Chapman, who would edit Austen's novels for Oxford University Press when
he returned to England, found himself chatting about Jane Austen with a
Jewish refugee from Iraq; recording what she said in his journal, he wrote
that the English village was the image of a lost past we all share. Chawton
Cottage has been restored in the image of that once universally acknowledged lost past of the imagination: the belated visitor marvels at the sinister iron cannons, souvenirs of predatory imperialistic journeys to the East
brought home by the two nautical Austen brothers, casually disposed now
among the domestic furnishings.

I would have seen more of Austen Country, as it was already being called in 1997, if I had had a car. And I would have had with me a copy of Maggie Lane's *Jane Austen in England* (1986; reprinted in 1995 and 1996 as "the essential background to the award-winning film 'Sense and Sensibility' with Emma Thompson and the top-rated TV series, 'Pride and Prejudice'"). But I was not prepared to drive on the left-hand side of the road to Bath, Brighton, and Cheltenham, Chatsworth and Stoneleigh Abbey, Manydown Park and Sevenoaks, Shrewsbury, Southampton, Lyme Regis, and Winchester, a small but complicated circuit. In Lyme Regis, that year, you could see an exhibit about the making of Roger Michell's *Persuasion*. And I could have gone to, for instance, Mompesson House on Chorister's Green on the grounds of Salisbury Cathedral (Mrs. Jennings's townhouse in the film of *Sense and Sensibility*) or Montacute House near Yeovil in Somerset (the real-life version of the Palmer estate). Cooperation between the Hampshire County Council and Cosprop, which made the costumes for the Meridian Television *Emma*, made it easy, in 1997, to visit an exhibition of costumes for the film at one of three locations in Hampshire, and an additional one in Dorset: I did not go there either. On the other hand, when I revisited Chawton in the summer of 2003, I did buy a paper dollhouse labeled "Jane Austen's House," which I brought home in a paper sack marked, identically, "Jane Austen's House."

What caught my eye the first time I entered Chawton Cottage was the miniature of a pretty young woman with dark hair, an oval of ivory set round with tiny diamonds, displayed in a glass case like the one at the National Portrait Gallery. "That's Jane's aunt Philadelphia," says the pleasant woman showing me round. "She's the one who went to India with the Fishing Fleet and had an affair with Warren Hastings, and the result as you know was Cousin Eliza." She cocks her head at me to see how I'll take this: she herself takes obvious pleasure in dishing the old dirt (most scholars have tended to hedge their bets on this particular factoid, and Deirdre Le Faye disputes it in her edition of the *Family Record*). This is the same woman who posted on a wall in an outbuilding a shockingly long list of "Jane Austen's Men" (Edward Taylor, Rev. Edward Bridges, Harry Digweed, Charles Fowle, "Mr Heartley," John Willing Warren, Charles Powlett, Tom Lefroy, the Rev. Samuel Blackall, "A Seaside Romance," and Harris Bigg-Wither, whom Jane agreed to marry, but then refused the next morning). She breezily explains it to me: "Some she liked, some liked her, nothing came of any of it but there was something there, on one side or another." Something like this new minority view of Jane

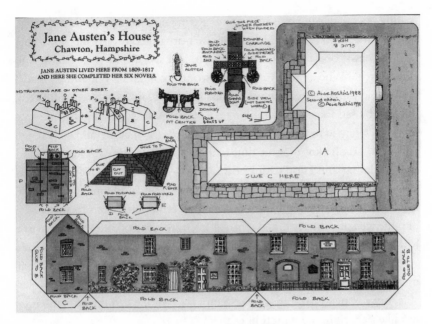

FIGURE 8. "Jane Austen's House" in paper. Courtesy English Village Designs, © 1988 by Anne Hoskins.

as a woman who knew and liked men would be the basis of the BBC-One biopic *Miss Austen Regrets*, aired on PBS in February 2008, in which Olivia Williams (Jane Fairfax, twelve years earlier, in *Emma*) plays Jane as a brisk, brave, and somewhat bibulous mature woman, who is manipulated into spinsterhood by her mother and her sister.[7] Phyllida Law—Emma Thompson's mother, Mrs. Bates of the American *Emma* in which Miss Bates was her daughter Sophie Thompson—plays Mrs. Austen.

Chawton Cottage in 1997 is full of brisk and jolly elderly Englishwomen who adored the *Pride and Prejudice* miniseries, and are having their fun being frank in its wake. I decide to buy a copy of *Darcy's Story* (it's in stock: someone explains to me that the policy here is to stock parallel narratives but not sequels). I say, "I'll take Darcy," and the clerk replies with a giggle, "I'm afraid seventy thousand women are ahead of you, dear." They know something, these women; they know what went on; the same thing always does go on, don't it though? (Mrs. Bennet to Mr. Darcy: "I assure you there is quite as much of *that* going on in the country as in town.") One woman shakes her head nostalgically as if recalling her own youth. "All those boys and girls, writing poetry, playing music, dancing, getting up their theatricals—they had a good time, didn't they?" They relish their privileged proprietary proximity to these new good times for Jane Austen, and specifically their nearness to Colin Firth. "When I met Colin," one woman confides, "I'm afraid I said a very stupid thing. I'd read about it, you know, so I said, completely innocent, 'It must be sad for you when filming a show is over, you all get to be such friends while you're making it.' He just looked down at me and smiled and said, 'Yes.' I didn't know at the time that he'd had an affair with Jennifer, during the filming. But I don't think he was angry—he could tell I was completely innocent." She casts down her eyes demurely. Colin and Jennifer had visited Chawton—they'd all of them come, for a little temporarily transformative dip into the well of innocence, and it had all been recorded on film. Sue Birtwistle had told them that *Pride and Prejudice* was her very favorite romance. Colin had looked at the original of the Hugh Thomson sketch hanging in the hall upstairs, the famous one where Darcy is looking down and saying, "Tolerable, but not handsome enough to tempt *me*," and he had drawn himself up just like that, right there in front of them.

Dazzled by the stars, the Chawton Cottage ladies also admire practical people like themselves, in real life—the successful producer Sue Birtwistle and of course Jane, as they imagine her. They know what she must have been like—energetic and merry and competent like them, transcribing Irish music for the piano in the days when she was sweet on Tom Lefroy. She had a keen eye, I overhear a guide telling a high school group: in the days when Sir Walter Scott was writing those long novels about people who lived a long time ago, Jane was nailing the folks she saw every day. Rich in social history, the novels tell you how people behaved then, how they still behave. The ladies tell me that in 1996 57,000 people visited Chawton Cottage, down from seventy-something-thousand the year before, but, on the other hand, double the twenty-something-thousand a year that came before the films were made. Now there are visitors like the young men who arrived the week before on motorbikes, dressed in black leather, and were up on everything in the novels—astonishing! Mainly British visitors, yes, but also Americans and lots of Dutch, Germans, and Scandinavians, and some Japanese (the astonishing young men on the motorbikes were Japanese); no, not many French. The boom has allowed them to expand sales, to pay the people who help out in the house, to do some needed repairs, get in the black. The practical, good-hearted, energetic, jolly woman (just like them) they imagine Jane Austen to have been is at the center of their happy industry. That she happened to be a genius and a great artist is unsurprising, in Chawton, nor is it surprising that tourists continue to come, or that Colin is now with an Italian woman, living in Italy, learning the language: he sent them a card.

The biggest portrait in Chawton Cottage, flashing to reflect a stray gleam of sun, is of Edward Austen Knight, Jane Austen's third-oldest brother, the one his parents handed over to rich relatives to raise (rather as Fanny Price's parents give her up for adoption, in *Mansfield Park*). He was obliged to change his name in order to inherit this property and much more. Edward finally generously settled his widowed mother and single sisters in this cottage, when they needed a home, and his full-length portrait dominates the parlor. It depicts an open-faced young gentleman in a fashionably languid pose against a classical background of columns: it seems meant as evidence that he made the Grand Tour, as he did. (Edward's dull journal of his tour, entitled *Jane Austen's Brother Abroad: The Travel Journals of Edward Austen*, edited by Jon Spence, achieved publication in Australia in 2007.) Buckling and cracking now, the portrait is too large for the wall. One is moved to reflect that his sister enjoyed neither a conventional privileged man's life like Edward's nor a conventionally amorous woman's life like that of her aunt Philadelphia, and that both these ordinary people had been conventionally represented on canvas, while she had not been. One thinks of those desperate recent biographies, allegedly of Jane Austen, which tell you more than you need to know about her brother Francis the admiral or Aunt Philadelphia's doctor husband Tysoe Saul Hancock, who struggled alone, in terror of tigers, in the Indian jungle. Facing the brilliant image of Edward Austen Knight as a gentleman, I think of the so-called Rice Portrait of a charming child, allegedly Jane Austen, and of the people who want to believe that the only commissioned portrait of that artist would show her as a demure young girl in a white dress, holding a hoop.

Staring at the likeness of her brother the squire, I recall what may have been the last paragraph of fiction Jane Austen wrote, in *Sanditon*. Charlotte Heywood is visiting Sanditon House, which old Lady Denham inherited from her first husband, a wealthy Mr. Hollis (all she got was a title from her second husband). Informed "that the whole-length Portrait of a stately Gentleman, . . . over the Mantlepiece . . . was the picture of Sir H. Denham—and that one among many Miniatures in another part of the room, little conspicuous, represented Mr. Hollis," Charlotte thinks to herself, "Poor Mr. Hollis!— It was impossible not to feel him hardly used; to be obliged to stand back in his own House & see the best place by the fire constantly occupied by Sir H.D." (*MW*, 427). I wonder what Jane Austen would make of her brother's portrait's prominence in the cottage dedicated to her memory.

Shortly after *Pride and Prejudice* was published, the exhilarated author wrote from London to her sister about a visit to an exhibition of paintings. She had been "well pleased," she reported, to see "a portrait of Mrs. Bingley, excessively like her." The former Jane Bennet was "exactly herself, size, shaped face, features & sweetness; there never was a greater likeness. She is dressed in a white gown, with green ornaments, which convinces me of what I had always supposed, that green was a favourite colour with her. I dare say Mrs. D. will be in Yellow." But a day later Jane had to tell Cassandra that visits to two other exhibitions had turned up no likeness of Elizabeth. Professing to be "disappointed," she explained, "I can only imagine that Mr. D. prizes any Picture of her too much to like it should be exposed to the public eye. — I can imagine he wd have that sort of feeling — that mixture of Love, Pride & Delicacy" (*Letters*, 212–213). Mr. Darcy would be more intensely possessive of his wife and his privacy, more aristocratically disdainful of publicity and display, than his pliable friend, whose character was so much less intricate. Trying to imagine sequels to her novels long before other people presumed to do so, Austen herself failed: she could only come close to imagining Elizabeth Bennet after her marriage, could only imagine a portrait of her secondary sister, Jane.

When *Pride and Prejudice* was the novel of the season in 1813, many people were curious about the anonymous author—"or *-ess*, I have been told," as Annabella Milbanke excitedly wrote to her mother. The novelist enjoyed the success and celebrity of her book, but claimed to be "rather frightened" when she heard of someone who "wishes to be introduced to *me*." She protested that it was not her aim to be a literary lion. "If I *am* a wild Beast, I cannot help it," she wrote. "It is not my own fault" (*Letters*, 212). Nevertheless she began to anticipate fame—with irony, also delight. She wrote to Cassandra: "I do not despair of having my picture in the exhibition at last—all white & red, with my Head on one side." Having gone so far as to imagine the colors and the pose, she undercut the silly idea with another equally silly one: "or perhaps I may marry young Mr. D'arblay" (*Letters*, 250). Her reference—meant I think to be hilarious—was to the nineteen-year-old son of the celebrated Frances Burney: evidently the ideas of marrying the young son of the older novelist and of having her likeness exhibited seemed to her equally comical. She must also have liked the sound of his surname.[8]

I returned to Chawton again in the summer of 2003 to celebrate the opening of the Chawton House Library. An international group of assembled scholars and Janeites—girls of all ages with competitive claims to a perfect right to Jane, snooty dowagers in pearls with county accents and upstarts from all manner of margins—gossiped in their separate groups under a big tent. One woman, who was wearing a white shirt she had embroidered all over with names ("Henry Tilney," "Augusta Hawkins," "Louisa Musgrove," etc.), drew me aside to show me in secret a picture that her manner indicated was contraband or worse. I failed to recognize the gentleman in the wig as "Tom"—Tom Lefroy, of course—whose portrait as a sober judge she had daringly photographed, against the house rules, in the Irish home of his descendants. Very few of these people imagine Jane Austen as she was described by those who had met her, as a "husband-hunting butterfly" or a silent, upright poker of whom everyone was afraid.[9] Neither do they think of her as sweet but vinegary and tragically thwarted "dear Jane." In their clear (if astigmatic) and adoring minds' eyes, the different images are complex and robust and complicated by images of themselves. They argue about whether or not she hated children (such as Mrs. John Dashwood's and Lady Middleton's spoiled brats) or sensibly feared the regular childbirths and pregnancies that killed her sisters-in-law or wore out a "poor animal" (as she wrote of her married niece, Anna). They speculate about whether she chose not to marry so as to have time to pursue her heart's desire, or, as others call it, her profession—writing novels. Past and present clash pleasantly as anecdotes are exchanged about the quirks of Austen family members and the interestingly eccentric American patron of the place, Sandy Lerner.

Lingering in England to visit friends for a weekend after the conference, I stumbled across a one-page story in a Sunday supplement about a young couple who meet while walking their dogs, Lizzy and Darcy. (My friend Ellen in New York named her dogs Darcy and Bingley; an acquaintance has a cat called Knightley.[10])

Getting a Life

In an Age of Personality, an Age of Celebrity, an Age of Biography, the focus is on a single character. The quest narrative of the hero or heroine is a story of growth and development ending in achievement, acceptance, fulfillment, and reconciliation—and realizing the self. In such an age, Jane Austen's novels—which interrogate and play with and more and less lightly undercut the narrative of romance—are read, first of all, for the heroine's plot. *Pride and Prejudice* gets pride of place: this heroine is unquestionably superior to her sisters, and the impact of their stories on her is not finally definitive: in the end she gets what she deserved from the start. Trying to imagine Jane Austen's life, the biographer—focused on the single individual, and obliged by the lack of documentary material to turn to the novels with more than usual need—looks first at that novel. *Mansfield Park* is another, different kind of story: not only is the heroine problematic, as so many readers have observed, but her character and fate are hard to separate from those with whom she is inextricably connected.

In the beginning of volume III of the novel, meek and mild Fanny Price asserts herself heroically against her intimidating uncle Sir Thomas Bertram, who has returned from his dangerous journey to Antigua, burned all the unbound copies of *Lovers' Vows* he could find in the house, and married off his eldest daughter, Maria, to a stupid man he knows she does not love, having persuaded himself she lacked "strong feelings." Sir Thomas in all his dignity enters the East Room, where Fanny sits in the chill without a fire, to congratulate her on the marriage proposal of Henry Crawford, who is waiting for her assent downstairs; inwardly, he is congratulating himself on having put her in the position to be able to make so excellent a match. Noticing the cold grate, which reminds him she has lived in his family as an abused poor relation, he pompously reassures himself by saying aloud that the rich Mrs. Henry Crawford-to-be will forgive her Aunt Norris for having made her suffer the cold. His mood is expansive: he is making everything up to her. When Fanny surprises him by saying it is "quite out of [her] power to return [Crawford's] good opinion," Sir Thomas replies, "I do not catch your meaning." He then manfully tries:

> "Am I to understand," said Sir Thomas, after a few moments' silence, "that you mean to *refuse* Mr. Crawford?"
> "Yes, Sir."
> "Refuse him?"
> "Yes, Sir."
> "Refuse Mr. Crawford! Upon what plea? For what reason?"
> "I—I cannot like him, Sir, well enough to marry him." (*MP*, 314–315)

The reader knows that Fanny is in love with her cousin Edmund. Fleetingly, that possibility crosses Sir Thomas's mind—he has worried before about "cousins in love"—but he puts it away: in the baronet who married a stupid beauty and let his daughter Maria marry stupid Mr. Rushworth, the capacity for denial adulterates shrewdness. Asserting his privilege as her elder and an uncle, he accuses Fanny of willfulness and ingratitude, and makes her cry by reminding her that Henry Crawford has been useful to her beloved brother William. After he finally leaves, Fanny reflects that "her uncle's displeasure . . . would abate farther as he considered the matter with more impartiality, and felt, as a good man must feel, how wretched, and how unpardonable, how hopeless and how wicked it was, to marry without affection" (*MP*, 324). In Fanny's view, Sir Thomas is simultaneously a terrifying tyrant and a good man, while Henry Crawford, having played with the affections of both Maria and Julia Bertram before deciding to make Fanny fall in love with him, is not. Or perhaps she can be charitable toward Sir Thomas because he has been charitable toward her, and because nobody is asking her to marry him.

Fanny's moral certainty and judgment are as unshakable as her will to marry her cousin Edmund, who is in love with Henry's sister Mary. When he returns to Mansfield Park, Edmund agrees with his father that Fanny should be glad to marry Crawford: the connection would strengthen his own suit. Hoping to help persuade her, he invites her to confide in him. The two walk together, and she confesses her thoughts and feelings, hinting about Crawford's flirtations with Maria and Julia, as she could not to her uncle, but holding back the main thing, her love for Edmund himself, which everything she says and does also expresses. The scene of shared incomprehension is as dramatic and almost as fine as the one in the East Room. It follows and depends on a more complicated, complicating scene in the drawing room, in which Henry Crawford picks up a copy of Shakespeare that Lady Bertram has set aside, and reads aloud various speeches from *Henry VIII*. Fanny, sitting near Lady Bertram, is determined to be interested in nothing but her needle-work, but "taste was too strong in her." Crawford reads so brilliantly, so good an actor is he, that Edmund, as he listens, sees how Fanny's "eyes which had appeared so studiously to avoid him throughout the day, were turned and fixed on Crawford, fixed on him for minutes, fixed on him in short till the attraction drew Crawford's upon her, and the book was closed, and the charm was broken." After Edmund thanks the gifted reader (hoping "to be expressing

Fanny's secret feelings too") (*MP*, 337), the two young men embark on a discussion of Shakespeare and acting, the importance of training in public speaking, and then of preaching, exploring connections between acting and Christian ministry as the novel has done before.

After a frightening, helpful series of family catastrophes, Fanny will marry Edmund and the couple will (ironically) inherit Mrs. Norris's parsonage, in the end: what that means about the meaning of *Mansfield Park* has been much discussed, as have the interestingly commingled themes of ordination and theatricals, the power structure and the slave trade, brothers and sisters and cousins in love, etc. Austen must have learned to read character and character reading character by reading Shakespeare (as this scene hints) as well as Richardson and other novelists, and by watching and listening to people play their roles on stages and in private; but how might a biographer document or track the process of her learning all that, or show how central and satisfying this way of understanding the world must have been in her life as it is in her work? Could Austen herself—not only her Fanny—have considered a man like Sir Thomas Bertram, who has cultivated ruinous relations to his own wife and children as well as to his niece and sister-in-law, and pursued dubious business in Antigua, "a good man"? Is he not, morally, as harmful and exploitative, as selfish and careless of others, as Henry Crawford? Does the narrator avoid judging him—as she judges Henry—because he is so powerful? Or on the other hand, is the important point that he, just like the slaves in Antigua, is a man—and an uncle? Jane Austen's sharp insight into character and ambiguity is bracing and dazzling, but her forgiveness here—if it is forgiveness—passes understanding. The pompous patriarch who is the prisoner of his own stiff civility, alienated from his affections and even from his own intelligence, is one of her finest creations: it might be useful to consider her genius and achievement, indeed her character, through the lens of this creation. But that is not literary biography's way.

S. Schoenbaum, the meta-biographer of Shakespeare, recalls being told that "trying to work out Shakespeare's personality was like looking at a very dark glazed picture in the National Portrait Gallery: at first you see nothing, then you begin to recognize features, and then you realize that they are your own."[11] The special interest in a woman writer that Byron's fiancée Annabella Milbanke shared with other literary women leads to what psychoanalysts call projection, which must motivate, or at least engage, all workers-out of personalities and readers of biographies. Single women, writing women,

Anglican women, childless women, tall women, women with sisters, satirical women, women who feel undervalued, women who dislike travel, men and women who dearly love a laugh, and people strongly attached to their natal families see themselves as if in a mirror in Jane Austen—along with all those women out there desperately hoping to find their Mr. Darcy.

There is no analogous glazed picture of Jane Austen, in the National Portrait Gallery or any other museum. The extant likenesses are only Cassandra's unsigned sketch of her impatient-looking sister and the two prettied-up Victorian engravings based on it that were made much later, in one of which she wears a wedding ring; perhaps the elegant daguerreotyped profile labeled "l'aimable Jane"; also, perhaps, the Rice Portrait, of a child, which belongs to a branch of the Austen family; and the favorite of most admirers, a watercolor by Cassandra dated 1804 that shows a dumpy Jane from behind, seated on the ground, wearing a blue dress and a blue bonnet with its strings untied. Evidently she's overheated; maybe she's overweight; very possibly her legs are in a not-genteel position; unquestionably, she's turning her back on us. Jane Austen is less intimidating than Shakespeare, and the biographer—and the reader—approaches the puzzle of her identity with less awe. The imaginary mirror, such as it is, being familiar and domestic, is much less grand.

Stephen Greenblatt begins *Will in the World* (2004), his biography of Shakespeare, with a chapter entitled "Primal Scenes." It does not refer, as you might expect, to what young Will saw through the keyhole of his parents' bedroom, but to the plays Shakespeare read and saw as a boy and the other spectacles he witnessed, which as Greenblatt sees it provided the foundation of his literary imagination and his work, and therefore of what matters about his life and makes his life matter. A biographer of Jane Austen might usefully begin similarly, with the plays performed in the Austen family theatricals and those she saw later on, in London—and of course the novels she read. But the many lovers of fiction who (as the bumper stickers you used to see in the 1990s used to say) would rather be reading Jane Austen have (influentially) preferred to take the opposite tack, and extrapolate the life from the work, looking for inadvertent revelations or repetitions in and around the text, or between the lines, and theorizing about the meaning of anonymous publication, the reticence of the narrator, the concern with manners, the focus on courtship, and the fastidious, elegant style. (Easier to extrapolate from the succession of the books is a meditation or debate about the heroine-centered novel: Does the novel make the heroine [NA]? Should a heroine express or

FIGURE 9. Cassandra Austen, *Jane Austen* (bonnet portrait), watercolor, 1804. Private collection.

hide the thoughts and feelings that make her one [*SS*]? Can she manage to please herself and everyone else as well, and reconcile the social with the inner life [*PP*]? Say she feels very keenly but cannot act—and is poor and dependent [*MP*]? But what if she is rich and can do as she pleases—will she also feel [*E*]? What if she fails to follow feeling, and lets the crucial moment pass—can she have a second chance [*P*]? It is not fanciful to imagine her books growing out of such an argument: the perspicacious Richard Simpson, in 1870, described her as a critic "who developed herself into an artist."[12])

More generally, the life of Jane Austen gets imagined as a novel—but one not by Jane Austen. Writers of more and less well-researched fictionalized biography or biographical fiction have invited readers to curl up with a story such as she herself might (!) have written: "A tear dropped on Cassandra's sewing and she murmured, 'I wish you would not talk so, you make me very unhappy.' Jane jumped up, ran to Cassandra, flung slender arms round her neck and cried out, 'Oh! I am a wretch to plague you so. You have troubles enough of your own. Between your Tom and mine we are a sad pair; but dry your eyes, your Tom will come back to you and as for mine, I have quite done with him. I shall not break my heart over him, I have had a tumble, and now I must pick myself up again and go on.'"[13] The assumption that keeps on going is that like every other girl she meant to marry—at the very least, as the narrator of *Pride and Prejudice* writes of Charlotte Lucas, that "without thinking highly either of men or of matrimony, marriage had always been her object" (*PP*, 122)—in other words, that she wrote what and how she did because first the desire and then the failure to marry obsessed her.

Some readers have been eager to find in the sequence of the novels a narrative of development, from the young woman who sought to define (and, surely, to be) an ideal heroine to the maiden aunt who looked on skeptically at young love—or from eager girl to nostalgic spinster—but it is hard to construct a convincing story for what we can make of this character. If we date the composition of *Northanger Abbey* correctly, to nearly two decades before its publication in 1818, the sequence suggests that complicated views were in place from the beginning. Of Catherine Morland the narrator writes that "when a young lady is to be a heroine, the perverseness of forty surrounding families cannot prevent her. Something must and will happen to throw a hero in her way" (*NA*, 16–17)—in other words, every girl is obliged to be a heroine, once you see her or set her at the center of a story, and gender and genre determine desire and action. In the first novel she published and in all the later ones, Jane Austen—like so many writing women before and after her—debates the relative attractions, to a man, of sense and sensibility, intelligence and what Emma Woodhouse kindly calls (in regard to Harriet) "tenderness of heart" (*E*, 269). ("Sense," throughout Austen's oeuvre, punningly, covertly signifies both the senses—the body—and the "good sense" of the mind.) Catherine, instructively, gets to be the heroine of a love story even though—or partly because—she is not only innocent but also ignorant. Henry Tilney, the cleverest of Austen's heroes, finds her attractive mostly because she admires him: the narrator comes out from between the lines to explain, "I must confess that his affection originated in nothing better than gratitude, or, in other words, that a persuasion of her partiality for him had been the only cause of giving her a serious thought." She adds, "It is a new circumstance in romance, I acknowledge, and dreadfully derogatory of an heroine's dignity; but if it be as new in common life, the credit of a wild imagination will at least be all my own" (*NA*, 243). Henry and his sister educate Catherine's eye and her taste, teaching her to love a hyacinth and putting her on the path toward having yet another hold upon happiness, the more advanced emotional capacity of loving a rose. "The mere habit of learning to love is the thing," Henry comments; "and a teachableness of disposition in a young lady is a great blessing" (*NA*, 174). The wisdom—and arrestingly Christian diction ("blessing")—belies the burlesque.

The sexual, intellectual, and moral confidence of the heroine of *Pride and Prejudice* is usually read as reflecting the high point of Jane Austen's own story, that is to say, the acme of her spirits about her own marital possibilities. Most critics go on from there to read *Mansfield Park* as her bitter, disappointed turn against brilliance—and exogamy. The story of exquisitely aware and responsive Fanny Price is not a conventional heroine's, being shaped and determined from the beginning by the stories of her mother and aunts, then by the choices and destinies of her male and female cousins and her dashing neighbor, Mary Crawford. The suggestion that people determine one another's characters and fates and can take one another's places undercuts the focus on the heroine's sole self, and her story. Fanny, the unlikely heroine, astonishingly triumphs in the inevitably tidy end, not only marrying her clerical cousin Edmund, the best man around, but also replacing his father the authoritarian Sir Thomas as the moral center of the novel universe (as she is herself replaced at Lady Bertram's side by her sister Susan). In her next novel, Jane Austen made a comic critique of her characteristic story about a poor girl's marriage for money (and status) by creating a rich heroine who is reluctant to wed. In the end Emma Woodhouse, who claims to have made the match between her governess and a neighbor and schemes to marry off her friend Harriet Smith, unromantically marries her avuncular thirty-seven-year-old bachelor almost-brother-in-law. Reading romance out of the sequence of narratives, many have concluded that Jane Austen "learned romance" too late—that as nothing had worked out for her, she dreamily imagined a heroine drenched in nostalgia and regret, longing for the hand-some sailor who got away—and marrying him, and escaping the confines of England for adventure on the high seas. The unfinished *Sanditon*, which takes place on the coast of England and elaborates modern themes of specu-lation and tourism—and also hypochondria—serves in this version of Jane's story as a sort of epilogue: although Virginia Woolf saw it as an exciting turn to new subjects and techniques of fiction, most biographical readings, shadowed by the end-stopped narrative of biography, have interpreted the (comically treated) theme of illness as reflecting the (tragic) preoccupation of the dying author.

The juvenile works that mostly remained unpublished until Chapman reluctantly brought out *Volume the First* in 1933 have convinced many read-ers recently that Jane Austen, like her own Catherine Morland, began as a bumptious eighteenth-century tomboy; the decorous narratives that follow them, they reason, show that she was "forced into prudence" (*P*, 30). In *The Madwoman in the Attic* (1979), Gilbert and Gubar, punning on the story that she covered her writing with a blotter when she heard the door squeak, argue that Jane Austen had a "cover story"—that the story her novels tell is a cover for the underlying emotional truths they conceal. Austen expressed her own personal feminist rage, they argue further, in the character of imperious Lady Catherine de Bourgh.

More recently, the American novelist Lore Segal finds a clue to the true Jane Austen in her language—the "rare passion" in which she writes of "the fate that looms before the elegant and accomplished Jane Fairfax," in *Emma*, what Segal describes as "the strikingly angry explanation that, lack of money having made independence impossible for her, she had 'with the fortitude of a devoted novitiate . . . resolved, at one-and-twenty, to complete the sacrifice and retire from all the pleasures of life, of rational intercourse, equal society, peace and hope, to penance and mortification forever' [*E*, 165]."[14] Segal's point is that the unusually strong language reveals Austen's identification with another poor unmarriageable Jane. But Jane Fairfax, seduced into making a secret engagement, is no more a self-portrait than Jane Bennet is. Like Sir Thomas Bertram, she is a complex person who demands and baffles judgment. It sometimes seems that to Jane Austen, who read so many silly novels, the very ideas of narrative and development might have been suspect, which might be why she looks back to a past before the story started, when Fanny and William Price danced together as children in Portsmouth, "when the hand-organ was in the street," or when Anne Elliot fell in love with Frederick Wentworth, when she was nineteen.

Reflecting their sense that she was conflicted or at least complex, Austen's biographers often posit a contradiction, or ambivalence, or split in their subject. Elizabeth Jenkins begins by contrasting the grace and beauty of an eighteenth-century fanlight window with the crudeness of the available equipment for personal hygiene in Austen's time; Jane Aiken Hodge, in *Only a Novel: The Double Life of Jane Austen* (1972), stresses the division between the writer's worldly life and her imaginative life, playing the role of the devoted maiden aunt in one dimension and satirizing Miss Bates in the other. "When Jane Austen was born, a star danced," writes Hodge, pleasantly entertaining the idea of Jane as Shakespeare's Rosalind, the witty and brilliant cross-dressing heroine of comedy, enchanted and fictive. (Jan Fergus's *Jane Austen: A Literary Life* [1991] takes a very different view of what "literary" means: her account of Austen's professional life insists—as Austen herself always did—on the importance of money.)

Most recent biographers have striven to debunk the "dear Jane" of legend by placing her more firmly in history, and therefore on the common ground. But biography is inevitably overdetermined, and interpretations of manners and morals tend to be anachronistic. And an ideological commitment to the notion of a distinctive self-realizing self, as well as ahistorical convictions about family dynamics and child-rearing practices, lead to strange interpretations and emphases. Was it ordinary—was it damaging—that Jane Austen should have been put out to nurse for so long, as an infant? Was it odd and destructive of family feeling that her deaf or mentally damaged brother, George, should have been sent away permanently to board with a village family? Some of her biographers (e.g., Tomalin) are too sympathetic with their subject, while others (John Halperin) dislike her too much. Park Honan and David Nokes have found more excitement than her own life story offers in the lives of her near connections: her two adventurous and successful long-lived sailor brothers; her aunt Philadelphia, who went out to India with the so-called fishing fleet to catch a husband, and caught the governor-general Warren Hastings as well; and Philadelphia's lively daughter, Eliza Hancock de Feuillide Austen, who danced at Versailles, met Marie Antoinette, married a faux French count who was beheaded during the Revolution, and later married Jane's brother Henry, who was ten years younger than she. There are other juicy anecdotes as well, about her variously scandalous aunts—Philadelphia Austen worked as a milliner, as a girl, before she was sent to husband-hunt in India; the grander Jane Leigh-Perrot was arrested and jailed for stealing a card of lace. And there is gossip about distant relatives like the wicked Lady Craven, or the adulteress who sharpened Jane's eye for the type. As Philadelphia's connection with Warren Hastings, who was tried at length in Parliament for his mismanagement of funds and people in India, provides spice for biographers who need it, so does the friendly relationship between the Austen sisters and their mentally impaired neighbor, the local great landholder, Lord Portsmouth, who studied with Mr. Austen as a boy, tangled with Lord Byron as a youth, and was married off by his greedy brothers, in middle age, to a woman—the daughter of his and Byron's solicitor—who tortured him, and helped to drive him mad. The search for gossip has been wide-ranging: *Jane Austen and Crime* (2004), by Susannah Fullerton, was inspired by the discovery that a Knatchbull hanged in Sydney, Australia, in 1844 was the half-brother of the husband of the novelist's favorite niece, Fanny Knight—the same Sir Edward Knatchbull in whose home Lord Byron's body was laid out in state, when it was brought back from Greece.[15]

Biographers have quarreled more and less fruitfully with accepted ideas and opinions: the arguments around the figure of the author Jane Austen are almost as interesting as the works themselves. Claire Tomalin has challenged the traditional picture of the country parson's isolated spinster daughter by showing that Jane met interesting people—French people, spies, and artists—in the cosmopolitan London salon of Eliza and Henry Austen. Park Honan and David Nokes make it clear that many people she either knew intimately or knew of had lives nothing like the conventional quiet, pleasant ones of the characters in her novels—in other words, that the constraints, etc., of the novels reflect her design, and not an impoverished experience. The question of class continues to baffle writers, especially Americans: in the television program "Biography," Jane Austen, whose family belonged to the pseudo-gentry, is flatly and misleadingly called "lower middle-class."

It is useful to be reminded of the nature of her links to the great and near-great, like Warren Hastings, the looter of India, whose young son was sent home to England and lived with the Austen family. Her few wry comments about hijinks in high society in her letters reveal that although she belonged to the gentry, she was far from being an inhabitant of the "world in masquerade." Nevertheless, like all readers of the newspapers in her time (and ours), Austen had personal views of the great:

> I suppose all the World is sitting in Judgement upon the Princess of Wales's Letter. Poor Woman, I shall support her as long as I can, because she *is* a Woman, & because I hate her Husband. . . . I do not know what to do about it;—but if I must give up the Princess, I am resolved at least always to think that she would have been respectable, if the Prince had behaved only tolerably by her at first.   (*Letters*, 208)

The tone is playful, but the sympathies are clear.

The word "respectable" that appears in this letter is an interesting favorite of Austen's—one of those double-faced words she likes to lean on, in the novels, that when pressed opens the gap between *seems* and *is*. "The family of Dashwood had been long settled in Sussex," *Sense and Sensibility* begins. "Their estate was large, and their residence was at Norland Park, in the centre of their property, where, for many generations, they had lived in so respectable a manner, as to engage the general good opinion of their surrounding acquaintance." This introductory paragraph raises questions: are the Dashwoods truly respectable, or do they only appear to be? (In fact the old gentleman is venal and ungrateful.) Has their "manner" (another double-faced word) of living pulled the wool over the eyes of the neighbors? How reliable anyway is the "good opinion" of a family's "surrounding acquaintance"? Jane Austen meant to amuse her sister by solemnly deliberating about whether she "must give up"—as if she knew her personally—Princess Caroline. But by saying that the princess would have been a better person, or maybe only a more "respectable" one (are moral worth and reputation the same?), had she had a different husband, she makes the point her novels insist on, that connections, marriage especially, have real effects on individual character. (Mr. John Dashwood, remember, was "not an ill-disposed young man, unless to be rather cold hearted, and rather selfish, is to be ill-disposed: but he was, in general, well respected; for he conducted himself with propriety in the discharge of his ordinary duties. Had he married a more amiable woman, he might have been made still more respectable than he was:—he might even have been made amiable himself; for he was very young when he married, and very fond of his wife. But Mrs. John Dashwood was a strong caricature of himself;—more narrow-minded and selfish" [*SS*, 5].) As *Mansfield Park* insists, and as all the novels make clear, some people's characters are weaker than others, and most of them are seriously affected, indeed altered, by the company they keep. And people's efforts to be or to seem respectable inflect both character and judgments of it.

Especially at their least private, and especially on the subject of people in high places, Austen's letters allow one to glimpse the writer weighing her words and savoring them, hinting that sound and syntax matter as much as what words signify. The biographer George Holbert Tucker compares her famous letter to James Stanier Clarke, the librarian who invited her to dedicate *Emma* to the Prince, with Dr. Johnson's famous letter to Lord Chesterfield. With a pen very delicately poisoned, she wrote:

> I am honoured by the Prince's thanks and very much obliged to yourself for the kind manner in which you mention the work. . . . Under every interesting circumstance which your own talents and literary labours have placed you in, or the favour of the Regent bestowed, you have my best wishes. Your recent appointments I hope are a step to something still better. In my opinion, the service of a court can hardly be too well paid, for immense must be the sacrifice of time and feeling required by it. (*Letters*, 312)

Her ability to handle and to dispatch the Regent's overbearing librarian, her insistence on going "on in my own *Style* and my own way," despite his invitation to write a romance on the house of Saxe-Coburg, suggest her strength of character. The scandals in high life of the time, reported in the papers, are foils to Austen's respectable novels, which implicitly, correctively respond to them. Seeing Jane Austen in context, it is impossible not to see that like Fanny, trapped in Portsmouth and dreaming of the elegant ceremony of tea at Mansfield Park, she was nostalgic for a world that seemed to be slipping ever further away. Even at Mansfield, the tea ceremony—presided over by the butler, suggestively named Baddeley—was a refuge for Fanny, an orderly ritual that made for a respite from the demands and chaos of a life lived alongside other people. It is wrong to read Jane Austen nostalgically, as representing Olde England in the golden age: she is rather, as Chapman wrote, the novelist of nostalgia for home.

"A shilling life will give you all the facts," W. H. Auden wrote—in a tone dismissive of both facts and biographies. Although the shilling disappeared years ago, short lives continue to proliferate, along with long ones—and facts slide into fictions in and around them. You can get the life story of Jane Austen these days in the brief Penguin life by Carol Shields, or the front matter of a mass market paperback, or a Wikipedia article. She was born on December 16, 1775, at Steventon Parsonage in Hampshire, the seventh child and second daughter of the rector, the Oxford graduate George Austen, and his wife, Cassandra Leigh. George was soon hard-pressed to feed his growing family: he farmed a little and taught boys who boarded in the house. Claire Tomalin vividly imagines the two little girls growing up with brothers and boarders, a crowd of noisy, door-banging boys, as in Fanny's home in Portsmouth.[16]

But Steventon Parsonage housed a more high-minded and literary family than the Prices. The Leighs had connections with Oxford as well as with the aristocracy; the Austens were also affiliated with the university. George was supportive of his writing daughter: in 1797 he sent out one of her manuscripts, "First Impressions," to a publisher. Mrs. Austen wrote amusing sociable light verse (Jane inherited the knack and the habit). For a short time the Austen girls and their cousin, Jane Cooper, attended a school in Oxford, and then in Southampton; they left after a typhoid fever epidemic, which killed their Aunt Cooper, who helped bring them home. A year later Jane and Cassandra were sent to the Abbey School in Reading; when they left school for good, Jane was nine. After that the sisters lived at home with their parents—after George's death in 1805, their mother—in the south of England, at Steventon in Hampshire, Bath, Clifton, Southampton, and finally Chawton, near Steventon. They helped with the housework: Jane was responsible for breakfast. Separately, by turns, partly in order to help out in times of sickness and childbearing, Jane and Cassandra made visits to their married brothers in London and in Kent. Although they were not widely considered remarkable in their time, Jane's novels—*Pride and Prejudice* especially—were admired and well received by readers, who included Richard Brinsley Sheridan, and by reviewers, including Walter Scott. But she did not live to be lionized before she died, on July 18, 1817, at not yet forty-two.

We read about other people, in biographies and novels, looking for bad or good examples, trying to escape our own lives and seeking models that might help us improve them. Master shapers of narratives about lives and selves, novelists are promising biographical subjects, women novelists most of all: the lives of Bronte and Eliot and Woolf, of George Sand, Izak Dinesen, Colette, and Edith Wharton continue to be chewed over. We read about them to learn how they came to be unique, creative, successful—and what their love lives were like. In the case of Jane Austen, the record is skimpy and full of holes, and there is no strong story line. A writer from girlhood, she had to have written a great many more letters than remain:[17] we have none written before she was twenty (we have a note Byron wrote when he was not yet eleven) and none at all from May 1801 to September 1804, her interesting late twenties. Few observers recorded their impressions of her. All this has strengthened the biographical force of literary criticism. Jean-Paul Sartre, in his biography of Flaubert, describes the boy Gustave, destined to be famous for pitilessly anatomizing his fictitious characters, intently watching through a window as his doctor father takes apart a dead body. The novels are the lens through which we look at the life and read the letters of a writer—and different biographers read those differently. Claire Tomalin interprets the emotional coldness of Austen's narrative voice as the result of Jane's mother's having put her out to nurse for certain critical months.

Under the circumstances, even textual analysis can slide into biographical reading. Among the few bits of evidence of Austen's practice as a novelist are the changes she made in the second edition of her first novel, from which the following sentence was dropped:

> Lady Middleton's delicacy was shocked; and in order to banish so improper a subject as the mention of a natural daughter, she actually took the trouble of saying something herself about the weather.   (SS, 384)

In the first edition of *Sense and Sensibility*, this sentence follows Mrs. Jennings's uncalled-for remark about a presumptive "natural daughter" of Colonel Brandon: Chapman explained that the author deleted it "in the interests of propriety." Claudia Johnson takes issue with him in the Norton Critical Edition (2002): "This is not quite right, because Austen actually retains the scandalous phrase. It might be apter to say that Austen curbed the irreverence of her satire on propriety." Tony Tanner had questioned Chapman's interpretation over thirty years before in a note in the 1969 Penguin edition, asking whether it was Jane Austen's sense of propriety or her publisher's that caused the alteration. He offered instead a "simpler explanation": that on second thought Austen decided Lady Middleton had not heard her mother's comment. "Jane Austen has just made it clear that Mrs. Jennings has lowered her voice expressly to speak to Elinor so that Lady Middleton might be expected to have remained unaware of the remark and her delicacy hence unruffled."[18]

But there is an equally simple, more plausible explanation. A scant five pages earlier, interrupting Mrs. Jennings's teasing about Elinor's putative boyfriend, Lady Middleton observes "that it rained very hard," to express "her ladyship's great dislike for all such inelegant subjects of raillery as delighted her husband and mother." One of the subjects on which Jane Austen was especially brilliant is the social usefulness of empty talk, and the way such talk exposes character. Especially talk about the weather: in *Pride and Prejudice*, after dinner at Rosings, everyone gathers "round the fire to hear Lady Catherine determine what weather they were to have on the morrow" (*PP*, 166). (Lady Catherine fancies that she controls the weather as Lady Middleton fancies she is a genuine lady.) But to use exactly the same gambit within five pages in a novel is to have rather too much of a good thing. In dropping Lady Middleton's second strategic change of subject, Jane Austen's goal I think was neither to condone propriety nor to soften her satire on it. She revised to improve the text; the dropped sentence is evidence only that she weighed every word.

Austen followed Fielding in declaring—in a novel—that "human nature" was her subject; she took up the role of novelist as Fielding the jurist conceived it, as a connoisseur of character and its judge. But unlike Fielding, who presided over the feast of human nature in the guise of a garrulous, generous innkeeper, and unlike George Eliot, who would expatiate in her own philosophical character during the intervals between the action, the Austen narrator rarely uses the first-person singular, giving us only a shadow of what the Victorian critic Edward Dowden, writing of George Eliot in 1872, called "that 'second self' who writes her books, and lives and speaks through them." Dowden continues, sketching an ideal—and very pure—authorial self in a humanist rhapsody:

> Such a second self of an author is perhaps more substantial than any mere human personality encumbered with the accidents of flesh and

blood and daily living. It stands at some distance from the primary self, and differs considerably from its fellow. It presents its person to us with fewer reserves; it is independent of local and temporary motives of speech or of silence; it knows no man after the flesh; it is more than an individual; it utters secrets, but secrets which all men of all ages are to catch; while, behind it, lurks well pleased the veritable historical self secure from unpertinent observation and criticism. With this second self of George Eliot it is, not with the actual historical person, that we have to do.[19]

George Eliot chose a nom de plume for her second self; Jane Austen did not. The difference begins to suggest a big difference between them. The "second self" Austen tantalizes us with is unnamed, elusive, and ambiguous; it invites us to imagine her ("A Lady") as ladylike and reticent, or as divided against or alienated from that lady self. It is telling that this kind of modern diagnosis does not ordinarily get mustered to account for the practice of her contemporary, Sir Walter Scott, the also anonymous novelist who was famous in his time as "The Great Unknown." When he finally came out as the author of *Waverley* and other novels in his "General Preface" of 1829, Scott made the point that "the mental organization of the Novelist" was "characterized, to speak craniologically, by an extraordinary development of the passion for delitescency!," or self-concealment. Scott confessed his "secret satisfaction in baffling" the extreme curiosity of the reader.[20] It is not hard to imagine that Jane Austen had a similar satisfaction. Playing with truth is part of the game of fiction.

An otherwise perceptive critic of Austen's novels, Scott was one of those who read Elizabeth Bennet's "confession" to her sister that she fell in love with Mr. Darcy on "first seeing his beautiful grounds at Pemberley" (*PP*, 373) as evidence of the heroine's materialism—and therefore of the unknown lady novelist's. Complaining, "But where is Cupid?," he concluded that while young ladies are all for love, older ones—like this lady novelist, presumably—are leery of it. Scott would have gleefully seized on Cassandra Austen's memorandum, which records that *Pride and Prejudice* was drafted by a young woman (suggesting it was revised and completed by a middle-aged one), to account for its mix of romance and anti-romance. But if rewriting enhanced it, Austen's characteristic irony rather than her aging is surely at the heart of the conjunction of romance and mockery of romance: looking at Pemberley,

Elizabeth is also looking with amusement at herself looking—as novel-readers as well as novelists do.

It seems to me a mistake to insist on her spinsterhood as the single always-operative fact of Jane Austen's life ("an old maid" who writes like a god, D. A. Miller calls her[21]). There is real risk, as well, in a biographical reading of, for instance, the theme the novels repeat, that one sister's story helps determine another's, which runs through the novels from *Sense and Sensibility* to *Persuasion*, and figures importantly as well in the youthful stories, where sisters—vastly less genteel, as Lucy Steele might say, than in the mature fiction—compete with one another outright. While it does reflect a circumstance of Jane Austen's personal life, it is also an aspect of the larger themes of the novels, the interdependence of characters in a community. The novels explore the ways that sister destinies determine one another and weave the fabric of society: Elinor Dashwood's sound good sense is a necessary reflex of her sister's (and their mother's) romantic sensibility, and the two oldest Bennet girls strive to correct the excessive silliness of their sisters. The first paragraph of *Mansfield Park* sums up the back-story: Miss Maria Ward of Huntingdon having had the good luck to captivate Sir Thomas Bertram, one of her sisters made do with Mr. Norris, to whom Sir Thomas could give a living, and the other married to disoblige her family (and in the end herself). The competing children and childlessness of these three braided unions are the makings of this novel about the second generation.

What should one make of that final sentence of *Sense and Sensibility*, the offbeat conclusion that Marianne and Elinor, living near one another after their marriages, "though sisters," continued to be loving friends? Biographers used to rhapsodize about the beautiful mutual devotion of the Austen sisters; more recent biographical fictions have tended to take a darker line, and see their twinned lives as crippled, awkward, and difficult, shadowed by mutual envy and resentment. Like virtuous virgins and predatory rakes, heavy fathers and scheming dowagers, the pairs or groups of sisters in Austen's novels are not first of all traces of true history but, rather, tropes that derive from the stories people tell—fairytales, folktales, plays, and other novels—as well as the families they live in: there's no prising them apart. Part of the problem in imagining Jane Austen as a character is that Jane Austen set the standard for conceiving character, and noticing how it reveals itself. The well-chosen detail, in her hands, is the essence of character. And we have precious few of those about her.

Nothing about mean and meddlesome Mrs. Norris, for example—not her having "found herself obliged to be attached to the Rev. Mr. Norris" once her younger sister married up, not her abusive treatment of Fanny, not her well-meaning, wrongheaded intrusions into the lives of her luckier nieces—makes her so memorable and real as her (offstage) wheedling of a cream cheese from the housekeeper at Sotherton, and then carefully bearing off the little prize. The smallness and banality of the detail make it count. Together with the bit of heath and the four beautiful pheasant's eggs she manages to acquire, it brings her character to vivid life—and also reflects the truth Jane Austen insists on, that so much depends on such little things. Like the half-glasses of wine and the very small eggs Mr. Woodhouse recommends, like Sir Walter Elliot's praise of Gowland's lotion for the complexion, the cream cheese that Mrs. Norris characteristically thrusts upon Fanny, making her hold it on the carriage ride home so as to give her cousin Maria more room, is worth paragraphs of character analysis or philosophical reflection. As Scott wrote in his anonymous review of *Emma*, this novelist's genius is for noticing the details.

We know too few details about Jane Austen: that she was slender and above the middle height, with hazel eyes (like her father's, and her Emma's), and that she fell short of being a beauty. Asymmetry, mentioned by some, is hinted at in Cassandra's sketch, and Sir Egerton Brydges remembered that her cheeks were a little too full. The quilt and the bit of lace at Chawton suggest that as one might have guessed—as James Edward Austen-Leigh insisted—she excelled at fine work with her hands, and was proud of the skill. We also know that she liked to dance, and enjoyed practicing on the piano. Too often recycled, what anecdotes we do have come to seem empty. Did she really fall down in a faint, in her mid-twenties, when told that she and Cassandra would be moving, with their parents, to Bath? If in fact she did, was it because she hated to leave the English countryside that nourished her genius, or because she hated Bath in particular, or living with her parents, at her age, as a dependent daughter who was never consulted?[22] Aren't all of those interpretations based on where we are and what we think we know?

Imagining that "Jane dreamed of rescue" from spinsterhood, the Canadian novelist Carol Shields repeats the most poignant romantic legend of all, that "once, idly, she covered a page of her father's parish ledger with the names of fantasy husbands: 'Henry Frederick Howard Fitzwilliam,' 'Edmund Arthur William Mortimer.' These were noble-sounding gentlemen with a ring of fortune about them," Shields comments—too credulously, it seems to me. As I imagine the literary girl writing them out, I hear her deliberate evocations of the history of England, and Shakespeare's plays, and romantic fiction, and comedies of manners: might she not have been joking to herself, or partly joking? The earnestly sympathetic biographer continues: "Then, out of a different longing, or perhaps terror, she wrote 'Jack Smith,' to be married to 'Jane Smith late Austen.'"[23] But it is hard to know how to interpret the emotions of the long-dead young writer of such a piece of "evidence." When Jane was nine, her mother wrote in a letter that "if Cassandra's head had been going to be cut off, Jane would have her's cut off too," a witty comment heavily overdetermined, in retrospect, not only by the legend of Scheherazade, the storyteller, but also by the reality of the guillotine, so active at the time. So is it fair to conclude that Jane Austen decided never to marry after Cassandra made the decision—that is, after the death of Tom Fowle, Cassandra's fiancé, in the West Indies? And did the sisters grow closer, or less close, as a consequence? Can we interpret the bits and pieces of a lived life as if it were a deliberate composition? Can we not?

The most overdetermined of all the anecdotes, romantics and anti-romantics agree, is the story that at twenty-seven (Charlotte Lucas's age, and Anne Elliot's) Jane Austen accepted and then rejected, within hours, a proposal of marriage. The man was the twenty-one-year-old landowner Harris Bigg-Wither, whose sisters were the intimate friends of the Austen sisters—a man "very plain in person—awkward, & even uncouth in manner—[with] nothing but his size to recommend him," according to another friend.[24] Jane changed her mind after a sleepless night, and arose to refuse him, and hastily leave his family's house, where the Austen sisters had been staying: and what do we know from that? Does the novelist describe the shape of her own life when she writes of Anne Elliot that having been "forced into prudence in her youth, she learned romance as she grew older?" (*P*, 30). Or is it wrong to read *Persuasion* biographically, and as a consciously valedictory utterance, or last word? Especially since William Deresiewicz has argued that Austen's second trilogy, *Mansfield Park, Emma*, and *Persuasion*, shows the influence of the Romantic poets,[25] an alternative quotation mischievously presents itself: the couplet in Byron's *Don Juan* about "the sad truth that hovers o'er my desk," which "Turns what was once romantic to burlesque" (IV, 3, 7–8). For reasons of temperament and taste, because of how she looked at things and the books she chose to read, romance and anti-romance were in dialogue in Jane Austen's mind from her earliest works to her last ones, as they were in Lord Byron's.

The private lives of people whose name is publicly known; the hidden secrets of the polished and the poised, and of well-bred virgins especially; what the writer failed or feared to spell out; the facts that mysteriously generate fictions—our ever more intense appetites for these are mutually stimulating. They are more ravenous now for many reasons, not only the vogue for memoir and "reality" television and the expense of spirit and space on personalities and would-be celebrities in the social media, but also the rise and sustained popularity of the novel in Austen's tradition, and its off-shoots and aftereffects, which include biography. What the nosy pertinacious reader craves about Jane Austen is what the novel that Jane Austen invented provides, not so much an account of the events of a woman's life as a suggestion of the flavor of her character and way of seeing, and of what the arc of such a woman's life suggests about life generally. My favorite anecdote—the inverse of the story about covering her paper with a blotter when the tell-tale door squeaked—is not an anecdote at all but a glimpse of her habitual existence. Her niece Marianne recalled that she "would sit quietly working beside the fire in the library, saying nothing for a good while, and then would suddenly burst out laughing, jump up and run across the room to a table where pens and paper were lying, write something down, and then come back to the fire and go on quietly working as before."[26] The watercolor that shows her seated on the ground, in a blue dress and a bonnet with its strings untied, facing away from the viewer, is the most expressive portrait we could have.

Bellagio, 1996: More Notes for an Austen Memoir

So deeply, earnestly, and gallantly did the heart surgeon from Oman look into my eyes that I can't remember whether he kissed my hand. "Ah, but where I save one life," he murmured, "you save hundreds!"

I blushed for both of us.

The surgeon was part of an international team of doctors, medical ethicists, anthropologists, and administrators gathered for a five-day conference at the Villa Serbelloni—the Rockefeller Conference Center in Bellagio, Italy—to devise "Strategies for Controlling the Traffic in Organs for Transplantation." I was at the villa for a monthlong residency to write about Jane Austen. My greater privilege, my longer period of support, might suggest that I was the more distinguished as well as the luckier guest at the villa, but the surgeon and I knew better. I was the elder, but there was no contest about our relative usefulness in the world and therefore, for all that it was so wonderfully out of this world, our status at the villa. The surgeon and his people were busy and concerned with urgent matters. They could manage only a week on the shore of Lake Como—unlike my group of scholars, artists, and writers, who seemed to have all the time in the world. From the way the Belgian leader of the conference rushed through the marble halls followed by his secretary, you would think the villa was a hospital and he its chief—and the rest of us the inmates, as one artist in residence caustically observed. The busy chief made us feel defensive. The surgeon from Oman, on the other hand, had beautiful manners: he was a pleasure to talk with even at breakfast.

Taking meals with people who come through the villa is the only thing required of monthlong residents, a tiny and usually pleasurable duty, a social obligation but also a moral one that incidentally can provide food for moralizing (as in Jane Austen). Even fleeting encounters with international experts in this and that serve to sharpen your sense of the world and your place in it. Being reminded of the grisly traffic in body parts between poor and rich countries fairly forced one to see oneself as overprivileged even under ordinary conditions, that is, even when one was not being served on pretty plates in a luxurious villa in Italy. Well before the "Bodily Organs" group arrived, many of us had whispered to one another that life here was not only too good to be true—at a pastoral remove from ordinary reality—but also too good to be deserved by the likes of us. One tended—or some of us did—to feel that no matter how promising and ambitious a work in progress was it couldn't possibly merit the reward of all this natural and manmade beauty, not to mention the servants.

From the way he shook out his linen napkin and ordered his eggs, I could tell that the surgeon from Oman had no such trouble. He had sat down across from me at the breakfast table after making a courtly little bow; his gallant riposte to my apology for being only a professor of English literature, when I introduced myself, made it clear he was practiced in the exchange of even unexpected pleasantries. In a fast world where a few hours can bring you from Oman or New York to Lake Como, a world where it's possible to slice into a beating heart or to sell your brother's kidney, some eternal verities persist, his manner telegraphed. Privately, I reflected that Jane Austen would have been diverted by the mutual politeness with which we acknowledged our differences and left them intact. Like Elizabeth and Darcy dancing at Netherfield, the surgeon and I were playing by the conversational rules, and consciously. "It is *your* turn to say something now, Mr. Darcy," says Elizabeth. "*I* talked about the dance, and *you* ought to make some kind of remark on the size of the room, or the number of couples" (*PP*, 91). There was little we could say to one another, and mutual pleasure had to come in the saying. So the heart surgeon from Oman, whose patients saw him as a god, pleased himself by deferring to a representative of The Humanities, and told me I saved more lives than he did by teaching people to read Jane Austen. Or so I imagined, for he couldn't possibly—or could he?—be laughing *at* me. Was his true conversational aim, like Elizabeth's when she's dancing with Darcy, to make further conversation impossible? His soft deep eyes and voice made it hard for me to believe that.

International exchange was encouraged at the villa along with interdisciplinary exchange, which can be harder, especially when the disciplines are not parallel. (He had no trouble reading Austen; I couldn't begin to tie off an artery.) And because of his schedule our interaction was doomed to be brief. It was a little bit different within the group of resident fellows. Two weeks together and shared memories of departed comical confreres and extraordinary pasta dishes had established some common ground between me and the Indian economist, the red-bearded novelist from California, the food writer with long pale nails, the Ecuadorian musicologist, and their more and less significant others. The small study groups that came through for a few days of meetings were always conversational hard going: small talk was difficult with specialists in sustainable development, global investing, or hospital restructuring, especially when they had little English or French. Jet-lagged, tired from focusing on the possibility of a future for life on earth, these experts tended to drift toward sleep in the evenings with soporific chat about the weather and the best connections to Milan. And at breakfast some preoccupied people didn't get beyond asking for the sugar, please.

But the doctor from Oman was urgent, vivid; bedroom eyes and bedside manner were both operative. Designed to level the interpersonal playing field between a doctor in expensive Italian shoes and a body he's evaluating for opening, his manner didn't contribute to my comfort. I looked down at my running shoes, then (inarticulate as Darcy dancing) mumbled that I had no ambition to save people's lives, only to amuse them. He corrected me: Jane Austen, he said sternly, is a great artist. Folding his napkin with elegant long fingers, he repeated that art saves people's lives. What would life be with-out art? We would be living as if we were already dead, life would mean so little. I was touched. Soon he reached for his fine leather briefcase, and was off to pursue the business of salvation in which he had so graciously, for a moment, included me. Surely he was one of those people who admire the novels for providing safe haven in a troubled world, an imaginary great good place where all's accustomed, ceremonious, where innocence and beauty may be born again without fanfare, and eternally preserved. A place like Mans-field Park—or the idea of it, the rituals of civilized behavior that Fanny Price yearns for in Portsmouth, I think, glancing out the window toward the rose-mary hedge surrounding the locus amoenus that is the villa.

I imagine the beautiful little boy he must have been, solemn in his navy blue school uniform in some rich exotic pavilion, being lectured by a pale man, an adventurous Oxbridge graduate who has nervously dared to follow Lord Byron's footsteps to the East, on the pretext of bringing enlightenment to the natives. The man introduces the boys to fabulous oddities: daffodils, parsonages, shrubberies, curricles, white soup. He presents Austen's novels to them as classics of English literature and records of English life in its finest tone, praising the naturalness of the characters, the purity of the language, the plausibility and elegance of the plots. He insists that the boys notice how the concern with manners persuasively underwrites distinctions in levels of moral awareness; he insists that aesthetic and moral values override what some of them object to as snobbery. He praises, equally, art and moral seriousness. The cleverest of the boys—the surgeon-to-be would have been one—hope to emulate the ways the best people talk and feel in the world of the novel, which this world just might resemble, if only our sense of life were perfected, as it might be by the arts.

Or would he have been introduced to Austen much later, in England itself, by a cultivated pipe-smoking professor of science who set an example by gracefully mediating between what C. P. Snow had called the two cultures? Perhaps a follower of the philosopher Gilbert Ryle, who famously acknowl-edged that yes, he did read novels—all six of them. Surprising myself, I pull up my moral socks and rebuke myself for thinking in stereotypes, a danger-ous, provincial habit that a residency at the Villa Serbelloni was meant to correct, and a habit Jane Austen herself so effectively questioned.

As I left the breakfast room, I tried to take his point, not much made in the circles I usually frequented. If the notion of the importance and saving grace of the literary classics still prevailed in pockets of high culture, humanities departments in the West had jettisoned it long ago. The prevalent view among my colleagues and students was that the classics functioned as cultural capital within an unfair economy. To people who thought about it at all, "Jane Austen" was shorthand for a Great Tradition conceived for their own purposes by dead white men, and for those stately homes of England's ruling class, monuments to ill-gotten gains like Sir Thomas Bertram's, that the National Trust was now pretending belonged to everyone. The splashy Jane Austen movies of the mid-nineties, just coming out the year of my chat with the surgeon, reinforced that view. (The man from Oman would have been too busy and serious to see those movies, but someone who arrived at the villa fresh from a screening of Douglas McGrath's *Emma* informed me that now he knew *that* one of her books, anyway.) My colleagues at home looked for literary value, if they continued to think it existed, in dark and difficult texts that spoke for the inarticulate and the powerless, fragmented or jagged texts that reflected things as they are. Most of my fellow scholars at the villa were writing about pollution, refuse, bloody conflicts; many of the artists boasted identities created by the horrors of history. The poet from Mexico City "identified" as a Nahuatl; the cultural studies man from Boston introduced himself as a son of Holocaust survivors; the glamorous children's book writer was "targeting" early adolescent girls of color. Lined up opposite my Jewish name in the printed matter distributed to residents, Jane Austen's name—"the homely quaintness of the Christian name, the cool elegance of the surname"—would seem to signal that I (following Trilling) was self-divided, warring against my ethnic identity. On the face of it I was retrograde and reactionary, if not merely silly and superficial.

I go back to my room and reflect that in certain circles, at least, Jane Austen is still safe as houses. I leaf through my notes on the great house. In Austen's novels, her critics write, the house is the ultimate commodity. (Variously, they cite other writers influenced by Richardson, on houses as imprisoning enclosures, and/or as images of the female body.) I make lists. In all the novels but *Emma*, the heroine's vulnerability is a function of her want of a home of her own, and her desire for one; her enemies are either the legal owners of substantial properties, the law itself, or both. In all the novels except *Persuasion*, his real property is surety for the hero's moral substance. Bad men (and women, too) defraud Marianne and Elinor Dashwood, and Anne Elliot, of houses that ought by right to be theirs. The heroine of a story Austen never finished, "Catharine; or, The Bower," is an orphan forced to live with her cranky aunt; she treasures the private place—more a gazebo or pavilion than a house—that she built with her women friends, who have been obliged to move out of the country. Except in *Persuasion*, the only completed novel that entertains the possibility of a heroine's lighting out for the high seas, a big house is the big prize: is the man who owns it only a synecdoche for it?

In the marble mansion in northern Italy, the macho novelist from California teases me about my project. "Admit it, she would have loved it here," he tells me; "wouldn't Jane have thought this place was really something?" His silken tones cover a barbed point, the commonly held belief that although she pretends to value higher things, deep down Jane Austen was cold and calculating (as Madame de Stael said, *vulgaire*), that she overvalued what Anthony Trollope, a comic novelist in her tradition and a less stringent moralist, indulgently called "the good things." Surely my interlocutor has in mind that famous moment when Elizabeth Bennet reflects that to be "mistress" of Pemberley would be "something." Many readers besides Scott have imagined that Jane Austen reveals herself at this moment—her prejudice, that is, in favor of wealth and power. When W. H. Auden praised her for showing "the amorous effects of brass," or money, surely he too had this scene in mind.

It has become a crux. David Nokes, in his 1997 biography, describes Jane's emotions on first seeing Godmersham, the great estate of her lucky brother Edward Austen Knight, in 1798, by imaginatively "quoting" from "First Impressions," the lost first version of *Pride and Prejudice*—which of course might have had no such scene in it:

> As Elizabeth, her heroine in "First Impressions," expressed it, on catching her first sight of Mr Darcy's mansion, Pemberley: "She had never seen a place for which nature had done more, or where natural beauty had been so little counteracted by an awkward taste." Nor could Jane quite suppress the thought that sprang unprompted to her heroine's mind "that to be mistress of Pemberley [or Godmersham] might be something!"[27]

In another recent biographical work of nonfiction, Elizabeth's famous reflection on first seeing Pemberley is relocated to the mind of Lady Byron, seeing Newstead Abbey for the first time years after her estranged husband had left her and England forever. David Crane expands on Annabella's (surely disingenuous) account of her feelings ("altogether those of gratification . . . I seemed to contemplate the portrait of a friend") by claiming they owe something "to Lizzy Bennett's [sic] visit to Pemberley in *Pride and Prejudice*, a novel Annabella admired."[28]

"Set her free, won't you," says the red-bearded Californian, urging me to follow my bliss, as he himself has done by breaking out of the confines of academic scholarship and venturing to the wilder shores of Creative Writing. "I can really see her here, can't you? Let yourself go. Go ahead and conjecture, put her in these wonderful gracious rooms: there must be some months or years of her life that are unaccounted for by her biographers. Imagine she up and fled the family parsonage and flew off to meet a guy at Lake Como; imagine her walking down these grand stairs."

We are walking down to dinner, he and his significant other both heavy-footed in their high-heeled, silver-studded cowboy boots. The stairs are plenty broad enough to accommodate Jane Austen as well. I can almost hear her refuse, in Elizabeth's words when Darcy asks her to walk with him and the Bingley sisters, saying that we three "are charmingly group'd, and appear to uncommon advantage. The picturesque would be spoilt by admitting a fourth" (*PP*, 53). An imagination in the grip of Jane Austen moves more logically toward self-consciousness than free flight. California suspects as much, and he is still hoping to nail me. With a glance at the lithe former graduate student clinging to his arm, he says: "Imagine she had a flaming love affair in a wild storm, just across the lake there, with Stendhal."

"Or Byron," his friend adds, pleased to be invited by his glance into the literary discussion. "Like in that Tom Stoppard play—doesn't he leave England for mysterious reasons? Or am I thinking of that novel by A. S. Byatt?"

"Byron doesn't actually appear in *Arcadia*, but yes," California drawls, then turns to me. "You know," he says earnestly, "she's right. Even the most serious scholar, these days, is perfectly free to try her hand at postmodern pastiche."

We are going downstairs to dinner: bound by the house rules to courtesy and collegiality, I smile.

The Road to Pemberley

Fictitious great houses in real English counties are the sites and in effect the substance of Jane Austen's novels. While in fact the ownership of houses in her own family's neighborhood was in flux in the years when Jane was growing up, the novels suggest that everyone who really matters is thoroughly grounded, or expects and deserves to be. *Sense and Sensibility* begins with the unfair expulsion of the deserving Dashwood women from Norland, the family home in Sussex; *Persuasion* begins with the words, "Sir Walter Elliot, of Kellynch-hall, in Somersetshire," identifying this Sir Walter as the owner of this house. Geographical specificity grounds the stories and insists on the real estates. Two of Austen's novels take their titles from the names of houses; Rosings and Sotherton, Hartfield and Donwell, signify as the names of characters do. The habitual Austen reader is able to rank even the houses at the margins of the stories—Lucas Lodge, Allenham, Maple Grove, Enscombe, Everingham—as to real elegance and moral heft. Their qualities are imbricated in the worth of the people who own and/or admire and want them, therefore in their rank and wealth and their character. When Elizabeth notices the perfect balance between nature and art in the house and grounds at Pemberley, we cannot but see it as a metaphor for the man who owns it and ultimately for her marriage to him.

With the exception of Sotherton, whose spaces can be mapped,[29] the imposing houses and extensive grounds are described only generally: there are no particular pieces of furniture, ample woods but few trees (save those leafy ones that will remain at Norland, and those threatened by improvers, at Sotherton and environs). Like the people, whose features are also unimportant, the houses have character in the most abstract sense of the word, a distinguishing quality we register and measure. The highest-ranking place is Pemberley: the park is ten miles round, and it brings in ten thousand a year. (The reiterated round number is perhaps a joke, as Bharat Tandon suggests numbers are in Austen, about the factual aspect of fiction and/or the metrical aspect of prose; certainly it serves here as a mnemonic. Mr. Rushworth gets twelve thousand a year out of Sotherton: money isn't everything.[30]) The name of Darcy's estate is first dropped familiarly by Miss Bingley at Netherfield Park, which her brother merely rents: she recalls it as the location of Darcy's great library, the work of many generations. Book II of *Pride and Prejudice* ends with the lilting promise, "To Pemberley, therefore, they were to go." Pemberley is Jane Austen's version of Paradise Hall in *Tom Jones*, of Christian's heavenly paradise in *Pilgrim's Progress*. Although Elizabeth Bennet inspects it thoroughly, in the company of Darcy's housekeeper, in the reader's imagination it shimmers like a mirage. Daphne du Maurier borrowed the fairytale music of the name for the first sentence of her popular gothic novel, *Rebecca* (1938): "Last night I dreamt I went to Manderley again."

For Jane Austen the woman, elegant houses were places to visit. She is caustic, writing to Cassandra, about the twenty-eight chairs in the library of her brother Edward's house in Kent, and about how rich everyone is in that county. Visiting, she enjoyed the comforts of away-from-home from a critical little distance. We follow her lead when we seem to time-travel and enter great houses, reading her novels.

By Austen's time, the modern practice of touring rich people's houses had been fashionable for many years. With money to spend, curiosity about the world, and the vaguer Romantic aspiration to feel new feelings in new places, visitors from the Continent were already touring England in the seventeenth century; young Englishmen of rank, often accompanied by their tutors, similarly toured the celebrated sights of Paris, Switzerland, and Rome. In this pursuit as in others, the rising middle class aped the gentry. Edward Austen Knight's grand tour of the Continent was intended to equip him for life as a squire. Richardson's middle-class heroine Clarissa Harlowe begins her fatal correspondence with the aristocratic rake Robert Lovelace because her uncle is about to accompany a young man on his Grand Tour, and asks her—the family's best letter-writer—to get his advice about where to go. Travelers' talk, memoirs, pictures, and maps identified the cities and monuments and views that a man who wanted polishing—a lucky young Edward Austen, for example—was obliged to take a detour to see. Seeing those sights would improve his judgment and taste, make him a gentleman in the new eighteenth-century style—not simply a landholder whose virtue derived from his possessions but a man of taste, a man whose social class was clear from his manners. Travelers brought back objects of art for their homes—sometimes, like Edward Austen Knight, paintings of themselves against a foreign or a classical landscape. Lord Byron would venture further, but most continental travelers, even in the early nineteenth century, were pleased to get as far east as Venice, where the aging Lady Mary Wortley Montagu had enjoyed receiving handsome young Englishmen and their tutors in her salon in the 1750s.

Decades before that, the journalist and novelist Daniel Defoe had made wide-ranging journeys of "the whole island of Great Britain" in his restless search for general information about business and progress and the physical world. His *Tour*, published in 1724–1726, was too eclectic and exhausting to be a model for leisure-time travelers, but the idea of visiting certain places in the nation grew incrementally in the years after Defoe died, along with national wealth and pride. Highly productive manufacturing towns were his main focus, but he was proud of the stately country homes of the aristocracy as well. "I think, any traveler from abroad, who would desire to see how the English gentry live, and what pleasure they enjoy, should come into Suffolk and Cambridgeshire, and take but a light circuit among the country seats of the gentlemen . . . and they would soon be convinc'd, that not France, no not Italy itself, can out-do them," Defoe boasted. He was particularly impressed by Chatsworth, the supremely civilized stately home the Duke of Devonshire had built in what was then a "howling wilderness" in Derbyshire (Darcy's county). In 1975 financial reasons obliged the Duchess, the former Deborah Mitford, to give it up to the National Trust for everyone to visit.[31]

In the course of the eighteenth century, as wealth increased and real and would-be English milords polished themselves by touring the Continent, their sisters and cousins and aunts and uncles developed an appetite for the designated scenic and architectural beauty spots of England, Scotland, and Wales. In the 1790s, when the Continent was closed to British travelers, tourism inside England increased. The passion percolated through the moneyed classes: Elizabeth Bennet's aunt Gardiner, who is married to a businessman, invites her to tour the Lakes, and Elizabeth's response to the invitation suggests how common such trips were at the turn of the eighteenth century. "Oh! What hours of transport we shall spend!," she cries, connecting motion and emotion in a pun that mocks the Romantic traveler. In advance she anticipates the profit and the pride of having consumed a fashionable entertainment, telling her aunt:

> "And when we *do* return, it shall not be like other travelers, without being able to give one accurate idea of any thing. We *will* know where we have gone—we *will* recollect what we have seen. Lakes, mountains, and rivers, shall not be jumbled together in our imaginations; nor, when we attempt to describe any particular scene, will we begin by quarreling about its relative situation. Let *our* first effusions be less insupportable than those of the generality of travelers." (*PP*, 154)

Elizabeth's desire to be a distinguished tourist, a distinctive and precise traveler—not a muddled, or argumentative, or boring one, that is, not like everyone else—suggests to the contemporary reader that not much has changed.

Another aspect of the culture of consumption, tourism, like the decoration of houses, was and is intrinsically competitive, being all about distinctions of taste and class. Ostentatious display was opposed by discriminating connoisseurship. Pride in what England had to offer was an aspect of competition with the Continent—and collusion with continentals, as well. "It is an irony often noted that the rapid growth of interest in views of British scenery was largely prompted by a foreign initiative," writes Malcolm Andrews, pointing to the "vast table-service" decorated with views of British beauty spots that was commissioned in 1773 by the Empress of Russia from the Staffordshire firm of Wedgwood and Bentley.[32] The beauty spots included country houses and gardens as well as ruins and natural scenes—"the celebrated beauties of Matlock, Chatsworth, Dovedale, or the Peak" (239), as *Pride and Prejudice* summarizes them, tucking a great house into a list of the natural wonders of Derbyshire. Elizabeth Bennet goes there rather than to the Lakes (Wordsworth's *Guide to the Lakes* was published in 1810; Hester Lynch Piozzi reported "a Rage for the Lakes" as early as 1789) because his thriving wine business prevents Mr. Gardiner from taking the longer tour. Anticipating the beautiful scenery, Elizabeth exclaims, "What are men to rocks and mountains?" (154)

But in Derbyshire, where her aunt wants to revisit the scenes of her youth, it is impossible not to think of one particular man. Defensively, in the dry tone she often takes when sparring with herself, Elizabeth thinks that she "may enter [Darcy's] county with impunity, and rob it of a few petrified spars without his perceiving me" (239). She thinks of him, a squire, as the owner of Derbyshire, and of herself as a sneaky thief. Derbyshire in Darcy's time was no longer the howling wilderness it had been when Defoe visited; and Austen was moved to protest, in her novel, that she was not writing the usual travel narrative. "It is not the object of this work to give a description of Derbyshire, nor of any of the remarkable places through which their route thither lay," she writes. "Oxford, Blenheim, Warwick, Kenelworth, Birmingham, &c. are sufficiently known" (240). When Elizabeth encounters Darcy, the two go through predictable conversational moves, talking "of Matlock and Dove Dale with great perseverance" (257), the way people did.

Visiting great houses is different from going to see lakes, mountains, and rivers that individuals don't own. That Elizabeth and her relations tour Pemberley without having been invited there has confused readers who imagine the house tour to be a fairly recent invention, as in its present form it is.

Tourism within England in fact began in the sixteenth century, reflecting the self-conscious greatness of the nation under the Tudors. For three centuries, it was

> the prerogative of the governing classes, members of the nobility and gentry. This is particularly true of the visitors to the great country houses, for their owners were willing to open their doors to whoever presented themselves on the tacit understanding that the low and common sort of people did not take such a liberty.[33]

In Jane Austen's time, this "governing" class was inclusive of people like Elizabeth Bennet, the slated-to-be-disinherited daughter of an educated gentleman, and the Gardiners, who had acquired the manners and taste and money of the gentry, without the land that was the economic basis of the ruling class. That Darcy graciously invites them to tour his park and house is not really evidence that love has converted him to democracy; rather, it suggests that the Gardiners go to Pemberley in the first place, and get admitted there, because money and education have made them his nearer equals. Elizabeth, who proudly notes their intelligence, taste, and manners as she listens to her uncle chat with Darcy, is happy to have these superior surrogate parents accompanying her. The scene contrasts with earlier ones where Mr. and Mrs. Bennet embarrass her, and prepares the way for her fairytale elevation into the ideal family of chosen young people that she and Darcy and Georgiana will compose at the happy end.

Gentleman and lady tourists desirous of seeing a great house customarily applied by letter or in person, and expected the courtesy to be extended to them, as if to a member of an extended family: tourists were annoyed when they found that a house was closed, or if they were refused entrance. Visitors expected to be shown around some of the rooms by someone like Darcy's Mrs. Reynolds: "The housekeeper [was] as familiar to the eighteenth-century tourist as they are to the visitors of today."[34] It was standard practice then as now to open some private spaces to the public so as to make visitors feel like guests. Family portraits were exhibited as family photographs still are in stately homes. The contradictions are more vivid now, as heterogeneous crowds pay good money to traipse through houses like Chatsworth. The show of hospitality has been described as a ruling-class trick: open to the public, the Great House appears to be what it's called, a portion of the

National Heritage, but it is in fact the property of a wealthy owner. Linda Colley observes that only in England is the public admitted to the private spaces of the ruling class.[35]

Things were subtly different when the middling and lower classes were not so subtly kept out. "Country houses could project a disconcerting double image—relaxed and delightful to those who had the *entrée*, arrogant and forbidding to those who did not," Mark Girouard writes about England in the early nineteenth century.[36] In *Pride and Prejudice* the double image is redoubled. While the Gardiners correctly assume they have entrée to Pemberley, kind Mrs. Gardiner is a little nervous (and a little overeager, in Mrs. Bennet's style) because of what she knows about her niece and its owner. Elizabeth keeps her counsel about Darcy's proposal, and convinces herself that she won't encounter him. But she is drawn to examine, in the portrait gallery, "a striking resemblance of Mr. Darcy, with such a smile over the face, as she remembered to have sometimes seen, when he looked at her" (250). In his absence, she fixes the eyes of the man in the picture on herself, reversing his "regard" and softening its expression, mastering the gaze, assuming the position in which she will eventually be able to change the man.

With the shift of sensibility during the late eighteenth century, the focus of travelers shifted from the outer to the inner world. Like Defoe, Dr. Johnson was curious to see what there was to see—but Johnson's confession that the emotional influence of the stark landscape of the Hebrides inspired him to write a *Journal* of his tour there is not something Defoe might have written. "That man is little to be envied, whose patriotism would not gain force upon the plain of Marathon, or whose piety would not grow warmer among the ruins of Iona," Johnson famously wrote of one of the Scottish islands, formerly inhabited by religious monks. The emotional effect of what Byron called the "genius of the place" fascinated Romantic writers; turn-of-the-century travelers actively pursued mind-altering trips. Ann Radcliffe, visiting it in 1794, settled down opposite the east window at Furness Abbey so as to invite fantasies:

> The midnight procession of monks, clothed in white and bearing lighted tapers, appeared to the mind's eye issuing to the choir . . . and the organ swelled a solemn peal. To fancy, the strain still echoed feebly along the arcades and died in the breeze among the woods, the rustling leaves mingling with them close.[37]

This account of her experience, published in 1795, might be the model for Catherine Morland's hoped-for tour of Blaize Castle and her eager acceptance of an invitation to Northanger Abbey. It is the kind of thing Jane Austen's mother had in mind on a visit of some days she made to Stoneleigh Abbey, which was owned by a member of her family. She reported, in a letter to Mary Lloyd in August 1806, on "the State Bed chamber with a high dark crimson Velvet Bed, an *alarming* apartment just fit for an Heroine." While she and Mary had perhaps heard Jane read the early version of *Northanger Abbey* that was sent to a publisher in 1803, she might have had the same thought even if she had not. Staying with rich relations, Mrs. Austen sounds the predictable note of the Romantic tourist:

> I expected to find everything about the place very fine & all that, but I had no idea of its being so beautiful, I had figured to myself long Avenues, dark rookeries & dismal Yew Trees, but here are no such melancholy things; The Avon runs near the house amidst Green Meadows, bounding [sic] by large and beautiful Woods, full of delightful Walks.

But her practical, housewifely side gets the better of her Romanticism:

> I will now give you some idea of the inside of this vast house, first premising that there are 45 windows in front, (which is quite strait with a flat Roof) 15 in a row—you go up a considerable flight of steps (some offices are under the house) into a large Hall, on the right hand, the dining parlour, within that the Breakfast room, where we generally sit, and reason good, tis the only room (except the Chapel) that looks towards the River,—on the left hand the Hall is the best drawing room, within that a smaller, these rooms are rather gloomy, brown wainscoat & dark Crimson furniture, so we never use them but to walk thro' them to the old picture Gallery. . . . Poor Lady Saye & Sele, to be sure, is rather tormenting, tho' some times amusing, and affords Jane many a good laugh—but she fatigues me sadly on the whole.[38]

Mrs. Austen and her daughter visiting Stoneleigh Abbey, or Jane visiting Godmersham Park, her rich brother's estate in Kent, would have had complicated relations to these places, which but for a stroke of fate might have been theirs. From the vantage point of a poor woman of the pseudo-gentry especially, the perquisites of good luck would seem peculiarly arbitrary, inviting one to imagine correcting it. The transformative happy ending of *Pride and Prejudice* that makes Elizabeth Bennet mistress of Pemberley and therefore "something" is such a stroke.

Like Mrs. Austen at Stoneleigh, Elizabeth looks at the windows of Pemberley House, but unlike Mrs. Austen she does not count them. Instead, she attends to the views of the park that they provide and frame. She and her relatives follow Mrs. Reynolds into the dining-parlour, "a large, well-proportioned room, handsomely fitted up," and after "slightly surveying it" she goes to a window to "enjoy its prospect." She notices that "the hill, crowned with wood, from which they had descended, receiving increased abruptness from the distance, was a beautiful object. Every disposition of the ground was good; and she looked on the whole scene, the river, the trees scattered on its banks, and the winding of the valley, as far as she could trace it, with delight. As they passed into other rooms, these objects were taking different positions; but from every window there were beauties to be seen" (*PP*, 246). As when she looks at Darcy's portrait, she seems to enjoy her own mastery of the art of perspective as well as the appropriation of all she sees.

To the extent that we read Pemberley as metaphorical, we read Elizabeth the tourist as a metaphor as well, a female version of Joseph Addison's fictitious Mr. Spectator, who distinguished between the metaphors of life as a pilgrimage and life as a theatre. On the one hand Elizabeth is a pilgrim and Pemberley is her destination; but we also see her as a spectator, who happily sees objects take different positions as she moves about. We share her curiosity and readiness to be engaged and moved by what is outside her, the "beautiful pyramids of grapes, nectarines, and peaches" (268), and the other natural but also artistic beauties of Pemberley. The way she looks at Darcy will make him smile back to her again: she becomes mistress of Pemberley by the force of her own imagination. In the happy end the place will be home to not only Elizabeth and Darcy and Georgiana but also Mrs. Reynolds and the rest of the servants. Visitors will come as well, and the Darcys will preside benignly over their little estate, being good to the poor. The emphasis is on the joy that trickles down to the multitude: the last phrase in the novel is about the Gardiners, responsible for "uniting them."

We get a glimpse of the domestic life of Charlotte and Mr. Collins at home, after marriage, but Austen never took the heroine's narrative past the wedding. She left it to others to imagine the story of the lives of the married Darcys (by now, many too many have obliged). She herself next undertook to write another, different, indeed a dissident variation on the heroine's plot, named after another great house, where domestic life is strained and uneasy. *Pride and Prejudice* chronicles the triumph of the individual; *Mansfield Park* responds that happiness and even character are always already contingent. That Jane Austen made this dramatic reversal upon herself reflects the seriousness of her project. The love story of Edmund Bertram and Fanny Price, shaped by the stories of their mothers, who are sisters, and the subsequent stories of their sisters and cousins, is wrapped up unromantically and unforgettably:

> Scarcely had [Edmund] done regretting Mary Crawford, and observing to Fanny how impossible it was that he should ever meet with such another woman, before it began to strike him whether a very different kind of woman might not do just as well—or a great deal better; whether Fanny herself were not growing as dear, as important to him in all her smiles, and all her ways, as Mary Crawford had ever been; and whether it might not be a possible, an hopeful undertaking to persuade her that her warm and sisterly regard for him would be foundation enough for wedded love.
>
> I purposely abstain from dates on this occasion, that every one may be at liberty to fix their own, aware that the cure of unconquerable passions, and the transfer of unchanging attachments, must vary much as to time in different people. I only entreat everybody to believe that exactly at the time when it was quite natural that it should be so, and not a week earlier, Edmund did cease to care about Miss Crawford, and became as anxious to marry Fanny as Fanny herself could desire.   (*MP*, 470)

It is *not*, of course "natural" for Edmund to cease to care about Miss Crawford and become as anxious to marry Fanny as Fanny herself could desire: on the contrary, it is artificial and conventional, required by the courtship plot. The heroine-centered plot of fiction promises the reader to take the protagonist toward the end that realizes her character: we root for Fanny to marry Edmund in spite of our awareness of his limitations and hers. Fanny's lack of sparkle has distressed many readers, and been justified by critics from Trilling to Patricia Rozema, but imagining a mild, meek heroine whose tenacity is her strongest suit is only one remarkable achievement of *Mansfield Park*. As the title intimates, this is not a heroine's story but a house's, and a family's. Its brilliant first paragraphs set the theme: that circumstances, and sister lives and neighboring lives, determine individual character and fate. Mansfield Park, the place, is outwardly elegant (if dull) but rotten at its patriarchal, imperialistic, selfish core.[39] Like its model, the mansion in Charlotte Smith's *The Old Manor House* (1793), it accommodates multiple lives that accommodate one another. Austen regularly undercuts her happy endings with irony that casts doubt on the possibility of happiness; in this novel more than the others, where characters so easily stand in for and replace one another, the narrator seems to mock the very possibility of the unique, complex, important individual self that romantic narrative makes so very much of.

It is a challenge to try to imagine Jane Austen biographically, which is to say in the light of her novels, and within the constraints of her narratives. She escaped or eluded the heroine's imperative to find and found a home and reify her character by choosing and being chosen by a man with an estate (or a ship) of his own, remaining her whole life within her natal family—more unchanging even than Fanny, who marries her first cousin, or Emma, who marries the brother of her brother-in-law. Almost always at home, Jane Austen was also always without a home of her own, moving from Steventon to Bath to Southampton to Chawton and, in the too-early end, to Winchester, with visits to London and Kent. She lived as a dispensable daughter who could be packed off to amuse an aunt in jail for stealing a card of lace, an available sister to be called upon to tend to a sister-in-law who was yet again giving birth; and as she looked around her, she could not help but be aware that pleasant settled lives on settled land, like those of the ancestral Dashwoods, were no longer in the cards, for most genteel people.

When we go looking for Jane in Austen-land today, we enact—or play at enacting—the paradoxes that inform her work.

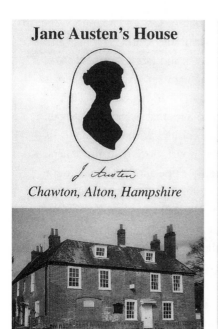

Jane Austen's House

J. Austen

Chawton, Alton, Hampshire

The Home of Jane Austen
famous writer
of 'Pride and Prejudice'

Chawton
Hampshire

FIGURE 10. Brochures for Jane Austen's house. Jane Austen Memorial Trust, *Jane Austen's House* (Chawton, UK: Jane Austen Memorial Trust/Jarrold Publishing, 1996).

CHAPTER 3

Neighbors

"There is nothing, Sir, too little for so little a creature as man. It is by studying little things that we attain the great art of having as little misery and as much happiness as possible."
—Johnson, in Boswell's *Life*

"For what do we live, but to make sport for our neighbours, and laugh at them in our turn?"
—Mr. Bennet, in *Pride and Prejudice*

W E KNOW JANE AUSTEN'S CHARACTERS BETTER THAN WE know our friends and relations, as John Wiltshire has observed. Macaulay compared her to Shakespeare, citing her creation of five clergymen, all young, unmarried, and in love, all members of the established church, who are impossible to mistake for one another. No one has ever claimed that Jane Austen invented character, as Harold Bloom claims Shakespeare did: her different genius was to teach us how to analyze and appreciate it, to read and savor and become a connoisseur of character, as she was, and to trace the fine line between character and caricature.

Alone with Elizabeth after the Meryton ball, Jane Bennet tells her sister how much she admires Mr. Bingley, who danced with her. "He is just what a young man ought to be," she says, "sensible, good humoured, lively"; she exclaims further that she "never saw such happy manner! So much ease, with such perfect good breeding!" Her quicker-witted sister responds, "He is also handsome, . . . which a young man ought likewise to be, if he possibly can. His character is thereby complete" (*PP*, 44). Elizabeth's echo of Jane's tendentious "ought to be" signals her awareness of the prim ambiguity of the phrase, also her own characteristic irony. Is the reader to understand that Bingley really is or merely appears to be what Jane (and everybody else) thinks a young man ought to be? If he is "exactly," is he therefore also *only* "just" such a young man? If he is as close to being such a young man as "he possibly can" be, does that mean he's trying too hard? And what does "character" mean if his good looks—his appearance—make Bingley's character "complete"?

In a letter to Cassandra of 26 June 1808, Jane writes of their sailor brother Francis: "We are all very happy to hear of his health & safety;—he wants nothing but a good Prize to be a perfect Character.—" (*Letters*, 132–133). Surely she does not mean morally perfect: she is evaluating Frank here from an aesthetic point of view, suggesting that her brother, enriched by a prize, will be a perfect sailor as a single young man in a novel such as Bingley might be a perfect match for a heroine, that is, perfectly suited to his role. (About the perfectly good heroines of moral novels, Jane Austen declared that "pictures of perfection make me sick and wicked"; she agreed with Mr. Knightley that charming girls should not be glibly imagined and acknowledged as perfect.)

From its first sentence *Pride and Prejudice* has focused on "a single man"—or people talking about such a man—and therefore in effect on Mr. Bingley, the man of large fortune from the north of England who has caused a flurry by renting a local great house, Netherfield Park. To take the house is to take up a promising role in the small community of landed gentry interested in any newcomer at all but especially in a young man available to be married to one or another of its abundant daughters. (There was a real scarcity of young men at the time Jane Austen wrote, during the killing wars on the Continent and in America, but to women with marriageable daughters, there is perhaps always a scarcity of eligible young men.) When Mr. Bingley enters society at the ball, he brings another young man with him—also single, taller, more handsome, reputedly much richer, and glacial in his manner, as becomes a man from even further north. Mr. Darcy is much admired, "till his manners gave a disgust which turned the tide of his popularity; for he was discovered to be proud, to be above his company." He refuses to dance with or even to be introduced to anyone outside his own party: "his character" is therefore "decided. He was the proudest, most disagreeable man in the world, and every body hoped that he would never come there again" (*PP*, 10–11). (The neighbors are free to hope thus and to condemn him: unlike Bingley, he is only visiting.) A man's "character," here, is what other people make of it: in this sense of the word, a servant is given a "character," or a letter recommending him, by a satisfied employer he's leaving. Darcy's "manners" to women—the particulars that compose his "manner"—cause Mrs. Bennet to be among "the most violent against him" after he slights her daughter Elizabeth.

Very early in the novel, we learn that Mrs. Bennet is no judge of character: "the experience of three and twenty years had been insufficient to make her" understand her own husband's, and she herself has blithely commented, apropos of a woman who thinks she knows her man, "One cannot know what a man really is by the end of a fortnight" (*PP*, 7). (Later, the much shrewder Elizabeth will echo her mother, telling Charlotte that Jane cannot be sure "of the degree of her own regard" for Bingley, "nor of its reasonableness," since "she has known him only a fortnight" [*PP*, 22].) Nevertheless, she is a gossip, dedicated to exchanging views as well as news with her neighbors, and she has no trouble at all pronouncing on Mr. Darcy's character after seeing him only once at a ball. By chapter 4, where Jane and Elizabeth talk over Bingley's character, it's clear that a man has at least two kinds or dimensions of character, one immediately apparent to others, the other not. The first dimension is manner and reputation, something within the power and purview of others to discern and also to determine. The plot of *Pride and Prejudice* depends on reputations: specifically, on Mr. Wickham's falsehoods about Mr. Darcy's character; on the truths that Darcy (in the service of his sister's reputation) and then Elizabeth and Jane withhold about Wickham; and near the end, on the "character" that his housekeeper Mrs. Reynolds, in a nice reversal, gives of her master.

By chapter 9, the plot has brought the young people together at Netherfield, then brought Mrs. Bennet there after them. The reader is developing her own estimate of the various characters, and is getting caught up in the relationships among them. As if to reflect this, and give the reader the cozy sense of interacting with the people in the book, character in the abstract becomes the subject of their conversation. Elizabeth initiates the discussion by presuming—as Marianne in *Sense and Sensibility* also does—on a comfortable, sisterly intimacy with the man who admires her sister; she tells Mr. Bingley that she understands him perfectly. "I wish I might take this for a compliment," he affably replies; "but to be so easily seen through I am afraid is pitiful." With half a bright eye on the silent Darcy, Elizabeth replies, "It does not necessarily follow that a deep, intricate character is more or less estimable than such a one as yours" (*PP*, 42). (She has half an eye also on her talking mother, whom she guesses Darcy is judging.) Amiable Bingley says, "I did not know . . . that you were a studier of character. It must be an amusing study," to which she replies with deliberate provocation (of course of Darcy) that "intricate characters are the *most* amusing," adding that, "They have at least that advantage." Smitten Darcy bites, making a caustic comment on the limited "subjects for such a study" in a country neighborhood, and Elizabeth responds that "people themselves alter so much, that there is something new to be observed in them for ever." Mrs. Bennet's mad conversation-stopper, "Yes indeed. . . . I assure you there is quite as much of *that* going on in the country as in town" (*PP*, 43), effectively kills any further talk of whether character is interesting because it is always changing. (One might conceivably defend Mrs. Bennet for sagely hinting at the truth that character is not essence but conduct: what goes on is what gossips talk about.)

Of Mrs. Bennet we know that "the business of her life was to get her daughters married; its solace was visiting and news"—not the news of the world of course but very local news of, say, the arrival of eligible young men in the neighborhood. Whereas clever people like her husband and her daughter Elizabeth are amused by the style of a letter that suggests Mr. Collins is "an oddity," therefore worth meeting—what we might call "a real character"—those with less ambitious habits of amusement gossip about what their neighbors *do*. Whether it is intricate or easy to see through, whether it is praised or blamed or considered as amusing for its own sake, character is everybody's business.

The young people in *Pride and Prejudice* tirelessly characterize themselves, the men especially: "not handsome enough to tempt *me*" (*PP*, 12), says boastful Darcy to his friend Bingley, stressing his own high standards, not the defects of the lady who falls short of them. The young women constrained to choose among the men respond to their insistent advertisements for themselves: Elizabeth claims she understands him after Bingley asserts, "Whatever I do is done in a hurry" (*PP*, 42). Darcy's pompous declaration, "My good opinion once lost is lost for ever," provokes her to escape to a more abstract level and remark mildly, "Implacable resentment *is* a shade in character" (*PP*, 58). She is in the habit of discussing shades *of* character and *in* character—with Jane, also with her aunt Gardiner, who will describe Darcy, in her account of Lydia's wedding, as "very obstinate," and go on: "I fancy, Lizzy, that obstinacy is the real defect of his character after all. He has been accused of many faults at different times; but *this* is the true one" (*PP*, 324).

The first volume of *Pride and Prejudice* ends with a marriage—Charlotte's to Mr. Collins—which (ironically) foreshadows the true love matches made at the happy end. This event causes Mr. Bennet to be gratified by Charlotte as a character, almost as he was by Mr. Collins—"to discover that Charlotte Lucas, whom he had been used to think tolerably sensible, was as foolish as his wife, and more foolish than his daughter!" (*PP*, 127). Like manner and manners and the choice of words, the choice of a life partner illuminates character: Charlotte's prudential choice, made deliberately and after knowing Mr. Collins less than a fortnight, is simply of an establishment of her own. In contrast, Elizabeth, after being rudely snubbed by Darcy in the beginning, characterizes him (inaccurately, projecting her own characteristic onto him) as "satirical" by way of riposte; then she works to determine his true character— as she puts it, to illustrate or "sketch" it, to "take [his] likeness" (*PP*, 93–94). (All we know about what Darcy looks like we learn in chapter 3, where "his fine, tall person, handsome features, noble mien" draw the attention of the ballroom, and the ladies declare he is "much handsomer" than Bingley" [*PP*, 10]. Like Jane Austen, like the reader reading, Elizabeth strives to "take" or "make out" his real character—not exactly the inner man, but those aspects of it that the man deliberately or involuntarily presents to keen eyes. Presumably a likeness that's taken in words may render a deep or intricate character that is hard to see, or to see through.) It is by taking his likeness, five chapters before the volume's end, that Elizabeth increases Darcy's "tolerable powerful feeling towards her" (*PP*, 94): he is flattered by the close attention, and by the accuracy of her perceptions. Sauced by its keenness and boldness, Elizabeth's interest in him provokes Darcy's interest in her: similarly, ingenuous Catherine Morland's far less critical and combative interest in clever Henry Tilney is what interested him in her. It is Darcy's intricate character that ultimately recommends him to Elizabeth; and her appreciation of it recommends her to him. In contrast, Bingley's "ease" and "happy manner," his susceptibility to being seen through, makes him the perfect match for the less searching Jane, whose characteristic "candour" is ingenuousness and lack of suspicion. For students of character, the less strenuously paired couple is less interesting: Jane's candour accommodates Bingley's complaisance in leaving her neighborhood and apparently forgetting her, because of Darcy's persuasion and/ or because he does not have the acumen and the self-confidence to know her and therefore to know she loves him.

Reading *Pride and Prejudice*, we assess and rank and judge the characters in the novel as they assess and rank and judge one another in order to make the most important choices of their lives. We are in something like the position of the neighbors, who also look on, and assess and rank and judge them, and moralize from their example. After Jane's engagement is made known, "The Bennets were speedily pronounced to be the luckiest family in the world, though only a few weeks before, when Lydia had first run away, they had been generally proved to be marked out for misfortune" (*PP*, 350). Reading people and people's lives is everybody's business, in Jane Austen's novels. Mr. Bennet has been roundly criticized for generations because he asks, toward the end of *Pride and Prejudice*, "For what do we live, but to make sport for our neighbours, and laugh at them in our turn?" (*PP*, 364). But laughter is a positive value and a salubrious one, in this comic novel where the heroine compares her happiness to her sister's by saying, "She only smiles, I laugh" (*PP*, 383). Reading, we laugh giddily, as if she had invited us, alongside Elizabeth at Mr. Darcy's not having yet learned "to be laught at" (*PP*, 371) (even though—secretly, soberly—we may wonder whether he ever will learn, and whether Elizabeth, and Jane Austen with her, might laugh at us, given the chance, as well).

Sometimes the narrator of Austen's novels sees inside the characters' heads; sometimes she does not. Describing the beginning of the walk that ends in Darcy's second proposal, when Elizabeth, Kitty, and Darcy are together, she writes: "Very little was said by either; Kitty was too much afraid of him to talk; Elizabeth was secretly forming a desperate resolution; and perhaps he might be doing the same" (*PP*, 365). The "perhaps" that fences her out of Darcy's mind puts the reader nearly inside Elizabeth's. Sometimes identifying herself with a character, sometimes judging her as if from above, Jane Austen plays out the tricky three-way relation among inner and outer and watchful selves. We imagine we come to know ourselves by reading novels and learning to know the novelists, as Elizabeth Bennet comes to know herself by reading Darcy's letter about himself. But among the novelists, Jane Austen—whose readers imagine themselves her intimates—is perhaps the hardest to know.

Near Neighbors

In a letter to her sister describing a dance, twenty-five-year-old Jane Austen laughed fairly savagely at just about all the neighbors who were there:

There were very few Beauties, & such as there were, were not very handsome. Miss Iremonger did not look well, & Mrs. Blount was the only one much admired. She appeared exactly as she did in September, with the same broad face, diamond bandeau, white shoes, pink husband, & fat neck.—The two Miss Coxes were there; I traced in one the remains of the vulgar, broad featured girl who danced at Enham eight years ago;—the other is refined into a nice, composed looking girl like Catherine Bigg.—I looked at Sir Thomas Champneys & thought of poor Rosalie; I looked at his daughter & thought her a queer animal with a white neck.—Mrs. Warren, I was constrained to think a very fine young woman, which I much regret. She has got rid of some part of her child, & danced away with great activity, looking by no means very large.—Her husband is ugly enough; uglier even than his cousin John; but he does not look so *very* old.   (*Letters*, 60–61)

It is the funny, intimate, gossipy letter of one sister to another—but Elizabeth would not write Jane, Marianne would not write Elinor, a letter so bad-tempered and heartless, so smugly censorious and glibly ribald, so relentlessly unkind. That it is not really malicious makes it more devastatingly critical and persuasive. Reading letters like this, one wonders about the relation to the novels (and the novelist's heart and mind) of this hard-eyed view, the experience it reflects of feeling alienated, and this habit of conspiratorial confidence as revenge. The Swiftian disgust for humanity is compounded by the implicit assumption that the writer's interlocutor will share the feeling (Cassandra has already seen Mrs. Blount and her husband, said or heard that Mrs. Warren's husband is old and ugly). Was being hard on the neighbors an Austen family trait, or a habit of the Austen "girls"? Does it reflect the resentment of powerless, dowerless young women? Definitely it is a far cry from Mr. Bennet's suave relaxed amusement, and it is much less tolerantly resigned than Austen's suppressed narrative hoot—or Anne Elliot's—at the "large, fat sighings" (*P*, 68) of fat Mrs. Musgrove, over whose tears for her deadbeat dead son Anne and Captain Wentworth begin to bond.

The description of the 1800 ball is most striking for its violent distaste for bodies, its conjunctions of details, and its determination to condemn (she regrets being "constrained to think" Mrs. Warren "a very fine young woman"). Of the characters in Austen's fiction, only the spiteful protagonist of *Lady Susan*, the short epistolary novel she never sought to publish (but made a fair copy of some five years after writing this letter), is comparably carping and critical of her acquaintances. But even Lady Susan is incapable of the dead baby jokes, the one about Mrs. Warren's having "got rid of some part of her child," and the more famous one about Mrs. Hall of Sherborne, who aborted after happening "unawares to look at her husband" (*Letters*, 17). The sexual disgust is as striking as the wit and timing; so is the wild imagination. Were Jane and Cassandra, in 1800, growing into a pair of fearful, condemning elderly girls giddy about sex and being beyond it? Was Jane pushing the envelope, in this letter, and was it to shock or to please Cassandra? Did the two encourage one another, buoying up one another's sense that the usual woman's life was not for them? Cassandra's letters are missing: how did she respond to the dead baby joke? Is this account of the ball the repressed underside of Jane Austen's novels, in which gatherings of friends and neighbors in the country are mannerly and mostly cordial? Or is this the voice of the "real" Jane Austen, the one that reflects her true, not very ladylike character? Of selfish domineering Mrs. Ferrars, in *Sense and Sensibility*, we are told that "a lucky contraction of the brow had rescued her countenance from the disgrace of insipidity, by giving it the strong characters of pride and ill nature" (232). Like her daughter Fanny, who is "a strong caricature" of her husband John Dashwood, Mrs. Ferrars is a delight to behold, at least for the reader of this novel, who (like an admirer of a caricature by, say, Austen's contemporary James Gillray) savors the reflection of character by physiognomy. As in the letter, the emphasis is on the pleasure-seeking eye of the satirical onlooker for whom insipidity is a disgrace because it is not funny enough. Because we know and hate Mrs. Ferrars, the wry gesture toward salvation (how lucky for her that she is not insipid!) seems almost redemptive. The complacency and seeming justness of the epigram characterizes the person sizing up Mrs. Ferrars, the narrator who relishes, equally, the tiny giveaway trait and the ability to register it, and of course the turn of phrase. There are signs of her in even the rowdiest of the letters.

In November 1798, a month before her twenty-second birthday, Jane Austen had written a more pleasant, less disturbing letter to her sister, in the usual condemning conspiratorial tone. Cassandra was in Kent, where the wife of their rich brother Edward had recently given birth to yet another baby; Jane was at home, and their neighbor sister-in-law Mary, their clerical brother James's second wife, had also produced a child, her first. In Jane's letter, which was as usual meant mainly to keep the sisters in close touch, she seems to mirror or model Cassandra's physical little distance, from home and perhaps from the dangerous reproductive imperative as well. After a teasing

FIGURE 11. James Gillray, *High-Change in Bond Street,—ou—la Politesse du Grande Monde*, 1796. Library of Congress, Prints and Photographs Division, LC-USZC4-8766.

boast of being the superior correspondent, she wryly summarizes the domestic news, about the health of their mother and Mary, servant problems and a disappointing ball, and the shocking amount she had just had to pay for stockings and linen, and her father for sheep. Then there's this, about the purchase of a novel:

> We have got "Fitz-Albini"; my father has bought it against my private wishes, for it does not quite satisfy my feelings that we should purchase the only one of Egerton's works of which his family are ashamed. That these scruples, however, do not at all interfere with my reading it, you will easily believe. We have neither of us yet finished the first volume. My father is disappointed—*I* am not, for I expected nothing better. Never did any book carry more internal evidence of its author. Every sentiment is completely Egerton's. There is very little story, and what there is told in a strange, unconnected way. There are many characters introduced, apparently merely to be delineated. We have not been able

to recognize any of them hitherto, except Dr and Mrs Hey and Mr
Oxenden, who is not very tenderly treated.   (*Letters*, 22)

One understands why many readers and writers—Virginia Woolf was one,
W. H. Auden another—imagined that had they met her they would have
been afraid of her.

Jane Austen's condemnation of *Fitz-Albini* and its overly present author
points toward the paradox of her own characteristic fiction. As enthusiasts
and critics agree, every sentence if not every sentiment in her novels is completely Jane Austen's: we recognize her distinctive voice, with those sly asides
to the reader tucked inside its cadences, as in the letter to Cassandra, and
we imagine we are her intimates and secret friends. Nevertheless, the novels
that convey the sense of a (very) particular person absolutely refuse to provide internal evidence of their author—it seems on purpose, in such a way
as to persuade one to crave and to concoct the person between the lines that
seems to have been generated by them. Late-twentieth- and early-twenty-
first-century biographies, biographical fantasies, and fictions of the novelist,
together with the many dreamy or overheated or condescendingly mocking
adaptations, continuations, and revisions of the novels, dramatic, cinematic,
and more or less literary, are signs of this yearning for Jane. She read Egerton
Brydges's new novel in 1798; nothing she wrote would be published until
thirteen years afterward, but she was already at work on drafting the early
novels. Her scorn for the novelist she condemns as inadequate because he
cannot escape himself—"Every sentence is completely Egerton's"—recalls the
high-minded moral and aesthetic confidence of Elizabeth Bennet, who at
"not one and twenty" is only a year younger than she was then.

You don't have to read more than half of its high-flying title to guess that
Arthur Fitz-Albini (1798) is nothing like anything Jane Austen would write.
It was dismissed in its time by the *Gentleman's Magazine* as a mere auto-
biographical fantasy, but praised by the right-wing *Anti-Jacobin Review*, in
what J. M. S. Tompkins would characterize as "a torrent of approbation."[1]
In the ground-breaking study she published in 1932, Tompkins described
Egerton's effort as one of many reactionary "fighting novels" directed against
the dangerous new philosophy of egalitarianism coming from France and,
more locally, from the radical author of *Political Justice*, William Godwin.
Writing, herself, at a dark period when a popular movement for eugenics
was rising to threaten civilization, Tompkins (who of course could not have

known Egerton personally) describes the eponymous hero of his novel as "a projection of Brydges's dream-self, the fine flower of centuries of specialized breeding." The elaborately and absurdly named Arthur Fitz-Albini holds on stubbornly to the old order and his extensive ancestral demesne but "falls a victim of his own noble susceptibilities in a coarsened world." While Jane, the novel's romantic heroine, "dies from the mere touch of vulgar malice," the hero drags on his life in refined melancholy.

Jane Austen's remarks on Egerton Brydges's novel do not notice its politics. Indeed, by taking the aesthetic high road, she effectively stakes a claim for superior refinement, or at least fastidiousness and kindness, therefore what might be called figurative if not literal breeding. Those unconnected characters introduced merely to be delineated—presumably, not integrated in the story—are recognizable knockoffs of neighbors she's able to name, and "not tenderly treated": she seems to disapprove on both counts. She herself disdains to treat Egerton tenderly: knowing him, she knew the novel would not be any good, she confides to her sister. (The relations between novelists and their neighbors, almost as interesting as those between personal history and fiction, continue to be problematic: interrupting a conversation at a recent Manhattan cocktail party about a woman who had won a literary prize, another woman writer remarked dismissively, "Why, she's a woman who lives in my building.")

Egerton (sometimes Sir Egerton, or Samuel-Egerton) Brydges was not actually living there in 1798, but he had resided some years previously in the Austens' neighborhood. In the late 1790s he still visited frequently to see their neighbor, his adored older sister Anne Lefroy. Because of the most recent Austen vogue and its biographical romantic emphasis, the sister's name is more familiar today than her publishing brother's: Mrs. Lefroy is that enemy of young love who—a year or so before *Fitz-Albini* came out—connived to send away her nephew Tom Lefroy, the boy Jane Austen might have married, who reminded her of the Tom of Fielding's *Tom Jones*. Years after the older woman's death from a fall from her horse, Jane Austen wrote an awkward, guilt-edged poem in her memory that suggests that her feelings for Mrs. Lefroy were still strong and ambivalent. "Madame Lefroy," she had styled herself, apparently to suggest Continental sophistication or Norman blood—a loaded move to make at that fraught political moment. The wife of a local clergyman, she had taken a special interest in the neighboring clergyman's second daughter, Jane. Cultivated and more than a little affected, ten years younger than Mrs. Austen, she must have struck a literary adolescent as a glamorous alternative to that brisk and busy woman. Surely what Jane Austen meant by the "family" ashamed of *Fitz-Albini* would have been Madame Lefroy herself—posing a piquant challenge to the younger woman's emotional and literary allegiances and ambitions, her moral scruples, and her characteristic eagerness to know the worst about the neighbors, especially those who wrote and were written about. ("That these scruples, however, do not at all interfere with my reading it, you will easily believe.")

In his middle thirties in 1798, Egerton Brydges had already published widely, poetry and fiction as well as essays on topographical and antiquarian subjects. He was especially interested in genealogy, in particular the history of his own family: he would spend years supporting his older brother's claim to the Barony of Chandos of Sudeley, which was eventually rejected (but a baronetcy was bestowed on Egerton Brydges in 1814). In 1812 Brydges would produce an edition of Collins's *Peerage*; in 1798 he had published, in addition to *Fitz-Albini*, "Reflections on the late Augmentations of the British Peerage," expressing the pity and contempt a hereditary aristocrat could not help but feel for the almost endless creations of the last century. (In fact, according to the obituary that would run in the *Gentleman's Magazine*, his "great-grandfather John Bridges was a grocer in Canterbury, and both his wives were grocers' daughters.") Egerton Brydges was also a biographer and a memoirist. The two-volume *Imaginative Biography* (1834) he published in his old age—about people ranging from the Elizabethan Lord Falkland (a friend of Lord Chandos) to his contemporary, the prolific and popular poet and novelist Charlotte Smith—takes it for granted that a famous person's life is there for the imaginative biographer to interpret, embroider, tweak, and indeed build on as he wishes. "By Imaginative Biography I mean, an Imaginative Superstructure on the known facts of the Biography of eminent characters," he explained guilelessly. Famous writers often slide into fiction: consider Lord Byron and his heroes, or Philip Roth and his.

Egerton Brydges seems not to have noticed the much younger and as yet unpublished novelist Jane Austen, or perhaps he was wary of his sister's sharp-tongued protégée: years later, after her death, he could recall only that she had "cheeks a little too full." The most interesting of his many literary works is a book about her contemporary and apparent antithesis, the passionate poet Lord Byron, whom he admired this side idolatry—or perhaps the other side. (The two men were not personally acquainted, although Byron seems to have noticed him in passing as a "strange" old man—using, curiously, the same word Jane Austen used about her neighbor's novel.) Shocked by reading in a newspaper of the poet's death in 1824, Egerton reacted Byronically: what Byron called "the lava of the imagination" boiled up in him, and for twenty-one days he wrote without stopping, he claimed, in an epic effluence of imaginative identification, bringing forth praise of the Noble Poet and gobs of verse, more or less accurately recalled, mixed with angry diatribes against the scurrilous mob of Lord Byron's detractors. Apologizing for quoting from memory, as he was living abroad away from his books, he also justified the practice as evidence that the poet's words (presumably, even when not exactly his) had penetrated to the inmost soul of mankind, and served as a glowing eternal monument to human feeling.

It's easy to dismiss Egerton Brydges as a Byron wannabe like so many hangers-on of the poet, early and late. A cynic might characterize his eulogy as an effort to hitch his wagon to Byron's star, and be numbered among the immortals alongside him, which might also begin to explain the priggish elderly Egerton's indifference to—indeed, his refusal to credit—Byron's scandalous sins. (At the time, aggressively moral men like Wordsworth were calling Byron's poetry immoral and vicious.) But moral and indeed literary fastidiousness melt in the blaze of fame like Byron's—while obscurity, on the other end, provokes very different responses. Jane Austen, a parson's unmarried daughter, a familiar kind of woman and his sister's neighbor in the country, was by definition of less interest to Egerton than the great lord who had bared his tortured soul, and kept aloof from the crowd that idolized him. While Egerton Brydges had probably not seen Jane Austen's letter to Cassandra, who knows what he had heard of her response to his novel? In general people tend to feel more or less the same way about one another.

One wonders what effect, if any, reading *Arthur Fitz-Albini* had on Jane Austen: did the title (together with the Norman coloration the author's sister assumed) inform her vision of Fitzwilliam Darcy? The Austen family were "great Novel readers & not ashamed of being so" (*Letters*, 26), as she boasted (with a sidelong glance at the neighbors and what they thought of novel-reading); they had a taste for books with tantalizing titles like Regina Maria Roche's *The Children of the Abbey* (1796), and may have enjoyed reading Maria Hunter's *Ella; or, He's Always in the Way* and Mary Charlton's *Phedora; or, The Forest of Minski*, both published in 1798, like *Fitz-Albini*. Austen is critical of many contemporary novelists in her letters; and she and her family, of course, did not read only novels. Jane knew ahead of time that *Fitz-Albini* was not worth buying, she tells Cassandra; while her father was surprised by its ineptness, *she* expected nothing better. (Arguably, rivalry with the neighbors begins at home; the place-specific category *neighbors*—not family and not quite friends—is imagined from inside it.) She knew what she would find: not much that was new, and not much of a story.

As if she had already imagined the intricate books she herself was to write, in which every element tells and fits as in a satisfying puzzle, she criticizes the novel for lacking coherence and integrity, and being short on plot. But she is most critical of Egerton's novel's wrong relation to real life, on both sides. "Every sentiment is completely Egerton's"—that is, not an imagined character's, and raw rather than transmuted by the imagination into something else. The actual people who are the basis for characters in what is supposed to be a fiction are not changed into imaginary people; they are identifiable versions of people the author—and at least one of his neighbors—actually knew. She condemns Egerton for writing as himself about the neighbors. She herself, to the everlasting frustration of her devotees, would not reveal her sentiments—her politics or her inner life—in the six novels she completed. She did not reveal much in her letters, either; even those written to her sister quash in advance, by their distance and tone of asperity, any hope a reader might have of self-revelation. The one that condemns *Fitz-Albini* begins with a mocking little moue of self-deprecation: "Having now relieved my heart of a great deal of malevolence, I will proceed to tell you that Mary continues quite well, and my mother tolerably so" (*Letters*, 21). And as everyone knows, Jane Austen's novels, unlike Egerton's, do not contain identifiable portraits of the neighbors, as *Fitz-Albini* so shamelessly did of the Heys and Mr. Oxenden.

"She drew from nature; but, whatever may have been surmised to the contrary, never from individuals," her brother Henry would insist in the "Biographical Notice of the Author" he published along with *Northanger Abbey* and *Persuasion*, shortly after her death—as if that fact were proof positive that her books are works of art. Henry's assertion and indeed his eagerness to seize the biographical initiative have been much remarked and commented on recently by critics who focus on the political and social context in which Austen's novels were written; his phrase "whatever may have been surmised to the contrary" has caused some eye-rolling and speculation. Who was whispering what about which characters in which novels, in 1817? Wild surmises about the relation of life and art were probably as common then as now:

certainly the belated reader, having noticed Egerton Brydges, can hardly avoid thinking of Sir Walter Elliot of Kellynch Hall, who reads no book but the Baronetage, shaking his head over the endless number of new creations. Or thinking that Egerton's sister Madame Lefroy sat unknowingly for the portrait of Lady Russell, in *Persuasion* — the prudent neighbor Sir Walter does not marry, although both are widowed, who wrecks Anne's youthful chance at love.

For the past two hundred or so years, no one has been able to read a novel by Jane Austen the way she read *Arthur Fitz-Albini*, that is, as an acquaintance of the writer and in a position to speak of her as Ulysses does in Tennyson's poem about "the great Achilles, whom we knew." Eager to know the truth behind them, belated readers of Austen's novels still collect bits and pieces that suggest what they suspect: do her wickedly observant second daughter's reports that she is "tolerably" well suggest that Mrs. Austen was an irritating hypochondriac, like Mr. Woodhouse and those comic characters she never got to finish off, in *Sanditon*?

Figurative Neighbors

The personal acquaintance of a writer reads the work with special attention, and looks in even the most fantastic fiction for suggestions of familiar things. On the other hand, writers we don't know personally become our familiars. Lending their minds out, they enter ours, and we come to think of them as persons one knows — not necessarily intimates, but neighbors.

Six years before she wrote the letter to her sister that mentions *Fitz-Albini*, in 1792, at the age of about seventeen, Jane Austen had written a story she entitled "Catharine; or, The Bower" — one of the so-called juvenilia that she took pains to make a clear copy of. The lonely young heroine of the story, sometimes called Kitty, tries at the beginning of the story to befriend a newcomer to the neighborhood by having a conversation about novels — "Books universally read and Admired," the narrator reminds us. Kitty brings up a popular novelist:

"You have read Mrs Smith's Novels, I suppose?" said she to her Companion. —"Oh! Yes," replied the other, "and I am quite delighted with them — They are the sweetest things in the world" — "And which do you prefer of them?" "Oh! dear, I think there is no comparison between them—Emmeline is *so much* better than any of the others—" "Many people think so, I know; but there does not appear so great a disproportion in their Merits to *me*; do you think it is better written?" "Oh! I do not know anything about *that*—but it is better in *everything*— Besides, Ethelinde is so long—" "That is a very common Objection I believe," said Kitty, "but for my own part, if a book is well written, I always find it too short." "So do I, only I get tired of it before it is finished." "But did not you find the story of Ethelinde very interesting? And the Descriptions of Grasmere, are not the[y] Beautiful?" "Oh! I missed them all, because I was in such a hurry to know the end of it—Then from an easy transition she added, We are going to the Lakes this Autumn, and I am quite Mad with Joy; Sir Henry Devereux has promised to go with us." (*MW*, 199)

A reader familiar with *Northanger Abbey*—or with Charlotte Smith's *Emmeline*—will recognize the conversation, in which one girl shows up the bad taste of another: it begs the question of whether novels are good for women by throwing the argument into the reader's court. Miss Camilla Stanley's language betrays her as a bad reader: her opinion is what "many people think," and her mindless gushing hyperbole—"the sweetest things in the world," and "quite Mad with Joy"—is the girlish idiom of the commonplace and unreliable Isabella Thorpe. Kitty, in contrast, prides herself on recognizing, and avoiding, what "many people think." She has a longer attention span than Camilla and a greater tolerance for passages of description (as opposed to plot); and she values books for being well written. (Whatever that means: "Oh! I do not know anything about *that*," cries Camilla, who likes to talk generally about "*everything*.") And presumably, therefore, unlike Camilla, she recognizes the differences between fiction and real life, and is not the kind of reader who moves by "an easy transition" from one to the other.

New views of English Romantic–period literature have led to a revival of interest in Charlotte Smith, the once highly regarded novelist and poet a generation older than Jane Austen who had been largely forgotten for nearly two centuries. It is on nothing like the scale of the Austen vogue, largely confined to academic circles, but there has been a good deal of interest there in Smith as a poet and a novelist, and a disappointed wife and the mother of twelve children. Renewed interest in both writers has been motivated by some of the same concerns, and indeed people curious about women's lives, women's writing, and feminist and radical politics at the turn of the eighteenth century are better served by the works of Charlotte Smith and her example than by the flickering semi-fictitious image of Jane Austen or her discreet, polished, lapidary novels. Disappointment with Jane Austen on this score has driven some to Charlotte Smith.

Born in 1749, married and a mother seventeen years later, Smith published her *Elegiac Sonnets* in 1784 and her first novel in 1788. By 1792, Jane Austen herself would have read not only *Emmeline* but also *Ethelinde* (1789) and *Celestina* (1791); in June of the year Jane Austen imagined Kitty chatting up Camilla Stanley about these woman-centered romances, Smith published *Desmond*, a novel about a man who travels to France, where he sympathizes with the revolutionaries there—but also with the upper classes whose property was being taken away. It is not known whether Jane Austen, who dated her copied-out story August 1792, was aware when she wrote it that many of Charlotte Smith's readers had turned against her because of the radical politics that *Desmond* could be interpreted as condoning. Before Smith's death in 1806, there would be six more novels, in addition to an ever-lengthening sonnet sequence, two long meditative poems, and assorted other publications—children's books, journalism, and a play. The prolific writer was well-educated and interested in natural history—botany, geology, and especially ornithology—and had begun her career by writing translations from the French.

Smith hoped that her poems would make her remembered among the English poets; she ground out novels only in order to put food on the table, she said, and claimed to like them no more than a grocer likes figs. The comparison is misleading: figs do not come in so many varieties. Instead of repeating a formula that paid off, as most writers for money do—and as she effectively did in her sonnets—Charlotte Smith was a daringly experimental writer of narratives. Her stories are not all domestic, and not only woman-centered. They take their protagonists to vastly different places, not only the Lakes and Paris but also Portugal, Calabria, and the untracked wilds (with implausible climates) of North America. Catastrophe strikes her characters in ingenious forms. In *Montalbert*, a young mother, not quite legitimate herself and not altogether legally married to an Italian Catholic, is trapped in an earthquake, with her baby, amid the ruins of Messina.

Smith, valued now for having renewed interest in the sonnet and for successfully experimenting with blank verse, influenced the poets and the novelists of her time and later. (Dickens was in her debt.) Formally, her fictions are varied—*Desmond* is a novel in letters, *Warwick* tells the story of his wanderings himself, and the narrator of *The Young Philosopher* can be caustic and detached in Jane Austen's manner, as here, when describing a character who must have impressed the author of *Northanger Abbey*: "Miss Goldthorp was a young lady naturally of a very tender and susceptible nature, and who, notwithstanding her aunt boasted of the care she had taken to prevent it, was very deeply read in romance and novels, by some one or other of the heroines of which she occasionally 'set her mind,' so that with a great versatility of character she rarely appeared in her own."[2] Smith is an ingenious composer of sentences. Describing the May–December courtship of a young woman by a military man, she writes, in *The Old Manor House*: "As to any suspicion that Isabella might think him of an age so disproportionate as to hear even his honourable offers with disdain and ridicule, it never occurred to the General; and he was pretty well assured, from the pecuniary circumstances of the family, that every other member of it would receive the remotest hint of an intended alliance with transport."[3] Suspense is built into the sentence: as Austen might do, Smith alters the standard syntactical structure, preposing the information, picking it up with the pronoun "it," and keeping the snapper—the ironic word "transport"—for the end. The choice of words is fastidious, calculated to suggest the General's complacent calculation; "disdain and ridicule" are planted early so as to get back at him, on reflection: it doesn't occur to him, but it seems true to us that he deserves both. "Pecuniary circumstances" is funny, as well—a genteel euphemism well-chosen to evade the truth. Austen surely learned from reading Charlotte Smith, especially *The Old Manor House* (1793), which combines elements of the gothic, the romance, and the sentimental novel, and anticipates the historical novel. The symbolic eponymous house is the first in the series of great but not altogether good fictional places in which pretty good people are immured—from Mansfield Park to Gosford Park and on to the lock-magnate's ugly country house in Ian McEwan's *Atonement*—structures that represent genteel family values and the cozy, sheltering image of home and England that is rotten at the core.

Although she took great pride in being Charlotte Smith of Bignor Park, in Sussex, and hankered after the pleasant ways of genteel country house living, as Jane Austen and Egerton Brydges also did, Smith espoused radical political causes: she was critical of nationalism and its wars, and she was a feminist.

Her own personal difficulties as a single mother seemed to her symptomatic of all women's, and she sympathized with Mary Wollstonecraft, condoning premarital sex and transnational marriage and strongly supporting change in the marriage and inheritance laws. She expressed sympathy for slaves (although she was not quite an abolitionist) and Catholics (especially French emigrants—her daughter married one), and boldly supported Wollstonecraft when she was mocked and condemned. In *Marchmont* she develops a historically grounded theory that anti-French feeling in England in the 1790s was nourished by memories of the Stuarts.

Her husband's fecklessness and the legal troubles that plagued her as she sought to get her father-in-law's estate settled on her children were the burden of her tales as well as their provocation: the plot of *The Banished Man*, based on her daughter's courtship, includes a character called Charlotte Denzil, who speaks the author's mind about lawyers, one of whom is named Vampyre. A public squabble with her publisher around her failure to deliver the novel in two volumes she had promised (and he had advertised) inspired her to add a satire on publishing to the conclusion of that novel. Reviewing it, *The British Critic*, in 1794, insisted that "private history should not be introduced for public perusal." It was something like Jane Austen's objection to Egerton Brydges's novel: Charlotte Smith had no such delicate qualms. Wollstonecraft and Godwin are legibly the originals for characters in *The Young Philosopher*, and the *Elegiac Sonnets* reiterate the well-known complaints of the domestically and emotionally burdened autobiographical sonneteer. A lady by birth, Smith was, years before Jane Austen, happy to figure in the literary world, pleased to mix with artists and writers— Cowper, Hayley, Romney—with whom she lived productively for a short time in a makeshift artists' colony. Although it was ambiguous and miserable, her marital status (arguably) gave her more freedom; but it was also a matter of character and taste, and of choice.

Reviewing a recent edition of Charlotte Smith's works, Gary Kelly asked why her novels were forgotten until "the burgeoning of feminist recovery in the last third of the twentieth century," while, by contrast, the novels of Jane Austen, "which build on Smith's, have much in common with them, also depart from them," were long regarded as classics, and have recently become a popular culture phenomenon.[4] One answer might contrast the continuing fascination with Austen's alluring authorial persona—"A Lady," anonymous and elusive, single and singular—with the mixed, only-human reaction to that overly explicit, nonfictional Charlotte Smith of Bignor Park in Sussex, who by writing poems about her lamentable loss of status distinguished herself from the Benjamin Smith of King's Bench Prison to whom she was irreparably married. Reading Jane Austen, we deliciously imagine being conflated with one or another of her heroines, or all of them, and also—even better—with her; Charlotte Smith, in contrast, is too many for us. She got behind too many kinds of protagonists, spread herself too thin instead of focusing narrowly, didn't have the time—working too hard, as she did, at too many other things, and counting—to play engagingly with the reader and invent a distinctive and consistent authorial personality of her own.

Country Village

Jane Austen's best readers have found certain passages in her works to be especially dense with secrets and hints about her motives, meanings, practices, and views. One occurs at the mid-point of *Emma*—in the middle of the ninth of eighteen chapters, in the second of three books; in the geographical and social center of Highbury, in the midst of Harriet Smith's shopping at Ford's store. Emma stands just outside the door of Ford's, looking "for amusement." The dramatic climax of what action there is will come later, at the picturesque elevation of Box Hill, but this well-known passage in the thick of things seems to be on many counts central:

> Much could not be hoped from the traffic of even the busiest part of Highbury;—Mr. Perry walking hastily by, Mr. William Cox letting himself in at the office door, Mr. Cole's carriage horses returning from exercise, or a stray letter-boy on an obstinate mule, were the liveliest objects she could presume to expect; and when her eyes fell only on the butcher with his tray, a tidy old woman travelling homewards from shop with her full basket, two curs quarrelling over a dirty bone, and a string of dawdling children round the baker's little bow-window eyeing the gingerbread, she knew she had no reason to complain, and was amused enough; quite enough still to stand at the door. A mind lively and at ease, can do with seeing nothing, and can see nothing that does not answer. (*E*, 233)

What Emma actually sees in the heart of Highbury surely fails to measure up to her hopes of amusement, although those are not high: while the people she expects to see—Mr. Perry, Mr. William Cox—are her social inferiors, the nameless creatures she does see are lower in the hierarchy of beings, indeed disturbingly beneath the village society she queens it over. The tidy old woman and the children, the horses, the dogs fighting over a dirty bone, and especially the butcher's tray of meat—all are a far cry from the characters whose manners and worth Emma spends her time considering.

The list of secondary and dead creatures begins to suggest that an ominous gloom threatens to inflect Emma's boredom—that her idle moment is redolent of mortality. She has, after all, been through a confusing time: the marriage of her governess to Mr. Weston, a small local landholder, and the consequent if late arrival in town of his attractive wealthy son (and as it seems fortuitously, of the competitively attractive and worthy Jane Fairfax) threaten the high place from which she has been used to look down. Having herself taken up Harriet Smith, she has had to think about Harriet's other connections, to advise her against marrying the farmer Robert Martin and to pronounce her friends the Coxes "vulgar." In her boredom and loneliness, Emma has finally been driven to visit Harriet's friends the Coles, who like the Coxes merely aspire to mix with the more established genteel families; and she has begun to get caught up in a nearly open rivalry with Jane Fairfax, who seems doomed to be a governess, a position or place that Jane compares to a slave's. Emma's sense of social place and of geographical place has become confused: chatting with Frank about Highbury, in the preceding chapter, she began to "feel she had been used to despise the place rather too much" (221). A mind as lively as Emma's is self-reflexive: suffering the low level of conversation at the Coles, she had found herself half-admiring Harriet for being satisfied with its banality. Irony is an aspect of her liveliness of mind: so how are we to read the reflections that go through her mind as she stands outside Ford's? And is it in fact her mind that's at issue, or her creator's?

Many critics have wondered whether this striking passage—frequently offered as a brilliant example of Austen's free indirect style—does not express Jane Austen's views as well as Emma's. Emma, after all, is an "Imaginist": she makes matches as the author of a courtship novel does. The passage describing what she sees from the doorway of Ford's lends itself to being read as an apologia for the famously cheerful accommodation to narrow circumstances that Austen's biographical brother and nephew praised her for, and her own boast of being interested in such trivia as the purchase of a sponge cake. Is this passage a justification for the famous lack of event and of "scope" in her novels, *Emma* especially? Is the author, in this strategically located passage, making it clear that she knows *Emma* is a novel about nothing?[5] Or is the point of the passage that Emma—nothing herself, a conventional character in a novel or at best a chilly young woman with a mind of winter, like the snowman in the Wallace Stevens poem—sees nothing that is not there and the nothing that is? And—to change registers from the metaphysical to the comic—does the description of what Emma sees outside Ford's signal to the author's secret friends that for the right-minded, lively-minded reader, as for a writer of the same stamp, nothing will do perfectly well—as it would not for the author of, say, *Fitz-Albini*?

Yes and no: it's hard to say whether Emma or the narrator is making the observations. It's just like this novelist to raise the big questions about the meaning of life and the capacities of lively minds, as it is just her style to stand in the doorway between her heroine's mind and her own: she pretty much invented the posture. Jane Austen's lack of interest in describing the particulars of right hand and left is well known:[6] the often-quoted descriptions of Pemberley (seen through Elizabeth's eyes) and of Donwell Abbey (seen through Emma's), and the rhapsody about the scenic cliffs at Lyme, are telling but dull set pieces. The busy scene that Emma contemplates from the doorway at Ford's is in comparison interesting. On one level grotesque, as I have read it, it is on another level the kind of view of a village street that might be turned out by a painter working in the genre of the picturesque. Sounding a little like Mary Crawford, Jane Austen declared in a letter that "my preference for Men & Women, always inclines me to attend more to the company than the sight" (*Letters*, 179). Her preference is for company and conversation, the interaction of men, women, and words, rather than the mutes Emma sees from her distance, a tidy old woman and a letter-boy as inarticulate as the horses and dogs beside them. (The recent films have distorted the Austen novels by making too much of interesting-looking horses and dogs, signifiers of the embodied life.)

Austen's attention to "the company" is also to its unarticulated motives and conscious and unconscious intentions—to her people's inner lives. Like Emma at the party at the Coles, who congratulates Mr. Knightley for arriving with appropriate dignity, in his carriage, instead of walking as he usually does, she enjoys noticing (or imagining) relations between behavior and character. "Nonsensical girl," Knightley says affectionately to Emma when she congratulates him for using his carriage; reading that, we share his warmth; but soon we discover that Knightley's carriage was intended for the comfort of Jane Fairfax and her aunt, and not as a show of the owner's dignity. The plot has thickened, and we are beginning to worry about the thickness of Emma's skull. But although (and because) she errs, her mind remains lively, like Elizabeth Bennet's mind, the liveliness of which (Mr. Darcy declares) made him fall in love with her. Mr. Knightley likes Emma's mind, too. His rebuke of her for teasing Miss Bates at Box Hill, a more serious version of his fond "Nonsensical girl," hardly signals the humiliation of Emma Woodhouse that a different, moralizing novelist might think necessary. Emma is rude and wrong, at Box Hill, for teasing Miss Bates, and Mr. Knightley is right again; as she has also underestimated Jane Fairfax's capacity to understand her, she underestimates her aunt's, and is heedless of the other woman's feelings. But like Emma and like Jane Austen, we have to laugh at the nattering Miss Bates—and forgive Emma because she means to be better.

As a lively young woman, Jane Austen herself was, like Emma, imprisoned in a country village, in a dull provincial society, and in the wearing banalities of women's domestic life. Riskier still, she must have feared, was the effect domestic life might have on her imagination. Writing of the contemporary novelist Jane West ("good Mrs. West," in her words), she wondered tartly how "Composition" was possible for a woman with a numerous family like hers, and (as the younger Jane put it) a head full of rhubarb and joints of mutton (*Letters*, 321). But for her, as well, domestic business threatened to seep into the mind. Sometimes it was, ironically, a source of metaphor: "Could my Ideas flow as fast as the rain in the Store closet it would be charming," she wrote to her sister, having been "in two or three dreadful states within the last week, from the melting of the snow &c." (*Letters*, 169). For Jane Austen, novelists like Jane West, like characters in novels and neighbors in the village, were people interestingly like and unlike her; it was amusing to regard them as one regarded Mrs. Ferrars, as meant to amuse.

Like many eighteenth- and nineteenth-century families, the Austens read novels aloud together: one of her nieces recalls listening in while Aunt Jane read her work in progress to her sister and friends, who could be heard chortling appreciatively behind closed doors. This intimacy encouraged some to write fiction. While she was composing *Emma*, Austen wrote a letter of advice to her eldest niece Anna, who was also writing a novel:

> You are now collecting your People delightfully, getting them exactly
> into such a spot as is the delight of my life; —3 or 4 Families in a Coun-
> try Village is the very thing to work on—& I hope you will write a great
> deal more, & make full use of them while they are so very favourably
> arranged. You are but *now* coming to the heart & beauty of your book;
> till the heroine grows up, the fun must be imperfect—but I expect a
> great deal of entertainment from the next 3 or 4 books, & I hope you
> will not resent these remarks by sending me no more.   (*Letters*, 275)

Sometimes cited as evidence that Austen preferred or even required a country village as the setting for her novels, it is not: when the Dashwood sisters
remove to London, in *Sense and Sensibility*, their lives continue to include
the same set of people. The country and the city offer equal opportunities
for characteristic action: in Austen, place, like character, is most interestingly
imagined as somewhere between the general and the particular, between
invention and literary cliché. But "the heart & beauty" of any book, in her
view, was the fun of it.

Austen was a tough critic of other novelists: in another letter to Anna,
written two weeks later, she would assert that "Walter Scott has no business
to write novels, especially good ones. . . . He has Fame and Profit enough as
a Poet, and should not be taking the bread out of other people's mouths," and
also allege, "I think I *can* be stout against any thing written by Mrs. West.—I
have made up my mind to like no Novels really, but Miss Edgeworth's, Yours
& my own" (*Letters*, 277–278). It is hard to gauge the shifting tone of the
accomplished aunt's critique of her niece's novel in progress. "I *do* think you
had better omit Lady Helena's postscript;—to those who are acquainted with
P.&P. it will seem an Imitation," she writes to her young competitor (*Letters*,
268); and again, "Milton wd have given his eyes to have thought of it," she
writes of a fictitious character's name she judges "a Nonpareil" (*Letters*, 276).
Interestingly, among her extant letters, the ones to her novel-writing niece
come closest in tone to her novels.

Country Village, Late 1990s

New ironies threaten to drive out the old ones. An essay posted on the
Internet in 2007 under the screaming headline "Jane Austen Must Die!"

argued that the popular vogue condescended to women, and ended with the challenging advice to "Pick up a book—one that has absolutely nothing to do with Jane Austen."[7] More recently, in an article in the *New York Times Book Review*, a "Los Angeles–based writer and critic" also committed to the cause of women deplores the fact that in fiction "female friendships remain strangely underexplored, unlike the search for true love (I'm talking about *you*, Jane Austen)."[8] Familiarity breeds contempt; simplifications trump complexity; writing has driven out reading; Jane-o-mania has gone on too long.

On the other hand, as the audience for things Jane-Austen has become larger, more varied, more vocal, and even more clubby and chummy, fans have made new friends and had more fun. At local and regional JASNA meetings, members have lifted glasses of sherry with the toast "To Jane" on her birthday; at national conventions, people have bought and sold books and bookmarks and book-shaped thimbles with pictures of Jane's characters on them, and played raucous games of "Jane Jeopardy." At one meeting I attended, a middle-aged speaker costumed in a purple turban and feathers and a matching Empire-style gown provoked thrills of recognition and gales of laughter by introducing herself with the words of Isabella Thorpe: "I know I look awful in purple, but it's your brother's favorite color" (*NA*, 218). The vogue has inspired fellowship and civility: at its margins, ladies in broad-brimmed hats have gathered in gardens across America for Austen-themed traditional teas, and high school students have been talked into tea-drinking. Even the French, who had never liked her novels, were caught by the wave the movies started: Jane Austen's novels were published in the prestigious Pléiade series for the first time in 2000.

In the late nineties, "Jane Austen" the adjective began turning up in private conversations. A lesbian friend of mine told me in confidence that a "Jane Austen romance" had converted her back to men, sure I would understand what she meant (I didn't). Another acquaintance quite as gnomically described a "Jane Austen moment" she had shared with a man at a party. A man someone introduced me to in Vermont produced an oil painting of Jane Austen based on existing pictures and his Janeite imagination: he offered it to the people at Chawton, and when they turned it down he and his wife made it the focal point of an English tearoom they opened. My own personal favorite Jane Austen moment occurred in my kitchen in Vermont in the late 1990s. Not especially genteel and not romantic, either, it recalled the theme the novels insist on, that talking about the neighbors and being talked about by them creates the sense and the substance of community. Those neighbors who comment like a chorus on the goings-on in the Bennet family, deploring their unlucky lot when Lydia runs off with a bungling fortune hunter and marveling at their good fortune when Jane and Elizabeth land their prize husbands, are still with us: reading, we measure our relation to the neighbors, gauge and take our distance from them as we learn to do, in our lives, from our own. "Charles Powlett gave a dance on Thursday," Jane Austen wrote to her sister Cassandra, "to the great disturbance of all his neighbours, of course, who, you know, take a most lively interest in the state of his finances, and live in hopes of his being soon ruined" (*Letters*, 25); and again, a couple of weeks later, "Charles Powlett has been very ill, but is getting well again; — his wife is discovered to be everything that the Neighbourhood could wish her, silly & cross as well as extravagant" (*Letters*, 26). And, rather more thoughtfully, "The Wylmots being robbed must be an amusing thing to their acquaintance, & I hope it is as much their pleasure as it seems their avocation to be subjects of general Entertainment" (*Letters*, 76).

There is just as much of *that* going on as there was in Mrs. Bennet's neighborhood: what the neighbors say about them still matters to people in apartment houses, offices, and academic departments, and certainly in country villages. Gossip fills our time, sets our standards, connects us with others, and defines us. What the neighbors say, what we expect they will say, what we say about them continues to organize people's lives — and of course who we think our neighbors are does. That Emma does not notice the farmer Robert Martin as her neighbor necessitates some explanation of the class system to twenty-first-century readers, but it's not hard to see contemporary analogues. In the pleasant village in Vermont where I spend summers, where everyone wishes everyone a good morning and a nice day, everyone wants to know everything about the pair of rich young men who have recently moved into the neighborhood, who have just made sport for their neighbors by parking a shiny new Porsche in their driveway. (Another Subaru Outback would not have the same effect.) The quality of laughter at the neighbors depends on their cars, characters, and caste, and on which of the neighbors are laughing. In a small town, still, everyone knows who everyone is, and who they think they are: the ladies who sponsor the chamber music society in my town, for instance, would never think of inviting Hester, whose husband collects the trash, to tea.

So when my mother did—she spent the summers with us there—it was with a glint of sly mischief. My mother was proud of her democratic politics and personal charm, and she was bored by the usual gossip about new cars and wives among the gentry who imagined themselves better than new-comers, summer people, people from "away"—flatlanders, as they used to say, like us. She was delighted to do what she knew the locals would not do. And of course, most important of all, she wanted to know the true details of the stale old scandal that everyone in the village had for years been taking for granted (but still snickering about)—that the man who collected the trash was married to his own aunt. She herself had been raised by aunts. Also, she liked Hester, especially after the upright, faded, girlish old woman remarked to her in passing that she'd never seen the sea: if history had gone differently and she herself had not had the bravery and the good luck to cross the ocean to America in the 1920s, my mother might have been in the same boat. Hester was a soft-spoken woman somewhere between my mother's age and mine; like us both she liked to talk. So I rustled up three teacups with matching saucers and we got right to it at the kitchen table— or Hester did.

"When Nathan came home from the war in Vietnam," she began, after the preliminary exchange of pleasantries, "he had no home to go to. Both his parents were dead long before he was drafted, and his only brother passed many years before. Our Billy used to hang around him, at school, and when he came back he came back here. My husband had passed some months ear-lier, and Billy still lived here in the house with me, and of course Wayne and little Carol Sue. It was a hard time, and Nathan was a help with the little ones, very tender; he was a great help to me. So eventually the two of us got together, and then we got married." She beamed, and then frowned. "That's when the people in the village stopped saying 'Hello' to me, folks I'd gone to school with, people I'd known my whole life. They were friendly enough with Nathan, who took over my husband's business of collecting rubbish, but they avoided me: crossed the street when they saw me, went down a dif-ferent aisle in the market, snubs like that. It went on for years," she said, and then, very mildly and demurely, "I think of it now, summers, when Nathan and I mow down at the cemetery: I mow over their graves, and I smile to myself as I think of how they shunned me."

Like all stories, this one invites the listener or reader to put herself in some sympathetic relation to the people in it—Hester and her neighbors, my mother and me. It is and is not like a story in Jane Austen: on the one hand, there is the country village and the woman who (like Emma) has never seen the sea, the anxieties about what the neighbors say and about being as good as or better than the neighbors, the social comedy of jockeying for position, the tragedy that one neighbor's gain is another one's loss, and the irony of inevitable fate. But on the other hand there's that American confusion of classes and generations, and a scandal too low-end, socially and morally, for an Austen novel. The human relationships at play, in and around my story and Jane Austen's, differ depending on exactly who is involved: if you happen to know Hester or her village or one near it or like it, if you knew my mother or know me, you will care more. It's a tricky business.

Commenting on the tragedies and comedies of individual lives, the neighbors (like parents and children and husbands and wives) have an impact on character—on human nature. Disapproval and disdain, exclusion from the group, injures a person's pride and self-love; resentment and rancor turn pleasant people sour; and civility and savagery are relatives. (Mr. Darcy to Sir William Lucas: "Every savage can dance.") Clever, sprightly Mary Crawford, who hopes to marry Edmund Bertram, cheerfully expresses her hope that his older brother Tom will die so Edmund will inherit the title and the estate. Jane Austen would have enjoyed Hester's situation and story, I think, more than such faux-elegant recent titles as *The Darcys and the Bingleys: A Tale of Two Gentlemen's Marriages to Two Most Devoted Sisters* (2009)—Jane Austen the student of human nature in country villages, the maker of those teasingly endogamous matches between Fanny and Edmund and Emma and Mr. Knightley, the cold chronicler of Mrs. Churchill's timely demise, the novelist who mocks whiney Mary Musgrove for claiming precedence over her pleasant mother-in-law.

George Eliot, whose thinking was strongly influenced by Austen's novels, imagined human society as a web and believed that sympathizing with imaginary characters in fiction strengthened the politically vital muscle of human sympathy. Of her last, broadest-ranging novel, *Daniel Deronda*, which is about—among other extraordinary subjects—the history of the Jews, she wrote that everything in it was connected to everything else there. Separation with connection, or sympathy with others who are not like you, just might be the theme of the novel in what F. R. Leavis called the "Great Tradition," the one that began with Jane Austen and flowered in the nineteenth century, when people in Europe and America, who had good reason to be worried about violence and war as well as ancestral voices prophesying war, began to fear for civilization as they thought they knew it, and began to revalue the vestiges or records or fantasies of a more civil and moral private life that are preserved as if in amber in the "classic" English novel.

FIGURE 12. *George Gordon Byron, 6th Baron Byron*, replica by Thomas Phillips, oil on canvas, ca. 1835. Courtesy National Portrait Gallery, London.

CHAPTER 4

Authors

Saw all worth seeing and then descended to the "Bosquet de Julie" etc. etc.—
our Guide full of *Rousseau*—whom he is eternally confounding with *St Preux*—
and mixing the man and the book—on the steps of a cottage in the village—I
saw a young *paysanne*—beautiful as Julie herself.
—Lord Byron, "Alpine Journal"

A S VIRGINIA WOOLF REFLECTS IN *A ROOM OF ONE'S OWN*, THE
subjects of women and fiction are tangled together. Richardson and
Rousseau had firmed up the knot between them in the eighteenth
century, and the women writers of the period complicated it. In *Nobody's Story:
The Vanishing Acts of Women Writers in the Marketplace,* 1670–1820 (1994),
Catherine Gallagher argues that the interest in women writers and woman-
centered narratives that burgeoned in the eighteenth century was perversely
enabled by the fact—the fiction—that novel heroines (unlike actresses) had
no bodies and had never actually lived, and therefore that their hidden inner
lives were fair game and safe subjects for speculation. Women who wrote and
acted for the stage, often the same people, flirtatiously worked and played at
concealing and revealing their private lives and parts, at being—on and offstage—public women, accessible. To write about women who had no bodies
was at once to beg the intriguing question the actress posed and also to exploit
it. To publish, of course, was to go public, to point toward, if not to exhibit
and reveal, one's private self. The genteel woman who wrote a love story about
a fictitious person and concealed her own identity and name—but specified
her sex and class, as the unnamed author of *Sense and Sensibility* did—was
gaming the system, promising to reveal all, exploiting the prurience that had

helped make Richardson's *Pamela* a best-seller, while remaining modest—as they said then, honest. The posture was replete with paradoxes.

The front matter of two unsigned first novels that bracket Austen's brief career as a publishing writer suggests the predicament of women authors in and around her time and place. Frances Burney's *Evelina; or, The History of a Young Lady's Entrance Into the World* was published in 1778 (when Jane Austen was three) with both a verse dedication "To —", the "author of my being," and a letter in prose, expressing "anxious solicitude," addressed "To the Authors of the Monthly and Critical Reviews." Both of these pre-texts express the young writer's anxiety about authorship. (To her private diary, Burney had confided "the terror of being attacked *as an author*": evidently she hoped to deflect attacks by courteously calling the critics themselves "Authors."[1]) Forty years after Burney's first novel was published, a much more startling fiction by an even younger woman, *Frankenstein; or, The Modern Prometheus* (1818), was published anonymously, with a disingenuous prefatory epigraph from *Paradise Lost* ("Did I request thee, Maker, from my clay / To mould me man?") and a more explicit proud dedication: "To WILLIAM GODWIN, Author of Political Justice, Caleb Williams, &c, These volumes are respectfully inscribed by THE AUTHOR." Mary Shelley boldly took the name "Author" and named her father as Frances Burney did not name hers—William Godwin, the celebrated political philosopher and novelist, who was even more famous in his time than the London music master Dr. Charles Burney had been.

Evelina is a woman-centered domestic novel about courtship that ends in marriage, which was by 1778 a conventional form of fiction for a woman writer to choose. In radical contrast, *Frankenstein* is a fantastic book about a man who creates a man without a woman's help: Victor Frankenstein rejects his own family, including the "sister" adopted by his parents who is also his fiancée, to devote himself to the arduous work of producing his hideous progeny. As if to emphasize his being the monster's only begetter, he tears apart the mate he began making at the creature's request. In an essay on Mary Shelley and her novel, the feminist critic Ellen Moers elaborates the anxieties evoked in both men and women by women's power to create another living being, and its relation to the power to author books.[2] (The feminist writer Mary Wollstonecraft died days after giving birth to her daughter Mary.) While ideas about both biological and authorial creation have radically changed since the early nineteenth century, anxieties about generation and originality linger, along with old myths—like the one that the Austen family was so genteel that Jane was constrained to publish anonymously.

By now, literary and social historians have richly documented the importance, brilliance, conspicuousness, and number of eighteenth-century women intellectuals and writers. While the dedications to Burney's and Shelley's novels reflect the continuing force of patriarchy in their lives, it is also the case that both these middle-class writers eventually did embrace the name of author as well as the career of writing—as raffish Aphra Behn and Eliza Haywood had done earlier on. Born to a different kind of father, having a different relation to him, Jane Austen surely had other personal reasons as well for choosing to publish anonymously. If some of her unwillingness to claim authorship outright was related to her position—and her anxieties—as a genteel spinster of a retiring temperament who was reluctant to put herself forward, another factor was her sense of humor. Authorial self-importance struck her as comical. Committed to the popular, "feminine," "low" genre of the courtship novel and its constraints, a reader of both serious books and popular fiction, a self-conscious and self-critical writer from the beginning, she was suspicious of the fashionable Romantic claim of originality.

As a girl, Jane Austen attached dedications to the stories she liked to read aloud to friends and family: she chose to sign them "The Author." She copied them out into volumes that she numbered I, II, and III, as if they were volumes in a single conventional novel. When her father sent "First Impressions" to a publisher, he described it as a work like *Evelina*. When she finally did publish, in 1811, she was middle-aged and her father was dead. Like Frances Burney and Mary Godwin Shelley, she did not put her name on her first novel. *Sense and Sensibility* was signed "By a Lady" (by accident or design "Lady A," in one 1811 newspaper advertisement). Her subsequent books were identified as "By the author of Sense and Sensibility, etc." This reticence, I think, is best understood as reflecting a skeptical view of authorship that is consistent with her sense of the world (and of the word "author" and its cognates). She critically, half-mockingly embraced the conventions of novels and novel-writing from her simplest, earliest works (like "Edgar and Emma," in *Volume the First*) to her subtlest late ones (*Emma, Persuasion*, and *Sanditon*). A Jane Austen imitator avant la lettre, she was interested in rewriting conventional plots and character types: she was less concerned to be Romantically original than to refine and enrich her chosen genre, to invest the novel form with more and subtler meanings. Early and late, she mocked the pompous role of author, which was being taken increasingly seriously during the years she wrote and published.

Jane Austen was in no position to read Keats's letter about "the Egotistical Sublime" or Wordsworth's long poem subtitled "The Growth of a Poet's Mind," any more than she could have read Roland Barthes or Michel Foucault on the hegemony of discourse and the "Death of the Author." She died almost a decade before the publication of Hazlitt's essay on Byron that objects to his drawing attention to himself. Hazlitt compares Byron's style unfavorably to Scott's more transparent style, and in solemn accents intones that "To be Noble and a Poet is too much for humanity." Written in 1824, the year Byron died—the news of the death of the author interrupted the composition—Hazlitt's essay begins to suggest, as Byron himself did, that the poet who seemed so much larger than life was an anomaly, more and less—or even other—than human.[3]

The notion of the great writer as both a godlike creator and the quintessence of the human is a Romantic idea that continues to fascinate readers: in its time—because it was her time—it would have had to engage Jane Austen. Recently, it has driven the imagination and the career of Richard Holmes, the contemporary "Romantic biographer"; his great predecessor was James Boswell, arguably the first groupie, who hung on and wrote down the words of General Paoli of Corsica, the philosopher Rousseau, and, at great length, Dr. Johnson. The revival and idolatry of Shakespeare in Boswell's time, spurred by Johnson's friend the actor David Garrick, may have marked the beginning of modern literary celebrity. By the beginning of the next century, there was widespread interest in the unique selves and personal lives of writers. William Hazlitt wrote autobiographical as well as biographical essays; he not only recalled his first encounters with the poets Coleridge and Wordsworth but also published an account of an episode in his own amorous life that is still embarrassing to read.

Byron himself grandiosely compared himself to his grandiose contemporary Napoleon, styling himself "the grand Napoleon of the realms of rhyme"; in a very different tone, his estranged wife made the same comparison, writing, "He is the absolute monarch of words and uses them, as Buonaparte did lives, for conquest without more regard for their intrinsic value."[4] A novelist fascinated by pretensions and posturing would have been very interested in the aggrandized Romantic self. "Pictures of perfection make me sick and wicked," Jane Austen wrote about the standard, implausible, flawless novel heroine (*Letters*, 335). Although hardly such a picture, Lord Byron paid portrait painters to record his striking beauty; his publisher had engravings of his likeness printed in his books. His self-importance would have irritated her.

Young and wonderfully handsome, the son of a rough Scottish heiress and the dissolute scion of an old family who was known as "Mad Jack" Byron, he inherited from a great-uncle, at the age of ten, a title and a dilapidated abbey in the north of England that was said to be haunted by monks. The publication of *Childe Harold's Pilgrimage, a Romaunt—Childe Burun's Pilgrimage*, in one manuscript—made him, overnight, a celebrity. It was a poem in two cantos, in Spenserian stanzas, about a privileged young man who had "felt the fullness of satiety" and traveled to the exotic East—from which Lord Byron had in fact just returned, poem in hand. In the elegant Whig circles that swirled through Holland House, in London, the young lord's lines about Harold and the "laughing dames in whom he did delight . . . [who] long had fed his youthful appetite" were hard not to read as self-referential—and provocatively specific. "Childe Harold basked him in the noon-tide sun, / Disporting there like any other fly," Byron wrote of his hero: it was thrilling and astonishing, at a time when peers had power and thrones were being shaken, to think that a Noble Poet could see and portray himself thus. It made him seem the more exceptional that Lord Byron spoke so directly and confidentially to the reading public, as a man like any other.

He acted out heroic roles off the page, in public and in private. Briefly, he took up a liberty-loving legislator's role in the House of Lords; by turns, he played the roles that playwrights and novelists had elaborated, of the well-born rake and the eligible young man. He dabbled in adultery, homosexuality, incest, and marriage, separating from his young wife and baby after a year. There were rumors and gossip, broadsides and caricatures. Byron wrote plays and sat on the board at Drury Lane Theatre, and after he left England for good in 1816, he took "the pageant of his bleeding heart," as Shelley called it, across the Continent, traveling in a special carriage he had ordered made on the model of Napoleon's. (When his companion and private physician John Polidori wrote of Byron's rape or seduction of a chambermaid that he "fell upon her like a thunderbolt," people were meant to remember that Napoleon was said to have fallen thus upon Italy.) Byron spoke as more than a metaphor for his country when he thundered against his brother peer Lord Elgin for stealing the Parthenon marbles; when he meddled in revolutionary politics in Italy, he did so as his nation's representative, alleging that "as a member of the English House of Peers, he would be a traitor to the principles which placed the reigning family of England on the throne" if he failed to support the new Neapolitan parliament.[5] When he died in 1824 it was at the head of a small army he had assembled, having lent his body as well as his money and famous name to the fight for Greek freedom that he had joined together with the brother of his "last attachment," Teresa Guiccioli.

Austen and Byron were contemporaries (she was twelve years older); accidents of biography might have made them, as many have been pleased to imagine them, secret friends, for all their obvious differences.[6] Their separate circles nearly intersected. They might have encountered one another early on, for example, in the Hampshire countryside, where he visited his solicitor John Hanson's family to enjoy the shooting. They might have met later, in Bath, or in London at the theatres and art exhibits that they both frequented or at a party for Madame de Stael to which both of them, allegedly, were invited (the story goes that he accepted, but she turned the invitation down). They had acquaintances in common—poor disturbed Lord Portsmouth, who always invited the Austen sisters to his balls, and the Scottish physician Matthew Baillie, brother of the playwright Joanna (Miss Milbanke's mother's friend), who had been called in to "treat" the boy Byron's lame leg by screwing it into a painful device and later, more successfully, tended Austen's brother Henry in an illness. For a few years the two writers shared a publisher, John Murray—"a Rogue, of course, but a civil one," in Austen's acerb judgment (*Letters*, 291). It would have been hard for her not to be aware, like everyone else in England, of that rogue of a different order, Murray's most important author, Lord Byron.

Jane Austen might have heard tell of Byron even before his years of fame, noticing (not without envy, surely) the juvenile imitations of Greek and Latin lyric poets that he had managed to publish before his majority. She would have relished the poet's bold angry satire against the critics who had attacked his first volume, and later on his other satires, which would have appealed to another witty critic of the same culture and society. Certainly she would have heard the gossip about his affair with madcap Caroline Lamb, Lady Melbourne's daughter-in-law, who dressed as a page boy to steal Byron's portrait from Murray's office. She might have got a whiff of the gossip about his marriage and the Separation, and Lady Byron's respectable "Policy of Silence" that made everyone so curious about his sexual secrets—including his affair with his married half-sister Augusta Leigh. Although Austen died before she could have read the 1818 novel by his former mistress that inspired Byron's terse critique in rhyme—"I read *Glenarvon* too, by Caro Lamb / God damn"—there are bits of Byron in the last novel she herself completed, which marries its heroine, in the end, to an ocean-going adventurer, a man of feeling with a piratical air, a satirical eye, and a scornfully curling lip.

In *Persuasion*, Anne Elliot and Captain Wentworth's sentimental friend Captain Benwick go "through a brief comparison of opinion as to the first-rate poets, trying to ascertain whether *Marmion* or *The Lady of the Lake* were to be preferred, and how ranked the *Giaour* and *The Bride of Abydos;* and moreover, how the *Giaour* was to be pronounced." When Benwick repeats, "with such tremulous feeling, the various lines which imaged a broken heart, or a mind destroyed by wretchedness, and look[s] so entirely as if he meant to be understood," Anne ventures "to hope he did not always read only poetry," and recommends "a larger allowance of prose in his daily study" (*P*, 100–101). The reader suspects that Lord Byron (along with Scott) is being laughed at. The allusion to "Lord Byron's dark blue sea," in the same section of that novel, is tantalizingly ambiguous, either mocking the poet's excessive claims of intimacy with the sea or acknowledging he had staked a successful claim to it. A giggle is more unmistakable in the second of two letters Austen wrote to her sister on 5 March 1814, just a month after Byron's *The Corsair* had sold a remarkable ten thousand copies—and led his publisher to offer him an astonishing ten thousand guineas. (When *Sense and Sensibility* sold out the year before, it brought her only one hundred and forty pounds.) The letter to Cassandra begins with an apology: "Do not be angry with me for beginning another Letter to you. I have read The Corsair, mended my petticoat, & have nothing else to do" (*Letters*, 257).

She does not mention Lord Byron in her very next letter from London in which she writes to Cassandra, "What cruel weather this is! And here is Lord Portsmouth married too to Miss Hanson!" (*Letters*, 261). The two exclamation points connect one "cruel" subject to another: Jane must have known of the circumstances of her titled neighbor's wedding. Lord Portsmouth, the Austens' mentally deficient neighbor in Hampshire, had been deliberately married off in his youth by his greedy brothers to a woman too old to bear him an heir; a widower by 1813, he was bullied into a second marriage to the daughter of the man who managed his money. John Hanson was Byron's man of business as well as Portsmouth's; as youths the peers had tangled in Hanson's house. Gossip had it that Mary Anne Hanson had been Byron's mistress, that he was making good on an old promise to make a lady of her when he gave her away to Portsmouth in the ceremony that Jane Austen would have read about in the papers. (Byron noted ruefully in his journal that he "rammed their left hands, by mistake, into one another," having drunk too much the night before.[7])

Jane Austen's name does not turn up in any of the voluminous letters, poems, and prose notes Byron wrote, although he did once boast he had read over 4,000 novels.[8] In a letter requesting a copy of Frances Burney's last novel, *The Wanderer* (in 1814—the year *Mansfield Park* was published) to help Lord Holland through the gout, he wrote, "I would almost fall sick myself to get at Me. D'Arblay's writings."[9] Elsewhere he claims that "when I do read, I can only bear the chicken broth of—*any thing* but novels."[10] To mock novels as an inferior feminine form was to take the standard masculine line, which Byron sometimes did and sometimes made fun of doing. "I am every thing by turns, and nothing long," he boasted proudly. Writing about his poem *The Bride of Abydos*, he expressed some anxiety about creating a female character—but his tone is coy. "I . . . have endeavoured as far as ye grossness of our masculine ideas will allow—to preserve her purity without impairing the ardour of her attachment,"[11] he explains to his journal. The ardor of his female characters has been admired by generations of Byron's readers.[12]

Byron and Austen both began writing in their youth by imitating romance—and mocking it. "Away with your fictions of flimsy romance," wrote the very young Lord Byron, in "The First Kiss of Love," published in his first volume of lyrics.[13] Of the awakened heroine of her youthful *Northanger Abbey*, Austen writes in the same vein that "the visions of romance were gone" (199). *Don Juan* begins, "I want a hero"; it goes on to disparage the military and political leaders written up in the newspapers, and takes, instead, a hero from "the pantomime," and popular legend. The narrator's alleged want or lack of a hero recalls the "want of a wife" in the first sentence of *Pride and Prejudice*—the lack misperceived as a desire, the perception of absence that generates the story. The opening of *Don Juan* is reminiscent as well of the challenging first sentence of *Northanger Abbey*, the declaration that "No one who had ever seen Catherine Morland in her infancy, would have supposed her born to be an heroine," which begins to fashion her into just that. The cool Austenian narrator can make an ordinary Catherine Morland a heroine; the cool Byronic narrator can make the pliant Juan a hero—in both cases by giving them substance (or words), putting them in a story, writing about them. Making a point of their authorial power, both writers insist as well, as W. H. Auden pointed out, on the power and the resonances of literary tradition and form.

Although for some reason she transcribed Byron's "Ode to Napoleon Buonaparte" when it was anonymously published in April 1814, Jane Austen did not reflect in print on either the Noble Poet's obsession with the emperor or other people's obsession with Byron.[14] But as a reader she had to have recognized Byron's knack of creating complicity with his reader, a gift she had herself. Byron's pose of aloofness and apartness, his satirical disdain and hints at dark secrets, made his readers feel his distance and at the same time feel like his intimates: in her different way, Jane Austen pulled off the same stunt. If his sexual promiscuousness helped to make Byron a literary celebrity, his confession of intimate thwarted longings ensured his readers' identification with him, and his fame. Generations have felt his personal attractions—and felt that he shared their secret desires to be extraordinary, rebellious, and original, good and bad, and sympathetically understood. If Jane Austen, in Byron's time, pointedly refused Byron, Byronism, and the Byronic authorial mode, like Byron she too forged a secret-seeming, successful personal connection with her readers, pointedly keeping herself personally out of it—as A Lady, or a mocking parody of one, might do.

It is impossible to name the many men and women who have tried to imitate or collaborate with or in some sense *be* Lord Byron—poets from John Clare and Laetitia Landon, and novelists who include his former mistress Lady Caroline Lamb (*Glenarvon* [1818]), his friend's wife Mary Shelley (*The Last Man* [1826]), and Benjamin Disraeli (*Venetia* [1837]), whose literary father had known Byron. Harriet Beecher Stowe, who knew and admired and eloquently championed Byron's angry widow—and condemned the poet and the male coterie that supported him—quotes his verses throughout *The Minister's Wooing* (1859), which she sent to Lady Byron to vet; Emily and Charlotte Bronte, who had only heard of him and read his poems, reimagined him in their saturnine heroes. Byron and his works have inspired ballets and operas, and personalities and performers of all kinds. When he heard of the older poet's death, the young Alfred Tennyson is said to have carved "Byron is dead" on a rock; very recently, there has been a biographical film by Nick Dear (2003), two volumes of a projected trilogy of Byron novels by the American writer Benjamin Markovits, and a new version of the life by the novelist Edna O'Brien. Byron is a symbol of lost literacy and grace, humanity and civilization, in J. M. Coetzee's *Disgrace* (1999), a bleak novel about a white South African professor of English literature who has been dismissed from his university job after a sexual affair with a colored student. Depressed and alone in a barren world at the end of history, the professor plans, sporadically, to write "a meditation on love between the sexes in the form of a chamber opera," which he will call "Byron in Italy," presumably a variation on Hector Berlioz's *Harold in Italy* (1834), inspired by Byron's poem. But the poet is too far now from the fallen world, not only for the wayward professor's students, who no longer read, but also for Coetzee's depressed, disgraced protagonist. The only notes of his opera he can imagine are the plaintive strains of a guitar played by Byron's last mistress, Teresa, lamenting her dead lover.

In 2003 John Murray's publication of Fiona MacCarthy's biography of Byron, at the end of Murray's long run as an independent publisher, was celebrated by an exhibition at the National Portrait Gallery in London ("Mad, Bad, and Dangerous") and a Byron-based marketing campaign on nearby Regent Street. Virginia Woolf's Byron-fatigue has gone over the top: the headline in the *New York Times Book Review* over an account of Edna O'Brien's 2009 biography was "Oh, Lord." On the other hand, the public's fascination with the Noble Poet (and fabulous sexual athlete) persists. Our Age of Celebrity, descended from the Romantic Age of Personality, is especially fascinated by the lives of English writers of Austen's and Byron's time. Like Regency style, the paradigm of Romantic authorship pervades the popular imagination; it may be the default setting for literary character.

Romantic Paradigm

Gender matters: the feminist point is hard to stop repeating. At twenty-one, Lord Byron, feeling free to exult in the prospect of leaving England for the Continent and adventure, wrote verses to a friend: "Huzza! Hodgson, we are going / Our embargo's off at last, / Favourable Breezes blowing, / Bend the canvass o'er the mast; / From aloft the signal's streaming / Hark! The farewell gun is fired, / Women screeching, Tars blaspheming / Tells us that our time's expired."[15] Compare Jane Austen's letter to her sister, written at the same age, describing the complex arrangements the family had to make so she could visit London with her brother Francis:

FIGURE 13. John Opie, *Mary Wollstonecraft*, ca. 1797. Courtesy National Portrait Gallery, London.

'Tho I have every Disposition in the world to accompany [Frank] . . .
I cannot go on the Uncertainty of the Pearsons being at Home: as I
should not have a place to go to, in case they were from Home.—I
wrote to Miss P—on Friday, & hoped to receive an answer from her
this morning. . . . My Father will be so good as to fetch home his prodi-
gal Daughter from Town, I hope, unless he wishes me to walk the Hos-
pitals, Enter at the Temple, or mount Guard at St. James. . . . I had once
determined to go with Frank tomorrow & take my chance &c. But they
dissuaded me from so rash a step—as I really think on consideration it
would have been; for if the Pearsons were not at home, I should inevitably fall a Sacrifice to the arts of some fat Woman who would make me
drunk with Small Beer— (*Letters*, 12)

The "fat Woman" is the bawd who entraps the country miss in the first plate
of Hogarth's *The Harlot's Progress*: irony is our young woman's only escape.
But on the other hand, many eighteenth-century women of the genteel
classes had lived more freely than Jane Austen managed to do. Indeed, Marilyn Butler has suggested that one of the most notorious of those women, the
feminist Mary Wollstonecraft, struck the Byronic posture before Byron did.[16]
   "If ever there was a book calculated to make a man in love with its author,
this appears to me to be the book," William Godwin wrote in 1798 about
Mary Wollstonecraft's *A Short Residence in Sweden* (1796).[17] Before Lord
Byron, Wollstonecraft set up as a Romantic author, a solitary wanderer who
seeks the reader's personal understanding and sympathy, pouring out her
feelings, focusing narrowly on her aloneness and desolation in a desolate
part of the world. If Godwin's poignant comment about her book sets up a
kind of paradigm of the ideal Romantic reader's response to such a Romantic
author, his complicated case was more than metaphorical. He had in fact, in
real life, to his surprise, fallen in love with the author of *A Short Residence*,
and even—against his principles—married her; and Mary Wollstonecraft was
very lately dead when he set down these words of praise for her book. If in
context the words are especially moving, they are also peculiarly to the point:
Wollstonecraft's book, a travel diary in the form of letters to an unnamed
correspondent, had in fact been calculated to make a man in love with her—
not William Godwin but her former lover, Gilbert Imlay, the father of one
of the two young daughters she left for Godwin to raise when she died
soon after childbirth in 1797. (Fanny Imlay would kill herself in her early

twenties; the baby, Godwin's daughter, would become the author of *Frankenstein* and other novels, and the editor of the works of her husband, Percy Bysshe Shelley.)

The *Short Residence* is based on the passionate letters—selected, rewritten, and adapted for publication—that Mary wrote to Imlay during an extraordinary journey to Scandinavia she undertook alone except for her baby and a maid. A travel journal meant to be informative, it describes a part of the world then unknown to most English readers and its harsh, sublime scenery (Mary repeats the word "sublime," and cultivates the feeling that the young Edmund Burke had inquired into in his 1757 essay). It also describes, from an anthropological angle, the curious customs of the northern countries, odd breakfasts of fish and spirits, for example, set out on white cloths by neat matrons. In accents that recall the lyric poetry of the period, it records, most memorably, the intimate effusions of a solitary wanderer, a sensitive, emotional, volatile creature who feels alone and abandoned in a cold, remote place and shares her feelings as if with an intimate friend or a lover. ("Oh, that the desert were my dwelling place / With one fair spirit for my minister!" Byron would write.) In the most vivid pages of the book, the writer describes herself as spiritually alone even when she has companions. Wollstonecraft describes, for instance, a journey through "a night such as I had never seen before" as the lone woman in a group of sleeping men—"fortunately they did not snore"—and her "voluptuous sensations" in the balmy air. Arriving at her destination shortly before five in the morning, she is pleased to record that "a dish of coffee, and fresh linen, recruited my spirits; and I directly set out again for Norway. . . . Wrapping my great coat round me, I lay down on some sails at the bottom of the boat, its motion rocking me to rest, till a discourteous wave interrupted my slumbers, and obliged me to rise and feel a solitariness which was not so soothing as that of the past night" (letter 5, 94–95). The wittily observed discourtesy of the wave points up the Romantic drama of the picture, of a lady huddled in her skirts at the bottom of an open boat on the ocean, sleeping in the darkness among rude men who do not speak her language.

More than once, the writer tells her unnamed correspondent of the comfort and pleasure she finds in writing to him; she is despondent, trying to pull herself together after a love affair (with him) gone wrong. The details of the relationship and the breakup are left unclear: for all the emotional self-revelation there is much that this writer fails to tell, and the purpose of her journey and her connection with her correspondent remain mysterious. Scholars still disagree about exactly why Wollstonecraft went to Scandinavia, which she evidently did as Imlay's business agent: he seems to have tired of her, and she seems to have responded with mixed desires to escape, amaze, and please him, perhaps even to seduce him from a distance with her eloquence. Audible throughout the *Short Residence* is the half-stifled cri de coeur of a wounded, brilliant woman, an exalted spirit who has dared to love hard. "Who fears the falling dew? It only makes the mown grass smell more fragrant," she writes boldly, ecstatically. And more boldly still, she observes that summer disappears in Norway "almost before it has ripened the fruit of autumn—even, as it were, slips from your embraces, whilst the satisfied senses seem to rest in enjoyment" (148).

The book is an outpouring in the tradition of Ovid's *Heroides* and of Heloise, the passionate nun; like two other books by women that were also published in 1796—Mary Robinson's sonnet sequence, *Sappho and Phaon*, and Mary Hays's novel, *The Memoirs of Emma Courtney*—the *Short Residence* fairly invited readers who had heard of the writer and knew something about her to look for links between the living woman's half-revealed private life and the intense intimate feelings written out for publication. (Mary Hays, an acolyte of Wollstonecraft, included her own lover's letters to her in *her* book.) The commendation of the author's widower made the book more scandalous—if, indeed, Godwin's comment about it can be disentangled from its literal context, his *Memoirs of the Author of "The Rights of Woman,"* which memorialized the radical feminist and acknowledged her illicit love affair with Imlay, the birth of her child, and her two suicide attempts. Godwin's memoir provoked a storm of hysterical abuse, savage diatribes against Wollstonecraft and the "unsex'd females," as the right-wing press called them, who followed her lead.

Wollstonecraft had begun her writing career conventionally, with a book about educating girls and a slim woman-centered novel—which, however, concludes unconventionally with a thundering rejection of marriage. From the beginning the autobiographical subtext is urgent, if not altogether legible. That the parents of the heroine of *Mary, a Fiction* (1788) have the same Christian names as the author's parents raises—as the title does—troubling questions about the truthfulness of fiction, and the arbitrary names, lies, and social fictions that constrain middle-class women's lives. The novel's plot is based on the passionate love between Wollstonecraft and her friend Fanny Blood, raising questions about the truth-to-life of the heterosexual marriage plot. The satirical point may be that romantic love between women is prefer-able; the more interesting point is that Mary herself is a fiction, conceivable only as a figure at the center of a marriage plot even though her passions point her in a different direction. *Mary, a Fiction* is not a good novel; Wollstonecraft lacked the novelist's interest in the complexities of personal relationships and of language. She wrote only one other novel, and gave it the title of a tract: *The Wrongs of Woman; or, Maria*. It was unfinished when she died soon after childbirth. In his *Memoirs* Godwin describes the pains she took in composing her narrative, which, with painstaking respect, he published together with the several different alternative endings she had left. The story of an unjustly accused, forcibly incarcerated young mother—and her more abused servant and friend—is presented, as the title suggests, as a parable of all women's lives: it is as if the writer had decided to coat her earlier polemic, *A Vindica-tion of the Rights of Women* (1792), in the sugar of romantic fiction. Like her first work of narrative fiction, her last one is sketchy, short on every ingredi-ent but plot. Her imagination of character was not a novelist's: it leaped from "Mary" or "Maria" to "women," blind to what might lie between particulars and abstractions. Her daughter Mary would be a more memorable, produc-tive, and successful novelist, if not a very much more engaging one.

More than her clumsy novels would do, the confessional-seeming *Short Residence* interested readers other than Godwin in the author. The young poet Robert Southey wrote to a friend, "Have you met with Mary Wollstone-craft's [travel book]? She has made me in love with a cold climate, and frost and snow, with a northern moonlight." The novelist Amelia Alderson (later Opie), who knew Wollstonecraft, understood that she had fallen in love with the author of the book and not the climate it described, and described her "tender sympathy" for "the interesting creature of feeling and imagination" conveyed in its pages.[18]

By the time she published *A Short Residence*, Mary Wollstonecraft was already a celebrity: the book was read as a document of a unique sensibility, proof of the value of sensibility generally and of Mary's in particular. The year it was published, Coleridge described to Hazlitt seeing Godwin and Wollstonecraft together, the philosopher making a point and the feminist responding playfully—representing, he said, "the ascendancy which people of imagination exercised over those of mere intellect."[19] Larger than life, espe-cially together, the implausible couple of writing celebrities seemed to be sym-bolic of the warring principles that were tearing apart society and authorial selves. Especially when set beside Godwin, where she in the end set herself, Wollstonecraft dramatically embodied a new kind of person. "The first of a new genus" is what she aimed to be when she set off to live by her pen in London. Perhaps she was. Both Elizabeth Bennet and Mrs. Croft, in *Persuasion*, echo some of Wollstonecraft's ideas; the figure of Mary Wollstonecraft, like Byron's figure, would have inflected Jane Austen's ideas of the writer's relation to readers.

Lustrous Mary Wollstonecraft did not aim merely to represent the creative imagination or its ascendancy, as another, more ordinary, beautiful, and accomplished woman might wish to do: the *Short Residence* conveys her more ambitious Romantic aspiration to dilate her own imagination to its fullest capacity, and to dissolve in it, taking the reader with her. The mood of the letters from Scandinavia moves up and down, ranging rapidly from exalted treeless heights to dark and dangerous depressions; the writer addresses a reader interested in anthropology and natural history, and then turns to the subject of her own sensations and emotions, taking for granted that these psychological phenomena are of at least equal general interest. In 1798, two years after the *Short Residence* appeared, Wordsworth would publish (with Coleridge) *Lyrical Ballads* and complete the two-part version of the great unfinished poem *The Prelude; or, The Growth of a Poet's Mind*. The compelling, seductive authorial voice of the *Short Residence* is an English Romantic voice tremulous with sensibility and eager for ever more intense experiences of self-enlarging, self-affirming consciousness of self. Wollstonecraft does not pretend to confess secrets she would not reveal to actual intimates, in the manner of Rousseau—she set him up as her antagonist, in the *Vindication*— who confided to the readers of his *Confessions* the deep desire to be beaten that he says he could never admit to a lover who was in a position to gratify it. Wollstonecraft, in Wordsworth's way, rises sublimely above such specifics and banalities as the mere mechanics of sexual, business, and travel arrangements, the details of who was who and where, to focus instead on her heightened sensations of spiritual expansion, higher things calculated to expand the responsive reader's own soul.

To write in the first person is to pretend to intimacy. Wordsworth would acknowledge that it was embarrassing that a man should talk so much of himself as he did, in *The Prelude*; similarly, the author of the *Short Residence* disingenuously apologizes for "being continually the first person—'the little hero of each tale,'" and claims that she tried to correct this, but that "in proportion as I arranged my thoughts, my letter . . . became stiff and affected." She turns on herself in the next paragraph, to invite or challenge the reader to like her personally: "A person has a right, I have sometimes thought, when amused by a witty or interesting egotist, to talk of himself when he can win on our attention by acquiring our affection. Whether I deserve to rank amongst this privileged number, my readers alone can judge—and I give them leave to shut the book, if they do not wish to become better acquainted with me." Mary's language of "rights" is characteristic; so is her egocentricity. Her imperious demand for an energetic sympathy that might match her own responsiveness is frank: her book is calculated to make the reader fall in love with its author partly because of that, and partly because it is addressed to a lover, and (like a letter in an epistolary novel) engages the reader's prurience. And like the heroine of an epistolary novel, Mary in all her vivid liveliness and amplitude of being remains out of reach, elusive, tantalizing.

In the first paragraph of letter 1, she writes as if to an intimate of the "other causes, with which you are already sufficiently acquainted," that "have so exhausted" her spirits—and not to the reader of her book, who is not acquainted with them. Still her bag of literary tricks is intended to engage: it includes the reliable appeal to the reader who will recognize a literary reference or echo. Richard Holmes points out the Shakespearean echoes in this passage:

> The cow's bell has ceased to tinkle the herd to rest; they have all paced across the heath. Is not this the witching time of night? The waters murmur, and fall with more than mortal music, and spirits of peace walk abroad to calm the agitated breast. Eternity is in these moments: worldly cares melt into the airy stuff that dreams are made of; and reveries, mild and enchanting as the first hopes of love, or the recollection of lost enjoyment, carry the hapless wight into futurity, who, in bustling life, has vainly strove to throw off the grief which lies heavy at the heart. Good night! A crescent hangs out in the vault before, which woos me to stray abroad:—it is not a silvery reflection of the sun, but glows with all its golden splendor. Who fears the falling dew? It only makes the mown grass smell more fragrant! (Letter 2, 75)

The twenty-first-century reader remains curious about what she did about laundry, or how Marguerite the maid and the baby fared. But the loftiness of the tone pulls the attention to higher things.

Wollstonecraft's great gift was for dramatizing her sole self, and perhaps by extension therefore her gift was for first-person lyrical narrative. In her personal life, she was given to dramatic actions, like carrying off her unhappily married sister Everina, and wetting her own clothes in the rain before throwing herself off Putney Bridge in a suicide attempt. William Blake was one of the many who marveled at her; he wrote a poem addressed "To Mary" in her voice, which begins, "Why was I born with a different face?" Her example—her writings, her story, and her face, in portraits—was presented, for the most part as a warning, to the next generation of women (like Jane Austen). It has continued to be inspiring. The early-twentieth-century American anthropologist Ruth Benedict described her feelings when first seeing, at the National Portrait Gallery, the likeness of this remarkable woman "who had saved her soul alive."[20] A portrait of Mary Wollstonecraft hung over Godwin's desk all his life: one wonders what the second Mrs. Godwin, who worked at her husband's side in their publishing business, thought about it.

Before Byron, Mary Wollstonecraft cast herself as the embodiment of human feeling, not an ordinary woman, an exile from social life, a solitary wanderer. Dr. Johnson had coined the term for himself; Wollstonecraft invested it with emotion and her personal charisma. A few years after the publication of the *Short Residence*, Charlotte Smith chose the term as the title of the last of her eleven works of narrative fiction. Smith's *The Letters of a Solitary Wanderer* (1801–1802) is a collection of gloomy tales retold by a philosopher tired of life, who observes the human scene and reflects on the wretchedness of other people's—most people's—life stories. The Romantic author's godlike detachment paradoxically engages the Romantic reader: he or she seems to be a quintessential but also rare and detached human self.

Jane Austen as we imagine her, the confidante of her sister Cassandra and a cozy circle that has widened to include us, her secret friends, was nothing like a solitary wanderer. Or was she?

In Love with the Author

And did you once see Shelley plain?
And did he stop and speak to you?
And did you answer him again?
How strange it seems and true!
—Robert Browning, "Memorabilia"

FIGURE 14. "Henry James," photograph, n.d. Courtesy of Print Collection, Miriam and Ira D. Wallach Division of Arts, Prints and Photographs, The New York Public Library, Astor, Lenox and Tilden foundations.

Falling in love with a writer, being possessed by an author's spirit or ghost, is the subject of Henry James's "The Aspern Papers" (1888), a story that pretends to be the account, written in the first person by a man whose name we never learn, of his obsession with a famous dead poet, Jeffrey Aspern, whose papers are rumored to be in the possession of an ancient lady living in Venice who had been the poet's mistress. Like the narrator and the poet and Henry James himself, the lady is an American. Off the scene there is a second Aspern admirer, an Englishman named John Cumnor, the narrator's friend, who has written earlier to the lady to request a look at the papers, and been turned down. Whether Cumnor and his co-conspirator are scholars, editors, publishers, or biographers is unclear: most importantly, the narrator is an amateur (with the stress on the Latin root of the word, "*amo*," I love). Cannily, suggestively, James does not set him to recalling or imitating the fictitious poet's verses: the man, not the work, is the object of his love. At a crucial moment in his Aspern adventure, the notoriously amorous poet's handsome face appears to him in a vision to offer, with a rakish wink, a man-to-man warning against women.

By then he is in need of it. At the advice of another American in Venice, a Mrs. Prest (personal names are pregnant), he has invented a ruse to get the papers, and presented himself at the palazzo under a pseudonym (unspecified). He has persuaded the difficult old woman, who wears a mask as if to shield her ancient eyes but possibly to obscure what remains of their dazzle, to rent him a room. And he has moved in and become entangled with both Miss Juliana Bordereau and—more dangerously—her awkward innocent middle-aged niece, Miss Tina (or, in the first redaction of the story, Tita). By the time the ghost of Aspern appears, the hint of a threatening proposition is in the air: having lied and sold (or rented) his soul in his quest for the Aspern papers, the narrator is invited to trade his body for those papers by marrying Miss Tina. The play of Jamesian themes is dense: Europe and America, art and life, spirit and flesh; the wretched lives of the impoverished spinsters, the lasting glamour of Jeffrey Aspern's world and the old Venice of art—Shylock's crass Venice and Portia's magical one; the past and the present; the vague indeterminacy of obscure nameless persons like the narrator, and the glamour of Jeffrey Aspern's great name. In a splendidly theatrical scene toward the end, the narrator rifles a chest for the papers in her dark room and the old lady rises up, shining a lamp on the criminal in the darkness, and shouts out accusingly, "Publishing scoundrel!" Then she falls back as if dead.

But Miss Bordereau only seems to have died: she lingers on. When she finally does die, the papers have been burnt, and they disappear for good along with her. Miss Tina gives the narrator the only memento left, which may or may not have as much cash value as papers have: a miniature of Jeffrey Aspern—a portrait of the poet that will hang over his desk all his life, as Mary Wollstonecraft's portrait hung over Godwin's. The play of oppositions and connections is elaborate and suggestive—image and word, material and immaterial, flesh and spirit, light and darkness, life and death, past and present, seeing and failing to see, the visible and the invisible (the fine eyes of Miss Bordereau that Jeffrey Aspern himself had looked into, now hidden by a protective eye-shade), romance as glamour and also as a lie, a misrepresentation—and above all of material and ghostly possession.

Almost as interesting as the story itself is the preface that James added for the New York Edition of 1907–1908, in which "The Aspern Papers" is bound together with three other equally tall stories, "The Turn of the Screw," a short story entitled "The Liar," and an even shorter one, "The Two Faces," about hypocrisy, betrayal, and manipulation among the exquisitely polite and privileged. Writing, like his narrator, in the first person, the author comes out from behind the scenes to tell the truths that suggested his fiction. The ancient lady, he says, is based on the historical Jane (sometimes Mary Jane, usually Claire) Clairmont, stepsister of Mary Wollstonecraft Godwin Shelley (being the daughter of Godwin's second wife) and sometime lover of Lord Byron. James recalls "the thrill of imagination" he felt, in Florence, on hearing "that Jane Clairmont, the half-sister [sic] of Mary Godwin, Shelley's second wife, and for a while the intimate friend of Byron and the mother of his daughter Allegra, should have been living on in Florence, where she had long lived, up to our own day, and that in fact, had I happened to hear of her but a little sooner, I might have seen her in the flesh." Had he heard the anecdote a year before, he observes, he might have met the lady; better, he concludes, that he did not. What James calls "the thrill of overlapping" might have remained a mere frisson, he confides, had he not heard as well of "a gentleman, an American of long ago, an ardent Shelleyite," who arranged to be Miss Clairmont's lodger "on the calculation that she would have Shelley documents," and failed to get them. The rest of the preface worries the ethical questions raised by literary biography—and associated conjunctions of art and life—that "The Aspern Papers" adumbrates: whether it is fair to conflate Byron and Shelley, or to imagine into existence "celebrities who not only *hadn't* existed in the conditions I imputed to them, but who for the most part . . . couldn't possibly have done so"—that is, an American Byron to match an American Miss Clairmont.

As his brilliant evocation of Venice suggests, James had a keen sense of the importance of habitat, as he called it, especially in relation to celebrity; and America had not produced a Byron. Some critics have applauded the patriotism or prescience that led James to imagine such an American poet, but as the author observes Aspern is "not even feebly localized, but I *thought* New York as I projected him." Defending the imagination by which he had displaced his character, he is reminded of imagining an English Sarah Bernhardt (with some traits of her predecessor, the French tragic actress Rachel) in *The Tragic Muse*. The relation of imagined characters and stories to true history, the relating of history as fiction, is the subject of "The Aspern Papers"—what he calls, in a metaphor taken from engraving, the connection between its "early 'state'" (as fact, gossip, and conjecture) and his artfully finished story. The magic of art can turn Shelley into Byron, an English poet into an American one, and Florence into Venice; the literary imagination is invited to conflate Miss Clairmont with Byron's last mistress, Teresa Guiccioli, who supposedly burned some of his letters—allowing the famous public burning of Byron's memoir in his publisher's fireplace to glimmer in the distance. The well-known story that Cassandra Austen burned a heap of her sister's papers happens to rhyme now, too.

"The Aspern Papers" plays with space and time: Jeffrey Aspern died young, but the muse that inspired him lived on, allowing the romance of "an overlapping"—of a modern person encountering a woman of the past—and inviting James to imagine "a final scene of the rich dim Shelley drama played out in the very theatre of our own 'modernity.'" For him in the 1880s, as he reflected some twenty years later, the Byron-Shelley era had the "air of the past just in the degree in which that air, I confess, most appeals to me—when the region over which it hangs is far enough away without being too far." It is startling to reflect, from here, on how close Henry James could legitimately feel, in the penultimate decade of the nineteenth century in Italy, to the Shelley and Byron dramas that had taken place there in the 1820s. As he points out in the preface, "the Byronic age" had not been so long ago when he himself had come to write in Italy, the land of the Anglo-American Romantic imagination of art. Middle-aged Americans who opened their copies of *The Atlantic Monthly* in March 1888 to the double-columned pages of the first installment of "The Aspern Papers" might have remembered reading "The True Story of Lady Byron's Life" in the same publication in September 1869. They (or their parents) might have been among the 15,000 subscribers who had dropped the respectable magazine, back then, in protest against the content of the scandalous "true story," or—more scandalous still—against Harriet Beecher Stowe's being the one to tell it. Its key sentence, a quotation from Lady Byron, was well calculated to shock: "Mrs. Stowe, he had incest with his sister." For many who had heard and might even still be whispering the rumors about Lord Byron, the conjunction of proper name and improper act was unspeakable and unthinkable.

Lord Byron was born a hundred years before the initial publication of James's story; he died in 1824, two years after Shelley; Robert Browning, some years before James, wrote his verses about meeting someone who had seen the younger poet. That closeness of a quarter of a century that James mentions is not something we can feel today; nevertheless, because of the numerous recollections and fictionalizations of Shelley and Byron especially, the Byronic period still seems, as it did to James, quintessentially Romantically and romantically literary, partaking of the nature of fiction, or romance.[21] The first furor of the Byromania that began in the poet's lifetime and turned into the Byronism that continues still had abated somewhat by the early twentieth century; James must have calculated that fewer people would recognize the names of minor figures in the Byron legend by the time he revised "The Aspern Papers" and altered into the more conventional "Tina" the queer original name of Miss Bordereau's plain niece, which was "Tita." (It playfully recalls the nickname of Byron's faithful burly gondolier, Battista, memorialized in *Don Juan*.) But "the Byron period," having been so much written about, in its time and later, was and is still burnished by a literary light. In his poems, Shelley had written of his friend Byron as "Maddalo," and "The Pilgrim of Eternity"; Byron had combined tropes of romantic fiction with his self-projections; fictions of Byron begat further fictions. For years after his death, people published, for profit, what they recalled or imagined of his conversation; his friend Dallas had himself painted with a portrait of Byron hanging on the wall behind him.

And the Byron connections lived on: Mary Shelley lived until 1851, Lady Byron until 1860, Teresa Guiccioli until 1873, and Claire Clairmont until 1879. The 1868 memoir of Teresa Guiccioli, by then the Marquise de Boissy, published in translation a year later, inspired Harriet Beecher Stowe to vindicate

Lady Byron. Stowe had been introduced to Lady Byron, who was also devoted to the abolitionist cause, in 1853, when the author of *Uncle Tom's Cabin* was touring Europe. In 1857, on another visit to England, she definitively fell in love with the English aristocrat, to whom she mailed, for prepublication fact-checking and approval, the manuscript of her historical novel *The Minister's Wooing*, which features not only lavish quotations from Byron's poetry but also the historical and fateful American political figure, Aaron Burr, imagined as a Byronic hero. In 1870, in a book-length version of the *Atlantic* article, she developed an argument that might rank as the first piece of feminist literary criticism, maintaining that she had sought to vindicate Lady Byron (who by then was dead, like her husband) for the sake of all women who were victimized, brutalized, and silenced by men.

Some readers are more susceptible than others to falling in love with authors; some authors are more likely objects of that kind of love than others are; and in literature as in life love has different guises. The example of Byron encouraged slippage between fact and fiction, and slippage between reader and writer. In his preface to "The Aspern Papers," James sketches a theory of fictionalizing based on metonymic displacements, contingency, and contiguity: to alter Florence to Venice, Shelley to Byron, London to New York, an English poet to an American one is to begin to transform an early to a later "state" in which its meanings are bitten more deeply into the "plate," or situation, or perhaps given meaning in the process. The craft of the author is a mode of noticing and making connections and resonances, and developing more. If for Henry James the peculiar romance of the "Byronic" period was precisely its nearness—it seemed possible to reach out and touch it, as if across the table—for us the relation is differently romantic. Like Byron himself, the Regency period has receded into a costumed past that fades into fiction. If Byron, with his rich and complicated self-contradicting life and oeuvre and more than usual number of personal secrets, is the paradigmatic subject for literary biographers, he is the focus par excellence of literary fictions (sometimes now called "factions").

"The Aspern Papers" is the queer opposite of credulous, or "straight," more orthodox literary biography that reduces the work to an illustration of the life, or a secret in it. In his biographical novel about Henry James, *The Master* (2004), Colm Tóibín does what the master himself did for Byron, brilliantly evoking the relationship between James and Constance Fenimore Woolson, an American writer living abroad who is thought to have sought—

like Miss Tina—a closer relationship than James was willing to have with her. Fenimore, as they called her—she was a grandniece of James Fenimore Cooper—killed herself, some said for love of Henry James; in the finest scene in Toibín's novel, the grieving James has himself rowed out toward the Lido, where he attempts, with great difficulty, to drown the dead woman's dresses, which billow up as if alive against the gondolier's pole.

The embodied poet is only delicately evoked in "The Aspern Papers": is Miss Tita or Tina not in fact the niece of Miss Bordereau but her child by Jeffrey Aspern? The question doesn't come up, in the story, and might not occur to some readers. The sexual body doesn't figure here as forcibly as papers do. The tale is a satire on a man obsessed with papers, but also a sort of admission. The belated interpreter feels pressure to find a homosexual subtext in the narrator's secret pact with Cumnor and more generally in the triangulated relation between men through a woman that is memorialized in the miniature of Jeffrey Aspern that will hang above the narrator's desk.[22] The miniature is worth money, but the letters are priceless, sought only by the obsessed—biographers, publishing scoundrels—who aspire not in fact to touch but actually to be Jeffrey Aspern. Like sex, money—the money exchanged between the narrator and Miss Bordereau, the money that might save Miss Tina from poverty, the money so valued by crass Americans—makes real connections that as always in James are opposed to ideal ones, but also are entangled with them. Venice is priceless but also pricey; its treasures enhance its value; it is a treasure, a real thing in which moral and aesthetic values are made manifest. The Aspern papers themselves, with their secrets, are material manifestations of evanescent emotions, connections, poets and lovers.

When Miss Tina confesses at the end to burning the papers—the scene is not described—the twenty-first-century reader—in addition to recalling the bonfire in John Murray's fireplace—might also think of a story told by the novelist Julian Barnes, the author of *Flaubert's Parrot* (1990). In a recent memoir, *Nothing to Be Frightened Of* (2008), Barnes describes an ottoman, or "pouffe," that, in his childhood, sat in his parents' parlor: the couple had stuffed it with the blue airmail letters, shredded, that had passed between them. "How to imagine that decision, and that scene?" Barnes writes. "Did they tear the letters up together, or did she do it while he was at work? Did they argue, did they agree, did one of them secretly resent it?" The author recalls the bits of blue paper escaping from split seams of the pouffe when he dropped his weight on it, as a boy, and he adds a later scene: "The collapsing pouffe was at some point chucked out. But instead of being put in the dust-bin, it was dumped at the bottom of the garden, where it became heavy, rain-sodden, and increasingly discoloured. I would kick it occasionally as I passed, my wellington ejecting a few more blue scraps, the ink not running, the likelihood of legible secrets being divulged even less. My kicks were those of a disheartened Romantic. So this is what it all comes to?"[23]

Child's Play

With the erotics of self-expression on their minds, second-wave feminists influenced by French Freudian theory wrote wittily and tendentiously about "the scene of writing," and—punning hard—"coming to writing." Confessional poetry, personal criticism, and popular books like *Fear of Flying* and *The Diaries of Anais Nin* informed a twentieth-century trend that continues, complicated now by even more concern with the intersections of truth and fiction. Over a hundred years earlier, feminist critics were recalling in the 1970s, the Bronte children, isolated on the heath, collaborated on charged fantasies about the imaginary lands of Glasstown and Angria that Charlotte recorded in her tiny hand. They had started out by telling stories about the toy soldiers that belonged to Bramwell, the only boy, but as he and his three sisters shared and elaborated on one another's imaginings, dukes more fiery than Wellington, Byronic seducers, and passionate beautiful ladies prolifer-ated to populate entire Gothic worlds.

Jane Austen's beginnings were nothing like that. Imagine, in contrast, a scene of writing in or around 1790—about the time Prince Frederick of Eng-land, Duke of York, married a relative with a name similar to his, Princess Frederica of Prussia. Jane Austen, somewhere between twelve and fifteen, sits with her quill pen before a sheet of paper, writing down first "Frederic and," then adding, with a sly smile, "Elfrida, a novel, Chapter the First." ("Elfrida" is not the same thing as "Frederica," and Austen may have written her story before she heard of the royal wedding: I purposely abstain from dates. "Henry and Eliza," another youthful sketch, was written years before her brother Henry married his ten-years-older cousin, the charming widow Eliza Hancock de Feuillide—who however may well have begun flirting with Henry before Jane put their names together.) Insofar as it is about anything, this very short, funny "novel" in five carefully numbered little chapters is

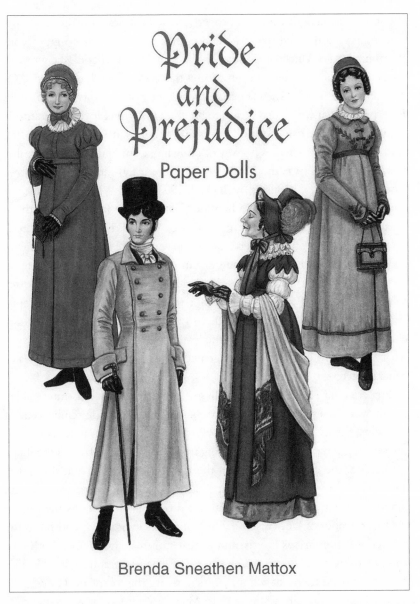

FIGURE 15. Cover of book of paper dolls. Brenda Sneathen Mattox, *Pride and Prejudice Paper Dolls* (Mineola, NY: Dover, 1997).

about the marvel of distinct and properly named entities, how they are separate and how connected (by the sound of their names; by marrying; by consanguinity). "The Uncle of Elfrida was the Mother of Frederic," she writes— then crosses out "Mother" and substitutes the more reasonable "Father."[24] Or does she do that only when she makes a fair copy of her story in *Volume the First*, prefacing it with a dedication to her friend Martha Lloyd, "in gratitude for your late generosity to me in finishing my muslin Cloak," signed "the Author" (*MW*, 3)? There is no way of knowing, now, and no matter, really: whether the Uncle was the Mother or (less absurdly) the Father, "in other words, they were first cousins by the Father's side" (4). What words describe the right relation of a hero to a heroine? Is it from the first—from birth—a function only of sex, their parents' and their own? What might their relation be "in other words"? It depends on the words that are said about them, and on the words they say. "Both born in one day and both brought up at one school," the narrative tells us, Frederic and Elfrida "loved with mutual sincerity but were both determined not to transgress the rules of Propriety by owning their attachment, either to the object beloved, or to any one else" (4). A plot is being hatched: the lovers won't "own"—accept, or say— what they feel; other people are watching; what they will or won't do is of general interest.

Frederic and Elfrida are "exceedingly handsome," also "so much alike, that it was not every one who knew them apart." They are reminiscent of the twins, Sebastian and Viola, in *Twelfth Night*—or perhaps not: "Nay, even their most intimate friends had nothing to distinguish them by, but the shape of the face, the colour of the Eye, the length of the Nose and the difference of the complexion" (4). Having carried that joke about sameness and difference as far as it can go, the Author drops that subject. As the title of the most famous of Jane Austen's youthful stories indicates, friendship is the subject of fiction just as love is, and as that story's form suggests, both love and friendship are best pursued by letter. The next paragraph begins, "Elfrida had an intimate friend to whom . . . she wrote the following Letter." The letter follows. Formally addressed "To Miss Drummond," it is a request for a bonnet to suit the complexion that is so like or perhaps unlike Frederic's. This request leads illogically to the sad story of the overly compliant Miss Drummond, who accepts two suitors because her "character was a willingness to oblige every one"(4), and is consequently obliged to kill herself; it goes on to stories about the daughters of her neighbor, Mrs. Fitzroy—also love stories. But while these have their (peculiar) points of interest, only the union of the titular Frederic and Elfrida can end the novel. In this very brief narrative, the crisis occurs after eighteen years, when Elfrida, jealous of his attention to the daughter of one of her contemporaries, "in a manner truly heroick, spluttered out to him her intention of being married the next day." The gallant Frederic replies, "Damme Elfrida *you* may be married tomorrow but *I* won't." The quibble cannot stand: it takes a marriage to end a novel, and it takes two to marry. After Elfrida has "a succession of fainting fits" ("she had scarcely patience enough to recover from one before she fell into another"), the heroic Frederic ("as bold as brass yet in other respects his heart was as soft as cotton") flies to her side and is "united to her Forever—" (11–12). One fatigued simile begets a sillier one. And narrative time is conclusively stopped by "Forever—." Like word games and charades and double entendres in Jane Austen's mature fiction, this story reminds us of the arbitrary nature of words, their power to make meaning and also—sometimes at the same time—to subvert it.

Jack and Alice, in the next story in *Volume the First*, in spite of being coupled in the title are brother and sister—not cousins, and not lovers. Part of the joke is that Jack hardly figures at all, after the title. The romantic adventures of "poor Alice," who has a drinking problem, are not at all happy. In the end she is alone, surprised that the man she loves, Charles Adams, "of so dazzling a Beauty that none but Eagles could look him in the Face" (*MW*, 13), has married her friend Lady Williams—to her consternation, as "all *her* fears were centered in his Cook" (29). The young Jane Austen enjoys defying her reader's expectations. Mismatches that defy disparities of age, beauty, and class—which Austen's mature novels effectively define as unthinkable by never acknowledging they might exist—occur regularly in what scholars call the "juvenilia."

The earliest writers who commented on these stories were shocked by their improprieties: when R. W. Chapman prepared to publish them, he admitted he would have preferred to burn them. When they are enjoyed and valued today, it is usually for their lack of decorum. Recent critics have exulted in evidence of the young writer's appetite: see, in contrast, old Mr. Woodhouse's denial of food to his guests. In "Frederic and Elfrida," two young ladies sit down "to Supper on a young Leveret, a brace of Partridges, a leash of Pheasants and a Dozen of Pigeons" (9). The heroine of "The Beautifull Cassandra" indulges herself in eating ices. When Eliza, of "Henry and

Eliza," begins "to find herself rather hungry," she is given "reason to think, by their biting off two of her fingers, that her children were in much the same situation" (37). In "Lesley Castle," in *Volume the Second*, a bride announces that her intended has been thrown from his horse and killed, causing her sister to lament having cooked the wedding feast, "Roasting, Broiling and Stewing both the Meat and Myself to no purpose" (113). The cook is mollified when the assembled guests agree that "the best thing we could do was to begin eating," and handily dispatch the edibles. In "The Visit," a little play, the titled characters genteelly request and pass disgusting dishes of tripe, liver, crow, and cow-heel and onion.

The youthful stories are sometimes read as well as evidence of young Jane's hunger to transcend constraints of gender. In "Henry and Eliza," for example, the heroine marries by the way and has two children, escapes from jail, sets sail "in a man of War of 55 Guns" (an impossible odd number, for guns on a balanced ship), and raises an army to destroy her enemy, "the Dutchess" (whose best friend is a bartender) (36). She is satisfied at the end because she has "gained the Blessings of thousands, and the Applause of her own Heart." But it is a mistake to read this as a simple wish-fulfillment fantasy. Eliza, who as a matter of course robs her benefactors, is a heroine only because her story grants her importance—as well as a sense of her own importance, which this writer hoots at. In "Love and Freindship," the romantic heroes Edward and Augustus exchange girlish exclamations ("My Life! My Soul! My Adorable Angel!") (86) as they "fly into each other's arms"—upending the hierarchical relation implicit in the standard pairing of love and friendship, and men and women, and questioning the usual assumptions about sentiment and gender that most writers of fiction accept, but most importantly of all making self-importance look ridiculous. The heroine of "The Beautifull Cassandra," the daughter of "a celebrated Millener," falls in love with a bonnet (in preference to a viscount), and leaves home. After "nearly 7 hours" of mildly rowdy behavior in London (for example, downing ices), she returns to declare, "This is a day well spent" (47)—raising the really big question of what kinds of young ladies, and adventures, and days are worth having and writing about.

In "The History of England" Jane Austen rewrites history into the kind of book Catherine Morland would like. Derived largely from Shakespeare, it acknowledges having a good deal of authorial invention in it, and puts women at the center: the heroine is the Queen of Scots. (Jane Austen must have been influenced by Sophia Lee's historical fiction, *The Recess* (1783), about the fictitious twin daughters of Mary of Scotland. "*The Recess* enjoyed enormous popularity for well over twenty years after its first publication," writes April Alliston in her introduction to a modern edition.[25]) Illustrated by the young author's sister, it is anomalous among her early efforts. Most of the early stories are heroine-centered fictions, notable for matter-of-factly chronicling pointless activities, and for more shockingly acknowledging sex, suicide, robbery, and disgusting meals. People are "carried home, dead drunk," and young wives run off, unsurprisingly, with the butler. Jane Austen's "deplorable lapses of taste over carnality" shocked E. M. Forster when her letters were first published;[26] recent readers have exulted instead, gratified to think that *really* Jane Austen was not at all genteel.

The youthful stories seem to me more interesting for their jokes about literary form than for their "shocking" content. They suggest the method of the writer we think of as Jane Austen, who turned and turned again on her chosen form (turning from the romantic pair of Frederic and Elfrida, for example, to the titular siblings Jack and Alice), and kept playing with the elements of fiction. They make it clear that her literary concerns and techniques are in effect all we know of her, all we can love that we are not making up. The stories, like the novels, are sophisticated, critical rewritings of fiction, combative efforts to set this writer apart from others whose conventional characters, implausible plots, and predictable sentences they gleefully miniaturize and exaggerate—and to one-up them. Like her six mature novels, most of them end with exaggerated tidiness, mocking by insisting on the marriage plot.

"The adventures of Mr Harley, a short, but interesting Tale," in three brief paragraphs, tells the story of a man's whole life, from youthful family difficulties to adult choices to the final solution of marriage—which is here the awareness of being already married. Anticipating the first chapter of *Pride and Prejudice*, the first chapter of "Edgar and Emma, a tale," is a dialogue between parents who cannot agree; the story is about the gulf between ordinary life and romantic expectations, like all Jane Austen's novels. But the end is tragic not comic, leaving young Emma to weep for the rest of her life for her one true love, the schoolboy Edgar, who failed to accompany his family to her parents' house on a visit. By subjecting it to condensation, exaggerating its conventions, and departing from them at whim, the youthful parodies acknowledge the heroine-centered novel as a literary form with a history and a definite shape, like the lyric or the ode. What sometimes seems like surrealism avant la lettre—as when one "short, fat & disagreeable" young lady dresses up as Envy for a masquerade, and proceeds to sit on the foreheads of the other guests, as they play cards—is parody as homage, to the novel and, more generally, to metaphor.

The young Jane Austen was drunk with the writer's power to make one thing lead to another—events in a plot, chapters in a narrative, words in a sentence. "In Lady Williams," she writes altogether too fluently, "every virtue met. She was a widow with a handsome Jointure and the remains of a very handsome face. Tho' Benevolent and Candid, she was Generous and sincere; Tho' Pious and good, she was Religious and amiable, and Tho' Elegant and Agreable, she was Polished and entertaining" (*MW*, 13). Lulled by the sentence rhythms, the unwary reader might nod off and not notice it makes no sense: the wary one will be delighted by the oversetting of expectations, the discrepancy between sound and sense, and the mockery of pompous formulations. Mary Waldron observes that Jane Austen "parodies the typical Johnsonian antithetical maxim" in this passage from "Jack and Alice": the parody is not only of Johnson, but of all emphatic prose under-written by its rhythms.[27]

Although "a verdant Lawn enamelled with a variety of variegated flow-ers and watered by a purling Stream, brought from the Valley of Tempe by a passage under ground" (*MW*, 5) mocks poetic language that's no longer fashionable, it's not hard to see what the author of "Frederic and Elfrida" thought was funny, or to think of modern analogues to that kind of cliché-ridden overwriting. Already, at twelve and thirteen, she approached the plot as a puzzle to be worked out, and not as a fantasy. "Frederic and Elfrida" and the other stories are not erotic or romantic, as, for example, the juvenile writing of the Brontes is. A lot of the jokes depend on the very young writer's view that grownups are funny. Charles Adams, the resplendent hero of "Jack and Alice," first appears at a masquerade, dressed as no less than the sun: "The Beams that darted from his Eyes were like those of that glorious Luminary tho' infinitely superior. So strong were they that no one dared venture within half a mile of them; he had therefore the best part of the Room to himself, its size not amounting to more than 3 quarters of a mile in length and half a one in breadth" (13). Of the six ladies who meet him there, only poor Alice John-son finds the super-sun-like Charles (whose first name and manly perfection recall Sir Charles Grandison's) irresistible, the others being "defended from his Power by Ambition, Envy, and Self-admiration" (15). The selfishness and self-regard of people in general and of sisters in particular is a recurrent matter-of-factly stated matter, in the stories as it is in the later novels. Egoism is the current against which love must contend. But the love story is obligatory: even The Beautifull Cassandra must fall in love, albeit with a hat, because she is a character in fiction.

If the very first thing we notice in the very first story is the young writer's interest in relations and relationships, and of course words, the second thing must be her evident pleasure in how one thing—or one word—leads logically or illogically to another. "Jack and Alice" begins, "Mr Johnson was once upon a time about 53; in a twelve-month afterwards he was 54, which so much delighted him that he was determined to celebrate his next Birth day." (One isolated inhabitant of "Lesley Castle" complains that she and her sisters "visit no one but the M'Leods, the M'Kenzies, the M'Phersons, the M'Cartneys, the M'donalds, the M'Kinnons, the M'lellans, the M'Kays, the Macbeths and the Macduffs" [111].) The young Jane Austen always numbered her chapters and took pleasure in the ritual of enumerating, and in numbers for their own sakes. The funniness, to a child, of a person's being over fifty is contagious even to the mature reader of "Lesley Castle," in which a young lady finely describes her father as "fluttering about the streets of London, gay, dissipated, and Thoughtless at the age of 57" (111). As Bharat Tandon suggests, Jane Austen's use of numbers is characteristic of her precision and the comedy that depends on it: he cites the play of five and ten in "the report which was in general circulation within five minutes after his entrance, of [Mr. Darcy's] having ten thousand a year" (PP, 10).[28] In Emma we are told that Harriet spends fourteen minutes at the Martins, instead of the promised quarter hour, but that novel also lavishly, mysteriously, acknowledges indeterminacy: Frank Churchill, his own father says fuzzily, is twenty-three or twenty-four; Jane Fairfax is eighteen or nineteen, Mr. Knightley is thirty-seven or thirty-eight, and Mr. Elton is twenty-six or twenty-seven. When the reactions of "an Imaginist" like Emma are described, we are told that "a linguist, a grammarian, a mathematician" (E, 335) would have also been staggered by the story of Harriet and the gypsies: the progression is perhaps suggestive.

The critics have traditionally told us that the young Jane Austen wrote to amuse and please her large, literate, and cozy family. That fact tends to obscure a fiercer one: that from the beginning, she had the greater reading public in mind. Slipping family jokes into her stories—"the Beautifull Cassandra"—and dedicating them to intimates who knew the books she sent up, she was also practicing techniques that would engage all readers, and imagining herself a mighty author. The dedications "to Francis William Austen Esq Midshipman on board his Majesty's Ship the Perseverance by his Obedient humble Servant The Author" (*MW*, 12), etc., suggest a jolly relation between siblings, and a family where formality was a joke. Jane Austen played, early on, at being a professional author. The awareness of her readers that was honed in the bosom of a reading family would continue sharp. In retrospect, the child's half-serious embrace of the convention of elaborate literary dedications seems to anticipate the tone of the too fulsome 1815 dedication of *Emma* to the Prince Regent.[29]

The most ambitious and probably the latest-written of her youthful stories, "Catharine; or, The Bower," is dedicated to her sister, whose "warm patronage" has won earlier works thus dedicated "a place in every library in the Kingdom" (*MW*, 192)—suggesting the author's aim at precisely such a place, or places. The big difference between "Catharine" and the other works is clear from the first sentence:

> Catharine had the misfortune, as many heroines have had before her, of losing her Parents when she was very young, and of being brought up under the care of a Maiden Aunt, who while she tenderly loved her, watched over her conduct with so scrutinizing a severity, as to make it very doubtful to many people, and to Catharine amongst the rest, whether she loved her or not. (*MW*, 192)

Catharine is created as a credible character in a fiction by being placed in relation first to "many heroines," secondly to "many people," and thirdly to herself. The "misfortune" that defines her situation and her character is the lack of love: by definition it triggers the marriage plot, which promises to solve it. Catharine's psychological density is a function of her relations to others, those around her and those in other books: that is what makes her a convincing character. Unlike Elfrida or Eliza, of *Volume the First*, she has an inner life.

In the ostensible act of diminishing her (as she will diminish Catherine Morland) as only a novel heroine, Austen-as-narrator aggrandizes this Catharine into humanity: to acknowledge her heroine as a heroine is to acknowledge the reader reading—to wink at and engage and establish complicity with her or him. The narrator takes for granted that we will take her own half-mocking view of Catharine, whose thinking about Edward Stanley she mimics:

The more she had seen of him, the more inclined was she to like him, & the more desirous that he should like *her*. She was convinced of his being naturally very clever and very well disposed, and that his thoughtlessness & Negligence, which tho' they appeared to *her* as very becoming in *him*, she was aware would by many people be considered as defects in his Character, merely proceeded from a vivacity always pleasing in Young Men, & were far from testifying a weak or vacant Understanding. (*MW*, 235–236)

Catharine, though "perfectly convinced by her own arguments," is—we suspect—far from the truth. Here, as in the first sentence of the story, a distinction is made between what "many people" think and what the heroine herself thinks. Catharine's sense of her own difference from "many people" and their way of thinking, her sense of Edward's being different from what they would think of him, work to make her a convincing character. However silly or flawed, she is a believable representation of a young woman, aware of the difference between the outsides and insides of people—unlike, say, the (merely notional or nominal) "Beautifull Cassandra."

The narrator of *Emma* will trace the heroine's feelings about a similarly thoughtless and vivacious young man—Frank Churchill—with more subtlety and drama, developing the technique of half-mockingly mimicking her thoughts:

He was silent. She believed he was looking at her; probably reflecting on what she had said, and trying to understand the manner. She heard him sigh. It was natural for him to feel that he had *cause* to sigh. He could not believe her to be encouraging him. (*E*, 261)

With access to many characters' different minds, this sure-footed narrator can tell a story in multiple voices. Jane Austen started out mimicking fiction writers, and learned in the process how to mimic the minds of whole neighborhoods so as to render them both ridiculous and real. Here, still mockingly, she helps us to a share of Mr. Weston's indulgent thinking about the likelihood of his son Frank's visiting Highbury:

Sixteen miles—nay, eighteen—it must be full eighteen to Manchester-street—was a serious obstacle. Were he ever able to get away, the day would be spent in coming and returning. There was no comfort in having him in London; he might as well be at Enscombe; but Richmond was the very distance for easy intercourse. Better than nearer!   (*E*, 318)

And here Austen the parodying ventriloquist throws the voice of the whole community as it embraces the new Mrs. Elton:

The charming Augusta Hawkins, in addition to all the usual advantages of perfect beauty and merit, was in possession of an independent fortune, of so many thousands as would always be called ten; a point of some dignity, as well as some convenience: the story told well; he had not thrown himself away.   (*E*, 181)

Noting the convenience of the round number—the precise amount that Meryton gossips say Mr. Darcy takes in a year—is a late variation on an old joke. Writing with awareness of what Jane Austen liked to call "the common phrase," this author uses it to convey at once a convincingly human fictional voice and her own judgment of it.

Only a Novel

The author Ian McEwan called *Atonement* (2001) his "Jane Austen novel." Unlike most productions of nineties-to-post-nineties Jane-o-mania, however, it is interested in Austen as a novelist first of all. Revaluations of her juvenilia, Claire Tomalin's 1997 biography, and McEwan's own characteristic perverseness led him to imagine her as a diabolically clever child. Setting his novel before the Second World War, he makes the child author a creature of her time, a sexual fantasist and a modernist, detached and cold. The prize-winning author of disturbingly grotesque fictions—"Ian Macabre," they called him—was, among other things, registering a protest against the dominant popular view of gentle, genteel, marriage-minded Jane.

The first section of the novel, set in a country house in England in the nineteen-thirties, is a brilliant blend of imitation and pastiche; the whole novel turns out to be an extended critical meditation on the novel in the Austen tradition, its sources and influences and its moral valence. The Austen connection was reinforced in the film version by casting Keira Knightley, the attenuated photogenic Elizabeth of Joe Wright's romantic *Pride and Prejudice* (2005), as the romantic heroine, Cecilia. *Pride and Prejudice* is faintly evoked in McEwan's story by the cross-class romance between Cecilia, the older daughter of the upper-class Tallis family, and Robbie Turner, the charwoman's son, who grew up in residence on the property, much as Mr. Wickham did at Pemberley. There are stronger echoes of *Mansfield Park* and *Northanger Abbey*. The novel takes its epigraph from the latter, Henry Tilney's harangue about the "dreadful nature of the suspicions" Catherine Morland has entertained about his family:

> "Remember that we are English: that we are Christians. . . . Does our education prepare us for such atrocities? Do our laws connive at them? Could they be perpetrated without being known, in a country like this, where social and literary intercourse is on such a footing; where every man is surrounded by a neighbourhood of voluntary spies, and where roads and newspapers lay everything open? Dearest Miss Morland, what ideas have you been admitting?" (*NA*, 197–198)

McEwan takes the quotation past the point where most people who quote it tend to stop—perhaps to stress the innuendo in "admitting"—to include the sentence of narrative that follows, the last sentence of the chapter: "They had reached the end of the gallery; and with tears of shame she ran off to her own room." Tears and shame and a flight from fantasy, as well as the perfervid imagination that confounds sexual-literary fantasies with the lives of the people one lives with, will be the subjects of *Atonement*.

And, of course, the house—the English country house that isolates groups of friends and families, and individuals in their separate rooms, the overheated house of sensational gothic fiction and the much less explicitly erotic but nevertheless affiliated tradition of Jane Austen. (The two have long been closely related: when the conservative critic William Gifford read *Pride and Prejudice* in 1815, he praised it in terms that surprise us now, for being nothing like a gothic. "No dark passages," he wrote approvingly; "no secret chambers; no wind-howlings in long galleries; no drops of blood upon a rusty dagger—things that should now be left to ladies' maids and sentimental washerwomen."[30]) The house of domestic fiction—Charlotte Smith's Old Manor House—is descended from the great good place of pastoral legend, but also its poisonous, threatening antithesis: Richardson's Harlowe Place responds to Fielding's Paradise Hall.

The American professor Lionel Trilling (and Edward Said, after him) misread the meaning of Mansfield Park, a house, fractured and unstable, that is built on the morally dubious foundations of patriarchal property laws and prudential marriages, but McEwan gets it right. Like Northanger Abbey and Mansfield Park, like Harlowe Place in Clarissa (Cecilia is trying to read that novel, in the heat), Tallis House, in Atonement, is pernicious in spite of its comforts and complacencies, customs and ceremonies. The family has not been in residence long: the house was built by the father of Jack Tallis, the current paterfamilias, who was a manufacturer of iron hasps and latches—ugly devices used to lock people in, and keep people out. The aesthetic and moral limitations of the house are, as always in domestic fiction, reflected in the human relations and fantasies that flourish in its interior spaces—rivalries, antagonisms, lusts. In the heedless, ambitious, selfish, dignified masculine manner of Sir Thomas Bertram of Mansfield Park, who also means well, Jack Tallis fails to cultivate his garden, ignoring family life and its toxins to engage in toxic affairs abroad—in his case, explicitly sexual and martial ones. Jack Tallis is having an affair with a woman in London, and he is also involved there in the government's progress toward war. The country house, safe and yet grotesque, is a satirical analogue to—among other things—the tight little threatened island of England. Jack Tallis, in the government offices, is preparing for a second devastating world war.

A sepia photograph of a country house of crumbling stone set on a parched lawn, with an ornamental fountain like the one that figures in the novel's plot, is on the dust jacket of the first edition of Atonement. Inside, there is a quotation from W. B. Yeats's poem "A Prayer for My Daughter": "And may her bridegroom bring her to a house / Where all's accustomed, ceremonious / How but in custom and in ceremony / Are innocence and beauty born?" Questions about innocence and beauty, peace and war, marriage and love, the home and tradition, and specifically about the relation of fiction—its tropes and traditions—to truth run through the belated Austen craze. Atonement is an homage to Jane Austen; the best point it makes is that the novel (not film) is the appropriate form for such a thing.

Literary references and allusions ripple through McEwan's fiction: there are quotations from writers from Auden and Austen to Woolf and Yeats, a letter allegedly written by Cyril Connolly, and evocations of Henry James—not only his house of fiction. Literature intersects intricately and violently with life. Cecilia, just out of the university and ready for love, is slogging through

Richardson's epistolary novel *Clarissa*; her life is ruined by a letter from Robbie, who gets arrested as a rapist (which the rake Robert Lovelace actually is, in *Clarissa*). Her younger pubescent dreamy sister Briony—the protagonist— has written a play for private theatricals to celebrate her brother's homecoming. Its heroine is called Arabella, the name of Clarissa Harlowe's sister as well as of the heroine of a celebrated send-up of romantic fiction, *The Female Quixote* (1752), which Jane Austen read and admired. (The discovery, in the 1980s, of the manuscript of an Austen family dramatization of Richardson's *Sir Charles Grandison* is somewhere in the literary background.) Thirteen-year-old Briony wrote the role of Arabella for herself, but she reluctantly agrees to allow her troubled, sexually advanced visiting cousin, who is a year older, to star in the play. (One recalls the ill-assorted cousins in *Mansfield Park*.) Before this can happen, Lola is raped (as Clarissa first and Lolita later are raped), in this case by a friend of Briony's and Cecilia's brother, a manufacturer of a candy made of chemicals, not real chocolate, called Amo (Latin for "I love," but also recalling ammo, for ammunition). Paul Marshall, a more sinister predatory version of the louche cosmopolitan Crawfords of *Mansfield Park*, will make a fortune when the government distributes his candy to soldiers during the war. He will survive, married to Lola, to prevent Briony from revealing the truth about what happened, long after all the good have died young.

Atonement is Briony's story—the story of an uncannily knowing child, more a version of Jane Austen the knowing innocent spinster of legend than of the joke-cracking author of the youthful stories and playlets. But like Jane Austen's six novels and the many novels and movies influenced by them, indeed like Briony's play about Arabella, Joe Wright's version focuses most of the time on the beautiful, nubile romantic heroine, and the question of her sexual and marital fate. McEwan's disturbing focus—after Freud, and Freud's great enemy Nabokov, after the feminist revaluing of Jane Austen's juvenilia—is on the sexual girl child. (Andrew Davies's dark 2008 adaptation of *Sense and Sensibility*, for the BBC, also emphasizes the sexual abuse of children, underscoring seventeen-year-old Marianne Dashwood's youth as well as the ruined Eliza's.) A precocious old-fashioned child, intense, meticulous, and fastidious (demonic, as played by Saoirse Ronan in the film), she recalls, more than Jane Austen, the legendary lonely little Brontes, whose romantic stories were spun out from their games. Cleverly and unfairly, McEwan conflates Brontesque erotic fantasy and Austenian precision, in Briony's play;

more interestingly, he daringly dramatizes the child's change from a dreamy writer of thin, stiff, semi-romantic little plays into a psychological novelist.

In the first section of *Atonement*, Briony looks out the window of her room to see her sister and Robbie standing on the gravel near an ornamental fountain. Cecilia bends to fill a precious vase she carries; Robbie attempts to take it from her hands; the vase comes apart; Cecilia strips to her underwear, strides into the fountain, and plunges to pick up the pieces. The rest of the novel follows from questions attendant on this perverse primal scene and the shock sustained by the child observing it. What did Briony see, and what did she want to see and therefore imagine seeing? How to tease apart the tangled strands of perception, desire, imagination, and language? Are there words with which they can be put together, like the broken pieces of the vase? Can Briony read, can she write, what she thinks she sees? How well can we read her? Misperceiving from a vantage point at once limited and overheated, misreading the written consequence of what she sees that quickly follows—Robbie's letter to Cecilia, which she intercepts—Briony is transformed, changed from a child into a sexual woman and from a play-writing prodigy into a novelist. The novelist, in McEwan's view, unlike a playwright takes but also confusingly mediates the characters and points of view of other people he or she knows: it is a question of genre, Briony begins to recognize (trying to describe her sexual-artistic epiphany to Cecilia, she (mis)pronounces a French word that Cecilia hears as the French name "Jean"). But she is more limited than she knows, and has begun to think and feel, and therefore she becomes destructive. The fantasist who manipulates conventional characters and the tiny toy animals in her room presumes to become that more complex character, the novelist, whose words—whose untruths—can have terrible effects on actual lives.

Briony's life is not at all like Jane Austen's. She is thirteen years old in 1935; she lives on into the World War and into her late seventies, enjoying financial success and fame as a modernist novelist; she breaks with her family; like Frances Burney, Madame d'Arblay, not like Jane Austen, she marries a Frenchman. As Henry Austen insisted rather too much, Jane Austen drew from nature but not from individuals; Briony, in contrast, enters into the consciousnesses of people in her house and family, confuses her own desires with theirs, and wrecks their lives. Nevertheless Austen's figure—suggestively distorted and fractured—is central to this novel, which explores the novel as a genre. Split between Briony and Cecelia, it begins to suggest Jane Austen was divided against herself, and/or obsessed with her older, softer, more sexually successful sister. (Cassandra was only three years older than Jane, but unlike Jane she had a love story.) Jane Austen shimmers throughout the story, a figure for sexual innocence and authorial achievement and detachment, and for the Great Tradition of the English novel, the mixed desires to know and to tell and to get a grip on the elusive and illusory, and for language and fictions, or lies. She moves like a ghost in and out of a novel about words and letters, writing and reading, the immense importance in people's lives of language and stories, and their only partial truth.

The preoccupation of nineties Jane-o-mania was with the maiden novelist's relation to the love stories she wrote. (An old maid, D. A. Miller sportively called her.) W. H. Auden phrased it more politely when he marveled that "an English spinster of the middle class" should know so much about "the amorous effects of brass," or money, the complexity of relations and attractions, the way desires confusingly collude. The recent celebration of the child Jane Austen, the author of the so-called juvenilia and possibly the demure young subject of the so-called Rice Portrait, rephrases this question. The notion of the virginal author of *Pride and Prejudice* as a preternaturally wise child—a bad seed, even, in Joe Wright's version of *Atonement*—seems satisfyingly and ironically to match the moral chaste Jane of earlier legend. McEwan's novel suggests that the Novel combines lies and fictions written to atone for telling lies, novels in different styles and drafts that take different points of view, and sexually explicit novels containing unspeakable arousing "dirty" words, written in a godless universe. The story of an amoral novelist, the antithesis of the familiar didactic Jane Austen of legend, *Atonement* is richly suggestive about why Jane Austen still matters.

When the police drag Robbie away on suspicion of raping Lola, which is a consequence of Briony's false testimony against him, Grace Turner, Robbie's mother, shouts, "Liars! Liars!" It is the end of part I, a half-acknowledgment of the lie it all has been, and—in this book—the end of the lie of the country-house novel. What follows are fictions about the same people, in different styles, and variously posed questions about the truth of fiction. The char's son takes the fall for the real rapist as a result of class prejudice: the novel in Jane Austen's tradition relies on and reaffirms these prejudices even as it disputes them (see Wickham, in *Pride and Prejudice*, a charming liar sexier than Mr. Darcy).

What truth does fiction tell, with all its lies? One of the two passionate letters Robbie writes to Cecilia—the one he unintentionally sends her, via

Briony—contains the shocking word "cunt." Jane Austen would not use that word, of course, nor would Briony's mother, who reads the letter; and that word is arguably responsible for all the hysteria and catastrophes that follow. Does McEwan—who dares to use it—indict the genteel or merely hypocritical refusal to talk straight about sex, to face facts and name things as they are, along with the genteel novel that represses such plain language, and seduces us by transforming sexual thoughts and feelings into fictions and lies? Is the (English?) inability to understand and articulate emotions like desire, and pride, and prejudice—one's own and other people's—at the psychosexual root of not only the Novel but also the War? Do innocence and lies and credulousness collude? Concluding the novel, realizing that one has been misreading the whole time and that to know the truth it's necessary to reread it, one is left with Jane Austen's question: what truths, general and particular, do novels tell us?

Defiantly critical of the genteel novel in Austen's tradition, beautifully imitative of it at the same time, McEwan's "literary fiction" (as publishers now call serious fiction) is richly reminiscent of the epistolary tradition—Richardson's—out of which it emerged. (*Sense and Sensibility*, according to Austen family tradition, was a novel in letters in its first version, *Elinor and Marianne*; family tradition are crucial in *Pride and Prejudice*, *Mansfield Park*, *Emma*, and *Persuasion*.) The two letters to Cecilia that Robbie types and mixes up are matched by the letter left by Lola's twin brothers when they run off; the letter of apology Briony doesn't write is matched by the letters from Cecilia to Robbie, and the letter from C.C. (not Cecilia but the literary man Cyril Connolly) to Briony. You can say things in letters you don't say in real life; letters can go astray, get mixed up. Letters, like novels, concretize those performative utterances that alter the world, words like "I love you," or "cunt," or "I saw him," or "Come back."

Clarissa, an epistolary novel that ends in a rape, inspired many of the novels that deny or repress the truth of sexuality and violence. Similarly, *Atonement* delights the reader with its aesthetically pleasing traditional symmetries and repetitions: the lie that Robbie raped Lola is believed because "everything fitted" (158). The expectation of pattern, symmetry, and fit helps make lies become true: the aesthetic is immoral. Part II is a critique of the old-fashioned pleasant lie of symmetry and pleasantness, a war novel, jagged and explicitly violent and horrible, featuring lower-class men and no women, set in France not in England, with the British army in retreat. Ironically, inevitably, it offers further symmetries and doublings, pairings. The end insists that this novel is altogether a lie, and simultaneously insists on its truth: Lola and Marshall, still living, would sue for libel and could, if Briony's story about the rape, the original crime, were published; Briony cannot and would not alter their names in any account. The novelist shatters, garbles, remakes, distorts reality; the shards of recognizable life in the fiction, along with the reminders of other fictions and the literary/linguistic heritage, make the fiction more eloquent and seductive. It is palpably a lie; nevertheless, or perhaps because of that, we read and even reread fiction looking for the truth it tells.

Ian McEwan's novel provoked arguments about whether the tricky narrative played fair with readers, whether the novelist played by the rules. Some people claimed to hear religious or legal resonances in the title; others ventured ingeniously that the subject was "at-one-ment." Is atonement possible for crimes that result from a complex history of social arrangements and circumstances? Mr. Collins comes to Longbourn to marry one of Mr. Bennet's daughters if he finds them "as handsome and amiable as they were represented by common report," the narrator of *Pride and Prejudice* tells us in accents that mock by imitating his. "This was his plan of amends—of atonement—for inheriting their father's estate; and he thought it an excellent one, full of eligibility and suitableness, and excessively generous and disinterested on his own part" (70). Probably McEwan did not have these thoughts of Mr. Collins's in mind when he chose the provocative title of his novel—but can the crimes of the imagination be atoned for any more than the accidents of inheritance can be? Are the truths of the imagination lies?

FIGURE 16. Action figure of Jane Austen. Photograph by Catherine Casalino, 2010.

CHAPTER 5

Why We Reread Jane Austen

Charmouth, with its high grounds and extensive sweeps of country, and still more its sweet retired bay, backed by dark cliffs, where fragments of low rock among the sands make it the happiest spot for watching the flow of the tide, for sitting in unwearied contemplation;—the woody varieties of the cheerful village of Up Lyme, and, above all, Pinny, with its green chasms between romantic rocks, where the scattered forest trees and orchards of luxuriant growth declare that many a generation must have passed away since the first partial falling of the cliff prepared the ground for such a state . . . : these places must be visited, and visited again, to make the worth of Lyme understood.
—*Persuasion*, chapter 11

It is hard that we should not be allowed to dwell as often as we please on what delights us, when things that are disagreeable recur so often against our will.
—William Hazlitt, "On a Landscape of Nicolas Poussin"

"And what are you reading, Miss——?" "Oh! It is only a novel!" replies the young lady; while she lays down her book with affected indifference, or momentary shame.—"It is only Cecilia, or Camilla, or Belinda;" or, in short, only some work in which the greatest powers of the mind are displayed, in which the most thorough knowledge of human nature, the happiest delineation of its varieties, the liveliest effusions of wit and humour are conveyed to the world in the best chosen language.
—*Northanger Abbey*, chapter 5

Indeed, one could argue that Austen's ideal reader *is* one who initially gets things wrong.
—Bharat Tandon, *Jane Austen and the Morality of Conversation*

MY FRIEND C. IS CONCERNED ABOUT HER OLDEST GRANDdaughter. Emma, born in 1995, is a great, an avid, an omnivorous reader, she tells me; she saw and loved all the Jane Austen movies, which her parents got for her on DVD. She's read and really enjoyed the other Austen novels, but she cannot and will not read *Emma*. No, the problem is not that the heroine who shares her name is a brat—there's a very annoying Emma in her class, and she doesn't mind her. And she says she does not object to what they say is the moral of the story, that you shouldn't manipulate other people or condescend to them, and that kids should be polite to older people (although she can't see going so far as to marry one). Can I explain? They have bought her several beautiful editions.

It is a grandmotherly question, dated by its preconceptions as well as its kind concern. If girls ever read Jane Austen, as cynics used to say they did, for the covert thrill of sexy romance masked as educational literature, they no longer do—at least not in our sophisticated, liberal urban circles. First of all, it does not seem obligatory, as it once did, to educate oneself by reading the classics: the prevailing cool view is expressed in the back-cover copy of the smash-hit mash-up, *Pride and Prejudice and Zombies* (2009), shelved in the "teen" section of your local mega-bookstore—that it "transforms a masterpiece of world literature into something you'd actually want to read." I'm not sure exactly what young Emma reads, but the covers of the other books piled in that super-sophisticated section promise laughs, sex, violence, grossouts, laughs at sex and violence and gross-outs, and weird spooky fantasy. What's now (deplorably) denominated "literary fiction" barely makes it to the tables in a dying book business where "romance novels" and "relationship books" by, e.g., Nora Roberts make dazzling profits. (Asked to account for her success, Roberts has explained that in hard times like ours, her books give one hope; presumably she was not quoting Lionel Trilling.) Overwritten and lush with adjectives, action, and explanations, predictable at every turn of the sentence and the bosom-heaving plot, mass-market romances are available and accessible to the curious teenager. They are easy to read, there are a lot of them, and tolerant parents and teachers and salesclerks—if they notice—tend not to disapprove of the girl who buys, borrows, quotes, or carries one, a girl who after all, unlike most girls, these days, is (they say proudly) a reader. The eager mass-marketing of Jane Austen–related books and films, from the by-now old movies of the 1990s through the continuing stream of sequels, etc., to the latest mash-ups, have confusingly confounded her works with popular genre fiction. I tell my friend that Austen's novel must seem slow and dull to a girl who has enjoyed the handsome, clever, richly colored movies, costume dramas calculated to persuade people to see her love stories as naïve, absurdly chaste romances of mostly historical

interest—dress rehearsals for the real thing we can finally truthfully write
and read about, and experience, today.

Young Emma probably reads for the plot, which is only normal, I tell
C.—and there's not much plot in *Emma*. It's the least romantic and the most
original and characteristic of Austen's novels. The problem for the modern
young reader is not only that there are no sex scenes and car chases: part of
the point of this book is how much little things matter, and it's most interesting to a reader who's read it before, and is already disposed to track the
echoes and parallels, the differences and, yes, the details. In the introduction to the latest Penguin edition, I remind her, Adela Pinch argues that the
novel is about nothing. My friend is a distinguished feminist professor, and I
can feel her turning off: she has read *Emma*, after all, and even some articles
about the novel, and she hardly needs me to tell her what it is about. She is
polite about the inadequacies of my aesthetic emphasis. Social scientists like
her have low expectations of their colleagues in the humanities: indeed they
count on us to dream on. Probably she thinks of me as one of those pleasure-
loving people in English departments who do not quite function in the real
world, and enjoy an alternative one a little too much. Maybe she's right: after
all, my take on Jane Austen is that everything in and around the books points
toward the mutual imbrications of realities and alternatives. I soldier on. I tell
her you have to be carefully taught, these days, to read Jane Austen, and that I
work to get my students to read for anything but the plot, and that her Emma
is too young to read *Emma* quite yet.

When I "teach" *Emma* to undergraduates, I work to alienate it. I read the
opening paragraphs aloud so the students can savor the slow, gradual elonga-
tion of the "e" from the short indeterminate grunt in the words it starts with
("Emma" and "best blessings of existence") to the long emphatic screech of
the "e's" in "real evils." If they seem attentive and I'm on a roll, I inform them
that the twentieth-century novelist George Perec wrote a whole novel entirely
without "e's," and that the "e" in Mr. Knightley's name distinguishes it from
the word it derives from (although the bluff middle-aged hero named after
the English Saint George is a modern version of the perfect, gentle knight,
a traditional gentleman farmer in a newly commercial society). I point out
that the dropped "e" in "Donwell Abbey" is what saves it from being too
simply, overly allegorically named "Done Well." (I might even go on a little
about "Norland" and "Morland.") If the students begin to say or want to
say that I'm making too much of too little I stop there. But with graduate

students, rereaders, I always manage to get to the conversation at Box Hill and Mr. Weston's game spelling "Emma" with the letters "M" and "A," minus the initial "e."

I want them to notice that the novel is a fabric of words, to see how Jane Austen insists that evil is real by her choice of words, and I want them to remember these words that sound at the very beginning of the novel. The best of them will hear the echo later when Emma considers the distressing possibility that Harriet might be "the chosen, the first, the dearest" of Mr. Knightley, "the wife to whom he looked for all the best blessings of existence" (422–423). Jane Austen's sentences sound and scan as those of few prose writers do. Sometimes, conscious of enjoying them a little too much, I worry that I am like those impious people in the couplet by Alexander Pope, those who "to church repair / Not for the doctrine but the music there." Music can expand the mind, as doctrine cannot. Stuart Tave wrote movingly of the amplitude of meaning in "the just and lovely words of Jane Austen [which] take power . . . not from a narrowness of meaning, fixed and single, but from a certain largeness of scope within which they can move in careful purpose."[1] Like most of her regular readers, I reread Jane Austen for the pleasure of the texts, to enjoy what Nabokov called "aesthetic bliss . . . a sense of being somehow, somewhere, connected with other states of being where art (curiosity, tenderness, kindness, ecstasy) is the norm."[2] I read her to borrow and enjoy her thinking about how language makes life mean and matter, her bracing sense that everything hangs on using it precisely and well. "Composition" is what she called what she did at her desk; and her famous effusion of praise for the novel, in *Northanger Abbey*, ends emphatically on the words "chosen language." A marriageable maiden's choice is the focus of the plots of her novels, and the novelist underwrites that theme by keeping us conscious of her own choices, of words. Zeroing in on those "e's" in the first paragraph of *Emma* and running with them, as I stand in front of my class, I find myself preaching that paying attention to each and every detail leads the attentive reader to the truth. That Jane Austen writes fiction, but she doesn't lie.

The novels emphatically scorn "the common phrase," fashionable slang (Mrs. Elton's "caro sposo"), the "thorough novel slang" of the time that Jane Austen deplored, bad grammar like Lucy Steele's, and pious moralizing clichés like Mary Bennet's. In *Sense and Sensibility*, when Willoughby thoughtlessly resorts to bluster ("Thunderbolts and daggers!"), he remembers Marianne's scorn and apologizes to Elinor, giving us a quick rare glimpse of his charm.

In a linguistically sloppier time, Austen's insistence on care with language is easily misread as school-marmish stress on correctness for its own sake, or as an equally old-fashioned charming fastidious emphasis on mannerliness and lack of profanity. (In the 1990s, one dowager at a Jane Austen Society meeting confided to me, wonderfully, that she adored the new movies because they had no "language" in them [her air quotes, to convey the innuendo].) But her care for language is neither only aesthetic nor merely moral, in the narrow contemporary sense that signifies high-minded opposition to blasphemous or sexually explicit language. Writing as a perfect lady liberated Jane Austen from the constraints of being one. She gave the following advice to her niece Anna, in a letter clearly designed to shock, about a character in that sober young woman's novel in process:

> Devereux Forester's being ruined by his Vanity is extremely good; but I wish you would not let him plunge into a "vortex of Dissipation". I do not object to the Thing, but I cannot bear the expression. (*Letters*, 277)[3]

Her language is principled and precise, respectful of the fact that both thought and feeling are intrinsic to their expression: she is a moral writer, but she does not moralize. It is impossible for me to believe she did not smile a little when she described Hartfield as a "notch" (slang then for female genitals) in the expanse of Donwell Abbey; and although the admirable recent editor of *Mansfield Park* disagrees, it seems to me that such a clever and conscious connoisseur of words had to be aware that Mary Crawford's remark about the talk of "Rears and Vices" at her uncle the Admiral's skirts the subject of sodomy.[4]

"You know I enjoy particulars," Austen wrote appreciatively, evidently in response to an especially vivid lost letter (not much more than this fragment remains of her response) (*Letters*, 288). The novels insist on the importance of details, like the rivet in Mrs. Bates's spectacles that Frank Churchill gets called in to fix. Walking with Harriet, Emma stops to tie her shoelace, then deliberately breaks it off as an excuse to bring Harriet to Mr. Elton's cottage. Later in the story, Mr. Knightley bends down to tie his shoelace: readers not yet aware that he is in love with Emma are led to think the effort of doing so causes his face to get red. On rereading, the matching episodes resonate wonderfully, comically, contributing to the beautifully patterned whole of the novel. It is not only in *Emma*, of course, that everything depends on the details. The reader is challenged to notice them from the very first paragraph of, for example, *Mansfield Park:*

> About thirty years ago, Miss Maria Ward of Huntingdon, with only seven thousand pounds, had the good luck to captivate Sir Thomas Bertram, of Mansfield Park, in the county of Northampton, and to be thereby raised to the rank of a baronet's lady, with all the comforts and consequences of an handsome house and large income. All Hunting-don exclaimed on the greatness of the match, and her uncle, the lawyer, himself, allowed her to be at least three thousand pounds short of any equitable claim to it.

The punning, alliteration, and off-balances (hunting done; *captivate* and *comforts and consequences, handsome house and large income*); the play of active and passive voices; and especially the punctuation signal mockery. My favorites are the commas that set off "himself." Kathryn Sutherland (who acknowledges that pointing, or punctuation, was often left to the printers in the period) argues that Austen uses two kinds of commas, the syntactical and the conversational: the three that follow the words "uncle," "lawyer," and "himself," would fall into the second category. Like the comma after "universally acknowledged," in the first sentence of *Pride and Prejudice*, they indicate a pause for an intake of breath, as if in conversation—and also, I think, a pause that suggests time taken to notice the lift of an eyebrow, for emphasis.[5] Like the energetically emphatic underlining in some of Jane Austen's letters and manuscripts, these commas indicate stress (in both senses of that word), and a giggle. Here they insist that marriage is a financial contract: Miss Maria's lucky arrangements were made by her uncle the lawyer (socially a very far cry from a baronet), a pompous man (*the* lawyer) clever enough to make nice distinctions. That Miss Maria's own uncle was obliged to acknowledge his niece had made a good match prepares the way for the story of Fanny Price and *her* much grander uncle Sir Thomas Bertram (who admires her figure and also cruelly tries to give her to that unexpected high bidder, Henry Crawford).

Austen's most suggestive comment about (or around) her writing practice occurs in a letter to her favorite niece Fanny—a response to a letter from Fanny reporting from London, where she was seriously considering a marriage proposal. The aunt describes her sympathy, and her inability to come up with useful advice about what Fanny should do about her suitor: "I am feeling differently every moment, & shall not be able to suggest a single thing that can assist your Mind. —I could lament in one sentence & laugh in the next, but as to Opinion or Counsel I am sure none will [be] extracted worth having from this Letter." Like an aunt in an epistolary novel, she brings literary sense and sensibility to the cases for and against marrying "Poor dear Mr. J.P."

> There *are* such beings in the World perhaps, one in a Thousand, as the Creature You and I should think perfection, Where Grace & Spirit are united to Worth, where the Manners are equal to the Heart & Understanding, but such a person may not come in your way, or if he does, he may not be the eldest son of a Man of Fortune, the Brother of your particular friend, & belonging to your own County. —Think of all this Fanny. (*Letters*, 279–280)

Briefly, she changes the subject to her own news, which is that the first edition of *Mansfield Park* has sold out and she is looking forward to a second one, being "very greedy." (She had already wryly observed that Fanny was "much above caring about money"—Fanny was in fact rich but her aunt's point is that no one is above money.) Having done with both their private lives, she adds a paragraph of assorted family news, then signs off—but comes back to add a postscript apropos of the letter's main subject:

> Your trying to excite your own feelings by a visit to his room amused me excessively. —The dirty Shaving Rag was exquisite! —such a circumstance ought to be in print. Much too good to be lost. (*Letters*, 282)

Too good to be lost, too good for preservation in the mere mock amber of a private letter, the telling detail "ought to be in print": thus Fanny's appreciative aunt, Jane Austen the proud member of a thriving print culture, successful author of *Mansfield Park* and two earlier novels.

Fanny's visit to her suitor's room recalls a classic in the annals of satire, "Cassinus and Peter" (1731), Swift's poem about the "two College Sophs of Cambridge growth" who are horrified to discover, in a lady's dressing room, paint, false hair, and, unimaginably, a chamber pot ("Nor wonder how I lost my Wits / O, Caelia, Caelia, Caelia sh—".) If either Fanny or her aunt knew Swift's poem, they would have known as well that the circumstances are not parallel: no woman, certainly not one daring enough to look, would be disillusioned or surprised to find dirty evidence of his toilette in a man's private quarters. It is important that Jane Austen does not seem to have been shocked by Fanny's visiting her suitor's room in order to "excite [her] own feelings"; what she finds "exquisite" is Fanny's noticing the "Shaving Rag." Fanny's keen eye for a telling detail is what makes her a "delightful creature," a very different creature than Harriet Smith, still stuck on Mr. Elton, who treasures the piece of court plaster that once stuck to him.

Registering Fanny's registering the shaving rag, delighting in it, Jane Austen longs to have the "circumstance" related to others, to preserve the tiny detail in print as bugs are preserved in amber. It is not the dirty banal thing itself but Fanny's seeing it that is "much too good to be lost," as the most keen-eyed observations will be unless they are written down and printed. James Boswell wrote that he would live no more than he could record, as he would plant no more corn than he could gather: registering and writing down this comically insignificant detail of her private life, Fanny reaps a kernel of general truth. By noting it in her letter to her aunt she makes it mean. The exchange about the shaving rag is between writers as well as women; it is as Swiftian as it is feminine. From it, you get a whiff of what it must have been like to learn at her feet how Jane Austen looked at things, and to try—for one's own amusement and edification, and for hers—to see and to write as she did. It begins to explain why not only her nieces and nephew but also later generations of readers and admirers have thought they could try their hand at trying on Austen's simple-seeming style.

Jane Austen does not tell us how to live any more than she told Fanny whom to marry, but she usefully reminds us to pay attention, to both the details of living and the words we use. She seems to me to be divided (not unlike Lionel Trilling) about whether it is in fact possible to reconcile the moral life with enjoyment of the best blessings of existence. Her politics, like her private emotions, are elusive. Did she not write much about the servants because she didn't think they mattered, or because she limited her characters to the class she knew best, or knew best how to skewer? The remark in *Northanger Abbey* that from talking about politics it is an easy step to silence is sometimes read as Austen's personal view—but it could be that of the people talking. (Does only Fanny consider Sir Thomas a good man?) When Elizabeth Bennet calls herself "a rational creature," and Mrs. Croft, in *Persuasion*, defends women as "rational creatures," as opposed to "fine ladies," does the novelist behind them deliberately evoke Mary Wollstonecraft—approvingly? Is it fair to discern, in the hints of anxiety about incest and endogamy in *Mansfield Park* and *Emma*, shadows of the debates going on at the time the novels were written, about so-called miscegenation—and of Jane Austen's personal views of that—mixed with her private anxieties about marrying and leaving home?

Austen is harder to catch in the ideological act than she is in the act of genius.[6] As I see it, she is most useful today, politically and morally, as an example of linguistic precision. If the formal exigencies of Jane-Austen diction and manners have the Balinese charm of remoteness, now, they function usefully as metaphors for the arbitrariness of social and linguistic signs. They encourage awareness that language itself is part of the problem, as some things should not and others cannot be said. Words as Austen deploys and weighs them reflect, obscure, and influence by mediating the subtle relations of signification to meaning—therefore of meaning to feeling, and of what is meant and felt to what must remain unsaid. "What did she say? Just what she ought, of course. A lady always does" (*E*, 431): this is what the reader is told about Emma's response to Mr. Knightley's proposal of marriage. In the face of this complexity, at the heart of it, in the elegant phrasing and timing and epigrammatic brilliance, there is the promise of mastery over language. "My Emma," says Mr. Knightley, toward the end, after his critical close reading of not-frank Frank Churchill's letter (and therefore his character), "does not every thing serve to prove more and more the beauty of truth and sincerity in all our dealings with each other?" (*E*, 446). If the language-loving reader's heart swells at this as at a patriotic anthem, the surge on second thought subsides. Although she wants to, Emma can agree with Mr. Knightley only "with a blush of sensibility on Harriet's account, which she could not give any sincere explanation of." For our heroine is still keeping a secret, therefore still being incompletely truthful and sincere: it is a function of her character and context, and also of the limits of truth in conversation, and furthermore of the English language. Some fourteen pages earlier, apropos of Emma's being baffled by the task of explaining her inconsistency, either Mr. Knightley or the narrator carefully reflects that

> Seldom, very seldom, does complete truth belong to any human disclosure; seldom can it happen that something is not a little disguised, or a little mistaken; but where, as in this case, though the conduct is mistaken, the feelings are not, it may not be very material. (*E*, 431)

Rereading Jane Austen, I don't believe that Emma and Mr. Knightley are real: I hardly believe Jane Austen was. But I believe this truth about truth in language, and begin to believe again in the beauty of telling the truth, and in the importance of trying to. We reread Jane Austen because she persuades us to be nostalgic for what we never knew, and because we want her clarity.

Understanding

The meanings of the words "understand" and "understanding" fall into three rough but overlapping categories. The first includes the verb "to understand," meaning to perform a solitary intellectual act, and the noun "the understanding," that is, the reason or mind or intelligence, or "power of the soul"[7] with which an individual comprehends or grasps ideas and meanings, and objectively observes and assesses other individuals. This is operative in reading novels of the sort that begin by characterizing an Emma Woodhouse as "handsome, clever, and rich," totting up her attributes in a tone that directs one to weigh them instead of being swept away by them, as one might be while reading another kind of book—say, a romance. In this sense of the word, Elinor Dashwood has "strength of understanding," Jane Bennet has an "excellent understanding," and Mrs. Bennet can be fairly dispatched as a woman of "mean understanding," meaning she is not very intelligent.

Austen appeals to readers who are inclined to value mental ability and to scorn stupidity, to rank people according to their intellectual powers: the capacity of minds is more interesting to her than the color of hair. Harriet Smith, unlike Emma, is "not clever," having no "strength of understanding"; Isabella Knightley is "not a woman of strong understanding," while her husband is a "very clever man." Miss Bates has "no intellectual superiority"; Mr. Perry is "an intelligent, gentlemanlike man"; Mr. Weston has "an active, cheerful mind." (Of Mr. Knightley, "a sensible man," more later.) When Emma thinks at the end of her story that she had wrongly "set up for Understanding" (427)—the word is capitalized—she is criticizing herself for having thought she was so smart. Emma's revulsion from her own intellectual arrogance is engaging: readers who think that Emma (like Jane Austen) is too smart for her own good have fastened on this moment, sensing an interesting reversal of Jane Austen upon herself, an instance of softening, even penitence or atonement.

People of understanding in this first sense of the word are equipped to get jokes and understand puzzles and witticisms that elude duller minds. "Do you understand?" Mr. Weston anxiously asks Emma after he spells out his simple flattering conundrum on her name, at Box Hill. ("Understanding and gratification came together," the narrator tells us.) Three pages later, smart-aleck Emma says defensively to Mr. Knightley about the joke she made at Miss Bates's expense, "I dare say she did not understand me" (374). To understand what is outside it—the cognitive function—is a function of the understanding, that inner capacity some people have more and some less of. "No doubt you were much my superior in judgment at [one] period of our lives," says Emma to Mr. Knightley; "but does not the lapse of one-and-twenty years bring our understandings a good deal nearer?" (99). This remains a question in the novel (and the world beyond it), and it begins to raise the question of whether and how, if the understanding grows more capacious in the course of living in the world, it grows more connected with the things and the people around it. Common sense and British philosophy would seem to suggest that it is so: Hume argued that experience is a factor in the operations of the human understanding. (Jane Austen does not, I think, think quite that way: in *Mansfield Park* she hints at a more tragic vision, writing of Fanny that "she began to feel that she had not yet gone through all the changes of opinion and sentiment, which the progress of time and variation of circumstances occasion in this world of changes. The vicissitudes of the human mind had not yet been exhausted by her" [*MP*, 374].) All the novels seem to insist on the importance of innate intelligence, and tend to contrast people of strong understanding with less acute people who have different virtues. Sisters like Elinor and Marianne or Elizabeth and Jane, rivals like Mary Crawford and Fanny Price, are paired, in part, to pose the question that Emma raises outright apropos of Harriet Smith, whether a strong understanding in a woman is a "charm equal to tenderness of heart" (*E*, 169). In *Northanger Abbey* there is a reflection by the narrator that "a woman especially" should keep it to herself that she knows anything at all.

The first meaning of "to understand," to comprehend, apprehend the meaning or import of, grasp the idea of, is illustrated in the OED by the familiar quotation from *Emma*: "One half the world cannot understand the pleasures of the other" (81). It is Emma herself who makes this observation to her father, in response to his saying, "I cannot understand it," about his grandchildren's enjoyment of being tossed in the air by their uncle. "You understand everything" (76), undiscriminating Harriet tells Emma, using the word in the same way. To observe that half the world cannot understand the pleasures of the other is to observe the word "understand" begin to slide, as "understanding" also slides, into the second category or dimension of its meanings, to signify not the intellectual power of an individual but imaginative sympathy between people. Here, for instance, is Emma contemplating, and then listening to Harriet describe, Harriet's visit to the Martin girls:

> After much thinking, she could determine on nothing better, than Harriet's returning the visit: but in a way that, if they had understanding, should convince them that it was to be only a formal acquaintance. (*E*, 185)

> They all seemed to remember the day, the hour, the party, the occasion—to feel the same consciousness, the same regrets—to be ready to return to the same good understanding; and they were just growing again like themselves, (Harriet, as Emma must suspect, as ready as the best of them to be cordial and happy,) when the carriage re-appeared, and it was all over. (*E*, 187)

"If they had understanding," they would get the point of the very short visit: such a quality is not intellect but social tact. Something of that kind of meaning colors Emma's flirtatious invitation, to Mr. Knightley, to look back twenty-one years to the beginning of the lifetime she has spent improving her understanding. To understand or have understanding of this kind is to add feeling to the "mere understanding" or intellectual power. In the main plot of *Emma*, as the hero and the heroine move from being friends and relations by marriage to being married lovers, from teacher and student to husband and wife, the movement from an intellectual to an emotional understanding is subtly mapped. Mr. Knightley, rebuking Emma in her adoring father's presence, makes the point that she sometimes *is* by saying she is "not often deficient either in manner or comprehension." He concludes with a clear emphasis, "I think you understand me, therefore." It is not yet midway through the novel and Emma only imperfectly does, although she thinks she really does. "An arch look expressed—'I understand you well enough;' but she said only, 'Miss Fairfax is reserved'" (171). Depending on being understood by the people they talk to, speakers like Mr. Knightley and Emma may encode their meanings by inflecting the words and looks they exchange, telegraphing "You know what I mean" in order to prevent others (like Mr. Woodhouse, here) from beginning to comprehend their meaning. Doing that, they make a connection that depends on silence and sympathy, and on separating themselves from those around them; their mutual understanding or complicity is a psychosocial, antisocial force, the force that forms couples, coteries, cliques, and classes.

Different from both the objective understanding of the mind and the sympathetic understanding that goes without saying is a third more trivial sense of the word, "understanding" meaning a specific assumption or set of assumptions or a formal arrangement or agreement that links and joins individuals who consent to it. Marriage is its ultimate form; an engagement to marry comes close. Mr. Knightley near the end finally has a strong "suspicion of there being something of a private liking, of private understanding even, between Frank Churchill and Jane" (344). If we conceal such an understanding from the community, the consequences—as this novel sees it—threaten our private agreement, and our individual selves. The trouble with every private understanding is that for both good and ill it is exclusive and in that sense anti-social, therefore not subject to being corrected. For we may be wrongly imagining that both of us see things the same way, or that something like a (socially sanctioned) contractual agreement binds us together. A related error takes place among more than two people when a "good understanding" (187) or pleasant consciousness of being a comfortable party encourages a sense of personal well-being: people being inveterately like themselves, sometimes some are left out, and sometimes they are not what they seem to be.

The three meanings of the word "understand" and "understanding" are discrete, but they slide into one another. For to comprehend the words or gestures of another person, to take in the signs he or she invests with meaning, is after all to begin to be that person's ally, accomplice, or confederate. Understanding what another might mean requires work by the understanding; it may require, and may lead to, a mutual understanding of more or less depth and feeling; its premise is the understanding—true or false—that you will know what I mean. The several kinds or dimensions of understanding influence and color one another; the separate, distinctive intellectual power of an individual is complexly involved with the people she lives with and the arrangements and conventions that inform social life, simply because she thinks and talks in language, uses words like "understanding."

In *Emma*, as the meanings of the word "understanding" are explored, misunderstandings proliferate. A world made up of families in a country village is a world where people literally speak the same language and think they do figuratively as well, so that a great deal goes without saying and is given to be understood. What is understood in that sense is inevitably sometimes misunderstood, or taken to be understood without positive or sufficient knowledge, for instance when all Highbury says, "I suppose you have heard of the handsome letter Mr. Frank Churchill had written to Mrs. Weston? I understand it was a very handsome letter, indeed. Mr. Woodhouse told me of it. Mr. Woodhouse saw the letter, and he says he never saw such a handsome letter in his life" (18). What we understand on Mr. Woodhouse's authority we understand only as he understands things, which is to say not very well. Frank Churchill's father uses heavy irony when he reports another letter from the same young man and says, "Mrs. Churchill, *as we understand*, has not been able to leave the sopha for a week together" (306). The italicized phrase suggests that what people have been given to understand is merely an excuse, and not the truth—and that he counts on his neighbors to mistrust distant Mrs. Churchill.

While mutual understanding is widely assumed to exist in, say, Highbury—that people so casually say "as we understand" attests to this—individuals there in fact, as elsewhere, talk at cross-purposes, and often mistakenly rely on other people's correctly reading between their lines. When Frank Churchill amuses himself by flirting with Emma in order to tease Jane, talking about the "true affection" of whoever bought Jane the piano, Emma says to him, aside, "You speak too plain. She must understand you." Frank replies, "I hope she does. I would have her understand me" (243). Emma is unaware of the secret understanding between Frank and Jane; Frank depends on Jane's overhearing him and understanding his meaning as only she can; rereading the novel, we are uncomfortably in on his game, distanced, as we were not the first time, from poor blind Emma.

In *Emma*, the love that the marriage plot celebrates as the acme of mutual understanding is also, as in all romantic comedy, a source of misunderstanding. When Harriet Smith falls in love yet again, this time with Mr. Knightley, she says to Emma, "I do not want to say more than is necessary—I am too much ashamed of having given way as I have done, and I dare say you understand me" (337). Emma is sure she does, but she doesn't. Fools like Harriet too eagerly assume, in emotional matters that tax the powers of speech, that they understand, or that others do; so do people of intelligence, like Emma. For although words are hard to interpret, so is silence. "Charming Miss Woodhouse! Allow me to interpret this interesting silence," cries tipsy Mr. Elton, in the carriage, coming back in the snow from the party at the Weston house. "It confesses that you have long understood me." Emma calls his words into question by repeating them: "No, sir . . . it confesses no such thing. So far from having long understood you, I have been in a most complete error with respect to your views, till this moment" (131). The sympathy Mr. Elton seeks and expects is very different from what Emma refers to when she says she has not understood his views: she's saying not only that she has no sympathy for his feelings, but also that she is horrified to learn of their existence. She means that she does not and cannot love him; and by so utterly misreading and misunderstanding her, he shows that he cannot love her as she needs and deserves to be loved.

False or foolish friends and lovers presume that understanding is easy, and sometimes misinterpret silence. Between true lovers, on the other hand, there is true understanding of differences. As Mr. Darcy's proposal echoes Mr. Collins's, Mr. Knightley's proposal to Emma echoes Mr. Elton's: "God knows," he says, "I have been a very indifferent lover.—But you understand me.— Yes, you see, you understand my feelings—and will return them, if you can" (430). (Unlike Mr. Elton, he wants not only to be understood but also to be loved back; unlike Mr. Elton, he has a sense of Emma's separate reality.) He reads her silence sensitively, and he charmingly despairs of finding language adequate to his feelings ("I cannot make speeches, Emma"). The narrator gracefully suggests that she does too, telling us of Emma's acceptance speech only this:

> What did she say?—Just what she ought, of course. A lady always does.—She said enough to show there need not be despair—and to invite him to say more himself. (*E*, 431)

Sure that the reader understands certain social constraints and conventions, and is in sympathy with related literary conventions of discretion and decorum, the storyteller withholds the love scene.

By acknowledging that this understanding on the reader's part exists— by naming it, or nearly—Jane Austen creates the complicity that makes for much of our pleasure in reading her. While misleading and mystifying us, in

Emma, she manages to create the conviction that we understand the sort of people who know how hard it is to express real feeling. Restrained language throughout *Emma* has been an index to truth of feeling, as "fine flourishing" language indicates that feeling is false, or betrays it by spelling it out. That Emma and Mr. Knightley communicate clearly in very brief exchanges throughout the novel promises the final mutual understanding between them that needs no language. "Seldom, very seldom, does complete truth belong to any human disclosure; seldom can it happen that something is not a little disguised, or a little mistaken," the narrator moralizes as the two declare their love, out of earshot. We are obliged to agree, having been shown how hard it is for people to make themselves understood. In *Emma*, some people lie, while others babble; some are naturally, others unnaturally, reticent; some are inarticulate. The urge to say something clever betrays some; their natural way of talking betrays others. People play word games, write charades, pose conundrums, manipulate children's alphabets, all in vain attempts at pretending they are the masters of a language that more often masters them. Like us, reading, they are obliged to understand within constraints.

Emma is about a young woman's struggles "to understand, thoroughly understand her own heart" (412)—to comprehend, support, possess, and in effect stand under so as to support the mysterious source of her being's energy. Her success in this private quest is signaled by her marriage to Mr. Knightley. Just as a community's life depends on the conventions and arrangements that presume "a perfectly good understanding between them all" (202), even when there is not one, a young woman's heart—whether or not she understands it—is affected by those around her. Instructively, it is when Emma suspects Mr. Knightley loves Harriet that "it darted through her, with the speed of an arrow, that Mr. Knightley must marry no one but herself" (408).

The comic novel that points to and laughs at failures of understanding depends—paradoxically—on the marriage plot, which ends in a mutual understanding understood as such by society. Jane Austen assumes her reader understands this plot's conventional nature, and by making this assumption she creates an understanding with that reader. This understanding allows us, at the end, once again to take the long comic view of Emma Woodhouse, handsome, clever, and rich. In the end she acts just as she must and ought to do, that is, she acts like a novel heroine, someone whose importance depends on the romantic plot. The heroine's marriage—one of several, as usual in comedy—is presented as a conventional arrangement from the literary and the social points of view. "Very little white satin, very few lace veils; a most pitiful business!—Selina would stare when she heard of it," Mrs. Elton, the malcontent, mutters from the edge of the scene (484).

The narrator has the last word: "In spite of these deficiencies, the wishes, the hopes, the confidence, the predictions of the small band of true friends who witnessed the ceremony were fully answered in the perfect happiness of the union." As "uniting them," the emphatic final words of *Pride and Prejudice*, also do, the last words of *Emma* emphasize the social spirit of comedy. The ending transforms Emma's wedding into an abstraction—a union—among other abstractions like wishes, hopes, confidence, and happiness. Doing so, it puts Emma and her life at a distance. Closing the book, we withdraw not at all in the spiteful spirit but nevertheless in effect as Mrs. Elton withdraws, understanding Emma at the end of the novel as we were called upon to assess her in the beginning—with the Lockean, Humean intellect that was called "the understanding." Part of the pleasure of reading is in this coming full circle—and also in being left out of the wedding party, free to take a clear comic view of the little bride and groom on the cake, and what little there is of satin and veils.

Jane Austen charms us by permitting us to share with her this detached view of brides and grooms. Separated from Emma in the end, we no longer share her subjective reality, her anxiety to understand the world and herself; but we perceive her understanding with Mr. Knightley sympathetically, seeing it as a distant analogue of our understanding with the narrator. So we can enjoy feeling detached and connected at once. To be an amused spectator of marriages seems, in the end, quite as delightful and companionable as marrying is. The reader can eat her romantic cake and have it, too, and even hedge her bets on Emma's happiness ever after—rather like Mr. Perry, who is prevailed upon by Mr. Woodhouse to acknowledge "that wedding-cake might certainly disagree with many—perhaps with most people, unless taken moderately," but who nevertheless occasions the "strange rumour in Highbury of all the little Perrys being seen with a slice of . . . wedding-cake in their hands," although "Mr. Woodhouse would never believe it" (19).

"It is respect for the understanding," Mary Wollstonecraft wrote in *A Vindication of the Rights of Woman*, "that keeps alive tenderness for the person."[8] By "understanding" she meant the mind; by "person" she meant the body; she was arguing that education for women would improve the state of marriage and therefore of the world. Austen modified this Enlightenment emphasis—

the dichotomous opposition of mind and body—with a Romantic insistence that emotional knowledge and sympathy, intuitive understanding of one's own heart and other people's, was as important as intellect, indeed was bound up with it. (Over time, Wollstonecraft grew more Romantic, too.) And to that other dimension of understanding she added yet another, with an emphasis that is not so much Romantic as novelistic, on the way social and linguistic and literary conventions inform both the head and the heart.

In the course of making what Henry James called an "ado"—that is, a novel—about Emma Woodhouse's marrying, Austen meditates on the meanings of the word "understanding," and on the extent to which people can understand that word and one another. Daniel Cottom writes that "this is the point of her satire: that understanding in general . . . is neither safe, nor certain, nor real. Understanding is the agreement we imagine between ourselves and others, and all of Austen's writing dramatizes the dangers in this presumption of agreement."[9] The novelist's game with the word "understanding," like the word games the characters play among themselves and against one another, serves to reinforce and support the theme of the novel, the paradoxical separation and connection between individuals, and between intellect and emotion, and between words and meanings. The three kinds of understanding are distinct and mutually dependent on one another, braided together.

England's Emma

Jane Austen began writing *Emma* in Chawton Cottage on January 21, 1814. At thirty-eight, she was already the author of several novels, two between boards and one that had been accepted for publication the following spring. Although her name was not on the title pages of any of her books, she was known as a writer among her family and friends, and in London her proud brother Henry had begun to make her authorship more widely known. As a very young girl she had written send-ups of genteel novels that double as startling works of realism—for instance, a story about a young girl struggling to get through a boring family visit while hiding her secret love. The name of this young person who fancies herself a tragic romantic heroine—and at the end of the story retires to her room, where she "continued in tears the remainder of her Life" (*MW*, 33)—is Emma. Another early Emma is in a romantic predicament in the even shorter story "The Adventures of Mr. Harley":

her husband has forgotten that he married her. The name also figures in two more of Jane Austen's juvenile works, "Lesley Castle" and "Sir William Mountague." In her twenties, she began but didn't complete a novel, "The Watsons," which also has a heroine—pretty, lively, and poor—named Emma. Around the time her own *Emma* was published, Austen drafted a "Plan of a Novel, according to hints from various quarters," mockingly compiling what she thought her neighbors demanded of a perfect work of fiction. It concludes thus: "Throughout the whole work, Heroine to be in the most elegant Society & living in high style. The name of the work *not* to be *Emma*—but of the same sort as S&S. and P&P." (*MW*, 430).

Emma insists by its title on the heroine, implicitly putting itself on the side of romance: it is the only novel she published that is named for the heroine. No question, it will be a woman's story. For the novel's first readers, the name would have evoked other Emmas in fiction—*Emma; or, The Unfortunate Attachment* (1773), by Georgiana Spencer, the Duchess of Devonshire, or Courtney Melmoth's *Emma Corbett* (1780), or Mary Hays's *Memoirs of Emma Courtney* (1796). Barbara Benedict records an anonymous title of the period, *Female Sensibility; or, The History of Emma Pomfret*, published by Lane.[10] People who preferred their scandal plain, not clothed as romance, and especially people who were connected, as Jane Austen was, to the British navy, might have been reminded by the name of a prominent, problematic national figure, Emma, Lady Hamilton. (In fact her name, originally, was no more "Emma" than it was "Lady Hamilton"; she had started out as "Amy.") This Emma, who was notoriously an adulteress, was the heroine of the love story of the nation's hero, Lord Nelson. The name would evoke the nation more comfortably for patriotic readers who recalled "Henry and Emma," Matthew Prior's "Poem, Upon the Model of The Nut-Brown Maid," which identifies its virtuous heroine—like Austen's heroine, she is her father's "Age's Comfort"—with a traditional English ballad, therefore with England. There is a reference to this popular poem in Jane Austen's next novel, *Persuasion:* "Without emulating the feelings of an Emma toward her Henry, [Anne] would have attended on Louisa with a zeal above the common claims of regard, for [Wentworth's] sake" (*P*, 116). In Jane Austen's *Emma*, Henry—the name of the author's favorite brother—is not the name of Emma's lover but of the aged father she is obliged to attend with zeal.

In a letter to Cassandra of 1800, Jane writes of a Miss Wapshire, "I wish I could be certain that her name were Emma" (*Letters*, 65), and in letter of 1808,

"There were only 4 dances, & it went to my heart that the Miss Lances (one of them too named Emma!) should have partners only for two." She goes on, "You will not expect to hear that *I* was asked to dance—but I was," by a gentleman with pleasing black eyes who "seems so little at home in the English Language that I believe his black eyes may be the best of him" (*Letters*, 157). Does an Emma deserve to dance every dance, as a Jane does not? The earliest recorded Emma, the mother of Edward the Confessor, was a Norman princess. The century-long war in which England and France traded accusations of producing more worthless romances than the other country came to a conclusion, of sorts, when Flaubert gave the name "Emma" to his romance-reading Norman bourgeoise, Madame Bovary. To what extent is Jane Austen's *Emma* about Emma, and to what extent does Emma, does *Emma*, represent England in or around 1814? Is this novel in dialogue with contemporaneous historical novels by Lady Morgan and Walter Scott? And to what extent are the heroine and the book representative of "England's Jane"?

In 1814–1815 Jane Austen's sense of audience was well-honed. She had collected the "Opinions" that people she knew had expressed to her about *Mansfield Park*; about her next project, she is said to have announced she was "going to take a heroine whom no one but myself will much like." Her worry about the heroine—real or feigned—extended to the whole novel. She expressed the fear "that to those readers who have preferred 'Pride and Prejudice' it will appear inferior in wit, and to those who have preferred 'Mansfield Park' very inferior in good sense" (*Letters*, 306). A month earlier she had written to Cassandra that John Murray, who was about to publish *Emma*, "sends more praise . . . than I expected" (*Letters*, 291). She seems to have thought she was doing something new. In London on a visit to Henry, she learned that the Prince Regent (of whom she strongly disapproved) admired her writing, and took this with aplomb. After the Prince's librarian invited her to dedicate the book to him, and after receiving yet another flattering letter from Murray, she purred from London to her sister in the country, "In short, I am soothed & complimented into tolerable comfort" (*Letters*, 289). When the librarian, Mr. Clarke, suggested that she write a romance about the royal House of Saxe-Coburg, she comfortably replied that, "I could no more write a romance than an epic poem" (*Letters*, 312). Completed three months before the winning battle of Waterloo, near the height of her nation's confidence and her own, *Emma* was her version of a national epic.

She finished it in March 1815, a year and a month after beginning it. It was in the middle of this period—the early fall of 1814—that she wrote the letter, responding to a manuscript novel her niece Anna had sent her, in which she famously declared: "You are now collecting your People delightfully, getting them exactly into such a spot as is the delight of my life;—3 or 4 Families in a Country Village is the very thing to work on" (*Letters*, 275). It surely reflects her delight in her work in progress. *Sense and Sensibility*, *Pride and Prejudice*, *Mansfield Park*, the as-yet-unpublished *Northanger Abbey* and as-yet-unwritten *Persuasion* cover much more territory, for all their narrowness, than *Emma* does. All the action of that novel takes place in a country village—Highbury, possibly an anglicized version of "Alton" (from the Latin "altus," meaning high), the name of the larger village near Chawton. London, Bristol, Bath, Weymouth, the north of England, Ireland, and continental Europe are talked about in the novel as distant places, dangerous to get to or be in. Mr. Woodhouse is reluctant to stir from his fireside; his son-in-law John Knightley can't understand why one would want to leave home to dine with a neighbor; the heroine has never seen the sea. (Chapman points out that Dr. Johnson had not, either, until he was fifty-six, and that George III had not seen it at thirty-four.)

Toward the end of the novel sulky Frank Churchill, looking over views of remote "Swisserland" in the snugness of Donwell Abbey, says to Emma, "I am sick of England—and would leave it tomorrow" (365). The sour remark damns him as Byronic—he also promises a self-expressive effusion from abroad—before his character is revealed as thoroughly bad; the contrast between Frank the would-be wanderer and Emma's own home-loving male relations could not be more dramatic. In the England of *Emma* tourists cut off from the Continent by the Napoleonic wars (they include an "Irish car party") are pleased to explore the local beauties of Box Hill. The reader is invited to think that only a fool or knave like Frank would want to leave England: we recall that he is said to be "aimable" only in French, not amiably English, having "no English delicacy towards the feelings of other people" (149).

When Frank comes to Highbury for the first time in his life and walks past Ford's with Emma, he interrupts her question about Weymouth and Jane Fairfax and abruptly announces that he has to shop. He says, "If it be not inconvenient to you, pray let us go in, that I may prove myself to belong to the place, to be a true citizen of Highbury. I must buy something at Ford's. It will be taking out my freedom.—I dare say they sell gloves." "Oh! yes, gloves and everything," Emma responds in the same key. "I do admire your patriotism. You will be adored in Highbury. You were very popular before you came, because you were Mr. Weston's son—but lay out half-a-guinea at Ford's, and your popularity will stand upon your own virtues" (200). Emma is being arch and flirtatious in response to Frank's archness. She is also, like Austen, aware that England is changing in 1814: propriety and manly virtue, once the province of the landed and well-born, have new commercial sources and manifestations. Inside Ford's, Frank reverts to their dropped conversation: "But I beg your pardon, Miss Woodhouse, you were speaking to me, you were saying something at the very moment of this burst of my *amor patriae*. Do not let me lose it. I assure you the utmost stretch of public fame would not make me amends for the loss of any happiness in private life" (200). If on first reading you admire the easy banter that makes Frank seem meant for Emma, the second time you register his evasiveness—and his pretentious and possibly even sarcastic and unpatriotic Latin. Jane Austen is approaching the big theme of England in her own way, noting the critical intersections between national and local, old ideals and the new materialism, what people say and what their words reveal.

A sense of national identity and pride is implicit in the way John and George Knightley greet one another—"'How d'ye do, George?' and 'John, how are you?'"—repeating one another's quintessentially English names in "the true English style, burying under a calmness that seemed all but indifference, the real attachment that would have led either of them, if requisite, to do every thing for the good of the other" (*E*, 99–100). The author of *Emma* characterizes John and George by how they talk; she listens to what all the three or four families that interest her say more than she looks at their village. Nevertheless we, like Frank Churchill, seem to know, as if we have seen them before, Ford's store, The Crown, and the small home of the Bates ladies, with its narrow stairs. In relation to them we easily imagine adjacent Hartfield in its pretty shrubberies, carved out of the larger estate of Donwell Abbey; Abbey Mill Farm, spreading out productively beside the Abbey; and the more and less dangerous walks and turns toward the vicarage and Randalls. There are gypsies around, and talk of turkey thieves to come, but Highbury and its environs are cozy and pleasant, easy to locate in the tradition of pastoral, which has typically been written, since Theocritus, by city people looking back at a country paradise cleaned up by the literary imagination.

On first reading, the pastoral Highbury that Emma comfortably contemplates as she stands outside Ford's waiting for Harriet to finish shopping seems a charming, quiet refuge from the world as we know it, even from other novels. But even at our first reading we have to ask: is it Emma, or the narrator, who reflects on the village scene? By bracketing the description of Highbury village with consideration of the perception of it, does not the narrator suggest (as Milton did) that the mind is its own place, and that it half-creates (as Wordsworth put it) the place it finds itself in? Is the narrator suggesting that Emma the Imaginist, whose too lively mind runs to spinning romantic stories, is or should be satisfied with contemplating the diurnal, unexciting, and real life of the village? What is the relation between this narrative that goes nowhere and its premodern setting?

The language of *Emma* calls attention to itself from the first page, which repeats the title. I pass over the dedication, "To His Royal Highness The Prince Regent," where the phrase "His Royal Highness" is written out three times: John Murray's fulsomeness can figure only lightly in my argument that by repeating sounds, words, phrases, and scenes, Austen insists that her novel is a fabrication of words, a literary work like a poetic epic, something more than a mere story or indeed a mere didactic tract. (But surely she must have been amused by the multiple "Royal Highnesses" in the dedication. And could she possibly have added, to balance the compliment to the nation's putative ruler, Mrs. Elton's peculiar promise to Jane Fairfax, toward the end of the novel, to be "as silent as a minister of state"?) In *Emma* the repetitions range from the staggeringly obvious to the very subtle. An example of the former comes toward the end of volume III, when the heroine sits with her father and is "reminded . . . of their first forlorn tête-à-tête, on the evening of Mrs. Weston's wedding day" (*E*, 422). Usually, a nice parallel reminding you that the linguistic whole has been deliberately fabricated is discovered only on rereading.

Repeating words and sounds, contrasting what seems and what is, what exists and what is perceived, the novel from the beginning calls attention to its language, characterizing it as indexical and referential and not at all transparent. By doing that, it stakes a claim for both the pleasures of language and the seriousness of this work of literary art. It is by stressing its heroine's significant imagination, by its play with point of view and all its authorial and linguistic self-consciousness, as well as by the subtlety of its moral and aesthetic distinctions, that *Emma* stakes its claim to difference from the ordinary run of novels. Like the poems of Jane Austen's contemporaries Wordsworth and Byron, it is concerned with the perceiving and creating imagination, with what the mind makes of persons and things.

The heroine's romantic name is immediately modified in the novel's first sentence by her downright, domestic-sounding English surname: the focus on the homebody-heroine is emphatic, comfortable (the word is right there for us to borrow). This novel is about a heroine who is decidedly not a picture of perfection, a book in which the word "perfection" is repeated so often as to become a crux. Mr. Weston poses the flattering conundrum at Box Hill, "What two letters of the alphabet are there, that express perfection?" (he means *M* and *A*), to which Mr. Knightley gravely rejoins, "*Perfection* should not have come quite so soon" (371). Emma's relation to some kind of picture is dramatized early on when Emma is called "the picture of health" by Mrs. Weston: Emma herself makes a portrait of Harriet, whom she hopes to make a heroine by making a match for her. (But Mr. Elton values it for the sake of the artist, not the sitter.) The gap between "real" people in life and in novels and the mere pictures of perfection that Jane Austen thought other people admired too much is in effect the subject of all her novels—pointing toward another, larger subject, the inevitable gap between any kind of novel and the world it seems to represent.

The first sentence of her story says, more or less, that Emma has everything going for her—as a heroine should. (Henry James echoes it in a review of a novel by Trollope, writing that the protagonist "is not handsome, nor clever, nor rich, nor romantic, nor distinguished in any way."[11]) That a man, not a woman, is typically described by the first adjective Austen applies to Emma has been remarked by those who are critical of her unusual confidence and independence of mind. Like her wealth, Emma's "comfortable home" puts her in a good position—no reason for her not to be happy and stay there, as she is disposed to do, enjoying some of the "best blessings of existence." That Emma only "*seemed* to unite *some of* the best blessings of existence" is not lost on the first-time reader; but the meaning of "in the world" is more problematic. What world is at issue, here? The reference in the title of Frances Burney's *Evelina; or, The History of a Young Lady's Entrance Into the World* (1778) is to a social world that thirty-eight-year-old Jane Austen might be said to have lived in for nearly twenty-one years. That worldly world may be evoked by the phrase—which also might refer to this world rather than the next. For the religious register (suggested by the phrases "the best blessings," and "the real evils") puts us in a serious place as it insists that place itself is serious. The point is reaffirmed by the repetition of "house" ("Woodhouse," "his house"), and the interesting word "situation," which will gain resonance later on in the story of job-hunting Jane Fairfax. Rootedness, house and home, are crucial here: *Emma* is about much more than Emma.

Beginning a chapter, the narrator introduces Mrs. Elton: "Human nature is so well disposed towards those who are in interesting situations, that a young person, who either marries or dies, is sure of being kindly spoken of" (181). The best way to appreciate that sentence—the way it steps back from the action to philosophize, temporizes with the phrase "interesting situations," pivots on the "young person" (pointedly not gendered), tendentiously parallels "marries or dies," blows up the parallel with the illogical "is sure of," and comes to social earth with the syntactically different but similar-looking "spoken of," ending triumphantly with a preposition—is to compare it with imitations. Here is Emma Tennant, also beginning a chapter, in her fan-fiction sequel, *Emma in Love* (1996): "Human nature is so well inclined to the receiving of compliments, that any amount of annoyance or interference will go unchecked, in order for the succession of pleasant remarks to continue."[12] The epigram is less sharp: the subject lacks weight. Similarly, Angela Thirkell, writing as an Austen wannabe, echoes *Emma* inadequately, in *The Brandons* (1939): "But human nature cannot be content on a diet of honey and if there is nothing in one's life that requires pity, one must invent it; for to go through life unpitied would be an unthinkable loss."[13] The most substantive difference might be the difference in weight between what people say to and about one another—Jane Austen's parallelism is bolder, her target more significant. There is also a difference in the music of the sentence, and the preciseness.

"A young person, who either marries or dies": English novels of the kind entitled *Emma*—or *Evelina*, or *Ethelinde*—are usually about young *women* who *marry*. (Cf. Byron: "All tragedies are finished by a death / All comedies are ended by a marriage.") The heroine's plot is in *Emma*'s case literally and outrageously that: here, as well as being possessed by the plot, the heroine hatches it, more than once. (Marilyn Butler observes that "the masterstroke" of *Emma* is "to make the apparent spring of the action not Emma's quest for a husband, but Harriet's."[14]) Of all the Austen heroines she is the only one to own, or nearly, a plot of land. Mistress of her father's house, Emma is free of the marriage market: unlike Elinor and Marianne, Elizabeth and Fanny,

Catherine and Anne, she does not have to sell herself to a man in order to get a home of her own. Being rich, she is not a commodity. Far from seeking to exchange her, her father wants nothing to change; the only lover who seeks to marry her for her money is easily shaken off early on. With her thirty thousand pounds and her nieces, her music and her crayons and her reading lists, she has, as she informs Harriet, "none of the usual inducements to marry." She goes on, enumerating them:

> "Fortune I do not want; employment I do not want; consequence I do not want; I believe few married women are half as much mistress of their husband's house, as I am of Hartfield; and never, never could I expect to be so truly beloved and important; so always first and always right in any man's eyes as I am in my father's." (E, 84)

But the marriage plot or the love story, which had pushed young women into narratives long before novels like Austen's were written, requires a mate for Emma. He is a member of one of the three or four families in her country village, more precisely a member of Emma's own family, her sister Isabella's brother, as they said then, and her own "brother" John Knightley's brother. It is hard to say whether the plot of *Emma* or *Mansfield Park* most cleverly foils the marriage plot by ingeniously eluding the obligation to exogamy.

> "Whom are you going to dance with?" asked Mr. Knightley.
> She hesitated a moment, and then replied, "With you, if you will ask me."
> "Will you?" said he, offering his hand.
> "Indeed I will. You have shown that you can dance, and you know we are not really so much brother and sister as to make it at all improper."
> "Brother and sister! no, indeed." (E, 331)

But yes indeed, as well. Marrying Mr. Knightley, Emma proudly reaffirms family connections already made, joins estates that are contiguous. She goes nowhere, stays the same, resists change. At the end she is as she was at the beginning, mistress of her father's house and still residing in it, having solved the problem of being both wife and maiden that baffled Frank Churchill's long-dead mother, who "wanted at once to be the wife of Captain Weston, and Miss Churchill of Enscombe" (16).

What happens to Emma, in *Emma*? In a sense, in the end, total victory is hers, as it is Elizabeth Bennet's. But the transformation is not so great. Her heirs, presumably, will inherit Donwell, while little Henry, her older sister's son, will have only Hartfield. But the general critical consensus, at least since Mark Schorer's famous mid-twentieth-century essay about "The Humiliation of Emma Woodhouse," is that Emma gets all that in the process of a plot in which she is taken down a peg.[15] Some argue that she comes to know herself by knowing she loves Mr. Knightley, rather in the manner of Elizabeth Bennet; some have even claimed that Emma is sexually awakened when "it darted through her with the force of an arrow that Mr. Knightley must marry no one but herself" (408). Others think she wants him only because she thinks he wants Harriet, whose "soft eyes" awaken her own most tender (homo)erotic impulses. Of course Emma only imagines Mr. Knightley's interest in Harriet—and on rereading one discovers Emma prefiguring all this early on, when, defending Harriet against Mr. Knightley's criticism, she says, "Were you, yourself, ever to marry, she is the very woman for you" (64). It is another piece of evidence of the obvious, that this novel, like Emma, stays where it begins.

It is interesting to compare Emma on this score with Elizabeth. When Emma looks at and reflects on the much less romantically named Donwell Abbey, in the same shopping frame of mind in which Elizabeth considers Pemberley, she is charmed less by its beautiful blend of nature and art than by its stability, being already, after all, well connected with the place:

> She felt all the honest pride and complacency which her alliance with the present and future proprietor could fairly warrant, as she viewed the respectable size and style of the building, its suitable, becoming, characteristic situation, low and sheltered—its ample gardens stretching down to meadows washed by a stream, of which the Abbey, with all the old neglect of prospect, had scarcely a sight—and its abundance of timber in rows and avenues, which neither fashion nor extravagance had rooted up. . . . It was just what it ought to be, and it looked what it was—and Emma felt an increasing respect for it, as the residence of a family of such true gentility, untainted in blood and understanding.— Some faults of temper John Knightley had; but Isabella had connected herself unexceptionably. She had given them neither men, nor names, nor places, that could raise a blush. These were pleasant feelings, and she walked about and indulged them.   (*E*, 358)

She walks over the gardens with some of the others, and they are drawn to a "broad short avenue of limes" that "led to nothing; nothing but a view at the end over a low stone wall with high pillars, which seemed intended, in their erection, to give the appearance of an approach to the house, which never had been there." The flaw, if it is one, is of a false entry, an entryway to a nonexistent approach. It is quickly smoothed away: "Disputable, however, as might be the taste of such a termination, it was in itself a charming walk, and the view which closed it extremely pretty." The prettiness is national in character, and an anthem ensues. "It was a sweet view—sweet to the eye and the mind. English verdure, English culture, English comfort, seen under a sun bright, without being oppressive" (360).

As in the Highbury village scene the focus is on Emma looking: here, Emma is taking in a synecdoche of England itself. Her relation to the land's proprietor—a man "untainted in blood and understanding"—confirms her possession of what she sees; her marriage will soon reaffirm it. The emphatic reiteration—"English verdure, English culture, English comfort"—persuasively insists, effectively praises, says, What could be better than England? But what on earth are we to make of that appearance of an approach which never had been there? It would seem that that, at least, had not been done well. That she notices the flaw and forgives it indicates Emma's continuing keenness and new generosity, perhaps, but the thing itself is baffling. The representation of the real estate is *done well*: the false entry is a reminder that it is not only, and certainly not most importantly, actual and material.

Is the point of *Emma* that although commerce reigns in modern Highbury, and buying seems to some to be the finest expression of patriotism, a superior old-fashioned agrarian England, when men were knights, belongs to a woman of mind and taste and imagination? That a woman like a novelist, like this novelist, owns England as much as the men who own the land do? Praising the land and the country village, casting aspersions on vulgar Bristol—Mrs. Elton's mercantile home town, where the slave ships docked—Jane Austen, they say, affirmed a virtuous, moral England, an ideal England of long ago at the moment it was changing for the worse.

But by its ambiguously ironic emphatic repetitions, *Emma* simultaneously celebrates and distances itself from the historical England of 1814, and from historical epics as well. The approach that never was there represents a place that never was there, except in the imagination: what *Emma* affirms is the imagination. Emphasizing Austen's irony and ambiguity, some critics have been led down the garden path, like Emma at Donwell, to consider the novelist's own putative ambivalence, her "regulated hatred" of the society she lived in. But interesting as it is, the subject of biography—the real life of the writer—is only one of several sources of the voice that charms us. Jane Austen was first of all a maker of works of art. To Cassandra she wrote, memorably, "I often wonder how *you* can find time for what you do, in addition to the care of the House; And how good Mrs West cd have written such Books & collected so many hard words, with all her family cares, is still more a matter of astonishment! Composition seems to me Impossible, with a head full of Joints of Mutton & doses of rhubarb" (*Letters*, 321). Cassandra did more of the housework; neither one of the sisters undertook marriage, a separate household, and all the attendant, dangerous "family cares" of a married woman like "good Mrs. West." "Composition" is what engaged Jane Austen: her *Emma* puts in precise and suggestive delicate balance the warring forces that enable a singular heroine, and a singular nation, simultaneously to change and stay the same.

Information

> For a man can employ his thoughts about nothing, but either the contemplation of things themselves for the discovery of truth; or about the things in his own power, which are his own actions, for the attainment of his own ends; or the signs the mind makes use of both in the one and the other, and the right ordering of them for its clearer information.
>
> —John Locke, *An Essay on Understanding*

> Mr Parker's Character & History were soon unfolded. All that he understood of himself, he readily told, for he was very openhearted;—& where he might be himself in the dark, his conversation was still giving information, to such of the Heywoods as could observe.
>
> —Jane Austen, *Sanditon (MW, 371)*

There is a scene in Douglas McGrath's film, *Emma* (1996), just as there is in Jane Austen's novel of the same name, where the heroine asks Jane Fairfax for the lowdown about Frank Churchill. She has never met Frank but she's heard a lot about him, and she knows Jane has met him at a seaside resort. Emma is as nosy as a novelist about private lives; in addition, the reader knows, she may have a secret reason for seeking "real information" (169) about Frank.

His father has recently—at her instigation, she imagines—romantically married her beloved former governess, connecting Frank's family, as Emma sees it, to her own. A further connection—Emma likes multiple connections—might just be possible: without ever having seen rich and eligible Frank, Emma has her eye on him.

In both the novel and the film, Jane barely responds to Emma's inquiry. As neither Emma nor the first-time reader (or viewer of the film) yet knows, she is secretly engaged to Frank. Emma thinks Jane is repellently reserved and the reader is persuaded to side with her: later, Emma will complain to Frank, in retrospect most inappropriately, that Jane is "so very unwilling to give the least information about any body" (200).

In the text the dialogue of the young women talking about Frank is presented from Emma's point of view, as if she is recollecting it. It unrolls in a single paragraph placed, as if for emphasis, at the end of a chapter; Emma's questions are written as direct speech, in quotation marks, and the first of Jane's answers in indirect speech, but also, confusingly, in quotation marks. This small significant asymmetry makes it even harder not to be on Emma's side, and as if inside her head:

> "Was he handsome?"—"She believed he was reckoned a very fine young man." "Was he agreeable?"—"He was generally thought so." "Did he appear a sensible young man; a young man of information?"—"At a watering-place, or in a common London acquaintance, it was difficult to decide on such points. Manners were all that could be safely judged of, under a much longer knowledge than they had yet had of Mr. Churchill. She believed every body found his manners pleasing." Emma could not forgive her.   (*E*, 169)

The next chapter begins by repeating that last line for emphasis: "Emma could not forgive her." By repeating the sentence in the narrator's voice, Austen suggests how irritating and annoying Jane Fairfax is to Emma, not only because she is not playing ball conversationally, but also because she is pulling moral rank by being discreet. She is also showing off her knowledge of the world to Emma, who has never been anywhere, while making a great point of distinguishing between manners, which everyone can see, and more intimate personal qualities accessible only to the perspicacious.

In the film the dialogue is presented directly, dramatically. At the point when Emma asks whether Frank is a "man of information"—to us the phrase seems as old-fashioned, pretty, and formal as the clothes the actresses are wearing—the Jane of the film replies, "All his statements seemed correct." The response is as evasive as what Emma remembers Jane saying in the novel, but here it depends on a mistranslation. The meaning of the old-fashioned phrase "a man of information" is clear enough to the moviegoer, who heard it before when Emma asked Harriet whether Robert Martin was such a man. But in this different scene the camera's close focus on the young women's faces brings the language into focus as well. The context in both scenes makes the meaning obvious: Emma is asking whether Frank (and before that, Robert) is a man worth a woman's talking to, a man with anything to say to a girl, a man one could imagine marrying. Conceivably, when she says, "All his statements seemed correct," Jane of the film might mean that Frank was correct or appropriate in his language, and therefore marriageable; but it is much more likely she means that what he said seemed accurate.[16] To an information-age Jane Fairfax, a "man of information" is a man who has his facts straight. This mistaken understanding of the phrase is a sign of the dangers of borrowing dialogue for a film from an old book that was written in what is after all a changing language. The word "information" in *Emma* sometimes does mean what it means today: data of public importance and general significance. But such "real information" as Emma looks for about Frank Churchill—facts about his family and history—is not quite the same as that. Nor is the "information" Emma wants to know if Frank is "a man of." Jane Austen's novel probes by repeating the phrase "a man of information," criticizing it perhaps as what she might call a "common phrase," or cliché (e.g., "Miss Frances married, in the common phrase, to disoblige her family" [*MP*, 2]). Her repetitions of it suggest the commonness of the word, and begin to suggest that the meanings of "information," still vexed, were changing at the time she wrote.

To the ears of a moviegoer of the late twentieth century or later, the phrase "a man of information" seems a genteel circumlocution, characteristic perhaps of the manipulative Emma. Trying to persuade poor Harriet Smith that the farmer Robert Martin isn't good enough for her, Emma says, tendentiously, "Mr. Martin, I suppose, is not a man of information beyond the line of his own business. He does not read?" Harriet struggles to defend her suitor: "Oh, yes!—that is, no—I do not know—but I believe he has read a good deal—but not what you would think any thing of. He reads the Agricultural Reports and some other books . . . —but he reads all *them* to himself. But sometimes of an evening, before we went to cards, he would read something aloud out of the Elegant Extracts—very entertaining. And I know he has read the Vicar of Wakefield." Harriet has a flustered sense that there is something wanting in Robert Martin, that is, something that Emma would want. She goes on: "He never read the Romance of the Forest, nor the Children of the Abbey. He had never heard of such books before I mentioned them, but he is determined to get them now as soon as ever he can" (29). Satisfied by Harriet's confusion, Emma can shift the focus to Mr. Martin's looks—as important as his information in reckoning a man's appropriateness for a discriminating young lady, which Emma is teaching Harriet to be.

Confusion is Harriet's element—as Mr. Knightley puts it, she is "not a sensible girl, or a girl of any information" (61)—but her confusion is worth pausing over here. Emma's questions define a man of information as a reading man, but even Harriet knows there are different kinds of books and different ways of reading. There are books intended to instruct and to delight, and useful Agricultural Reports, as well as books for leisure and ladies like Vicesimus Knox's popular "Elegant Extracts," and Goldsmith's popular moralizing novel. Under Emma's tutelage Harriet has become aware of a third kind of books—popular novels like Ann Radcliffe's *The Romance of the Forest* and Regina Maria Roche's *The Children of the Abbey*—and therefore perhaps of another way of reading. Harriet seems to be aware that if Robert Martin deserved to be called a man of information he would read fashionable gothic novels for himself, for pleasure. In the film Harriet's mention of a title, *The Romance of the Forest*, gives the audience a rough idea of what scholars have been documenting: in the eighteenth century, a romantic novel by a woman promised to feminize and polish a Robert Martin. Neatly evocative of a still-familiar genre, the title of the Radcliffe novel is the pretext for a bit of business in the film that's not in Austen's *Emma*: Martin, cast here as a comic dolt, first admits, under the trees, that he can't remember its name, and later boasts that he's managed to get the book.

The little anecdote reflects historical truths that educated moviegoers were aware of by the mid-1990s. Scholars for some thirty years had been working to show that in England in the second half of the eighteenth century, there was an enormous growth in printing presses, literacy, and the publication of new secular books, especially novels by women. The value of reading popular new books was debated then as now, with Dr. Johnson, for one, defending it as a social and socializing practice. "We must read what the world reads at the moment," he allegedly declared. "It has been maintained that this super-foetation, this teeming of the press in modern times, is prejudicial to good literature, because it obliges us to read so much of what is of inferiour value, in order to be in fashion, so that better works are neglected for want of time, because a man will have more gratification of his vanity in conversation, from having read modern books, than from having read works of antiquity. But it must be considered, that we have now more knowledge generally diffused; all our ladies read now, which is a great extension."[17]

In *Northanger Abbey*, which satirizes literary fashion, mocking not only novels but other profitable publications "with which the press now groans," Catherine and Isabella Thorpe "shut themselves up to read" novels together (*NA*, 37). (As a girl Catherine preferred "running about the country" to "books—or at least books of information—for, provided that nothing like useful knowledge could be gained from them, provided they were all story and no reflection, she had never any objection to books at all" [15].) Isabella's boorish brother John denies any knowledge of any novels except two famously risqué ones, *The Monk* and *The History of Tom Jones*. (In the most recent television rendering of *Northanger Abbey* [2007], Catherine herself reads *The Monk*—a symptom of the tireless sexing up of Jane Austen.) But Henry Tilney, who also knows something about fabrics, professes wild enthusiasm for a woman's novel like *The Mysteries of Udolpho* (by the author of *The Romance of the Forest*), which he claims to have read with his "hair standing on end" (106) the whole time. Henry says he sometimes reads novels together with his sister, who—more sophisticated than poor Catherine—misunderstands her when she refers to news of the latest horrible thing "just out" in London, thinking she means a riot (like the Gordon Riots) and not a new novel (112).

The author of *Northanger Abbey* sends up but also defends novels by and about women as works "in which the greatest powers of the mind are displayed," etc. (37). But what is the effect on the mind—and the body—of reading them? Writers since Montaigne have debated the physical effects of reading both stories and what Jane Austen might have called works of reflection. Arthur Young, writing in the 1770s, complained that in "an age schooled by *Sir Charles Grandison*," readers were unwilling to give up "the pleasure of being amused for the use of being instructed," in order "to receive real information."[18] But how might novels contribute to making a man a man of information?

A proper answer to the question would require the analysis of ideas that were current in Austen's time about what there was to know and the ways of learning it, and about theories that the self and society could be improved by reading. One might begin with the Protestant practice of reading the Bible and other religious literature for "the information of the soul," or spiritual value. But civic value was also an objective of those who argued for the extension of literacy. Charles Hoole, in 1660, wrote that reading should be taught even to "such children as are intended for Trades, or to be kept as drudges at home, or employed about husbandry; their acquaintance with good books will (by Gods blessing) be a means to sweeten their (otherwise sowr) natures, that they may live comfortably toward themselves and amiably converse with other persons."[19] Good books, presumably, taught adherence to the Good Book. Jane Austen's first readers would have been familiar with the intersecting and sometimes contradictory arguments about the spiritual and social, intellectual and civic uses and perils of various texts, the development in tandem of national literacy, a national literature, and the nation itself, and with it the idea of the informed citizen whose reading equipped him to function in the public sphere.[20] The history of reading practices in the long eighteenth century is outside my scope here: my subject is Jane Austen's uses of the word "information" as an index to her thoughts about reading and personal development, and to some salient differences between her time and our own.

In the first decades of the nineteenth century the word retained the sense of its root, *formation*, naming an inner process like education—sometimes close to the (equally problematic) German *Bildung*. The meaning is retained still in the phrase "for your information." It was once much more alive: the protagonist of *Gulliver's Travels* (1727) makes an instructive distinction between facts and the mental process of receiving them when he repeats his Master Houyhnhmn's argument "that the use of speech was to make us understand one another, and to receive information of facts." (One may still, similarly, *receive* as well as *have* intelligence.) Unfamiliar with lying and false representation, Gulliver's Master quickly understands the evils of mis-information and disinformation, too: he explains, "now if any one *said the Thing which is not*, these Ends were defeated; because I cannot properly be said to understand him; and I am so far from receiving Information, that he leaves me worse than in Ignorance."[21] Elizabeth Bennet uses the word this way when she asks Darcy, toward the end, about what he told Bingley about Jane's feelings for him: "Did you speak from your own observation . . . when you told him that my sister loved him, or merely from my information last spring?" (*PP*, 371). The word "information" as Swift and Austen used it in this sense signified something between data or news and the imparting and receiving of it. Austen therefore often uses the word, as we no longer do, apropos of data of a local, trivial, or private kind, as when Fanny Price looks forward to "direct and minute information of the father and mother, brothers and sisters, of whom she very seldom heard" (*MP*, 234). For us "information" tends to be data of greater general interest and consequence—although it also includes gossip about a man's family, character, and reputation. (These days, "real information" about "what he truly was"—data scrounged up and presented as "hard facts"—can ruin a person in the public eye more thoroughly than it could ever have ruined a Frank Churchill). Jane Austen points out that we would do well to take note that information's truth is jeopardized as it is passed on. Anne Elliot gently corrects her friend for believing gossip that came to her thirdhand: "Indeed, Mrs. Smith, we must not expect to get real information in such a line. Facts or opinions which are to pass through the hands of so many, to be misconceived by folly in one, and ignorance in another, can hardly have much truth left" (*P*, 205). Like all language, information is colored and shaped by the minds that receive and contain it, and pass it on.

Over time, the meaning of the word "information" has moved—as if to parody by inverting a common rhetorical figure—from the container to what it contains, or from the effect to its cause, like "horror" in the phrase "horror film." On the edge of change, Jane Austen points to the dangers of this. Because as one person informs another facts slide into opinions, public opinion of individuals and types—what we, today, call "information"—cannot as Austen sees it be relied on. Reading through her works, one senses a shift in her attitude toward the newspapers from her first published novel, in which rude Mr. Palmer puts up the newspaper to avoid the people he's with, to *Sanditon*, left unfinished when she died, where Mr. Parker believes what he misreads in the papers. But it is more complex than that. At Mansfield Park, the young people lounge about idly reading Quarterly Reviews; Tom Bertram picks up news about both the horses he bets on and the war from the newspaper; in Portsmouth, gross Mr. Price inflames himself by reading the gossip in the papers about adultery in high life. It would seem that the new popular publications attract only the worst people—but Edmund Bertram studies the papers too, and the exemplary Mr. Knightley also reads newspapers. Jane Austen wickedly tempts the reader to simplify.

It's clear she thinks that public opinion cannot be relied on. In *Mansfield Park*, Edmund answers Mary Crawford's put-down of the clergy by saying that her knowledge of them, gathered from talk at her uncle's table, is unreliable, and Mary defends herself: "I speak what appears to me the general opinion; and where an opinion is general, it is usually correct. Though *I* have not seen much of the domestic lives of clergymen, it is seen by too many to leave any deficiency of information." (Mary's uncle is an admiral who has lived an irregular life, bringing his mistress into his home.) To which Edmund says: "Where any one body of educated men, of whatever denomination, are condemned indiscriminately, there must be a deficiency of information, or (smiling) of something else" (110–111). The repetition, the smile, and the insinuating "something else" suggest the word had something like a double meaning: Edmund's hint that prejudice or a want of respect, rather than a deficiency of information, is involved points toward an older meaning of "information," the process of moral development or education, the "information of the soul," that creates what *Emma* calls "right-minded and well-informed people" (*E*, 164).

Distinctions between a mind and its contents, a man and what he says, are hard to make. When Mrs. Bennet is dispatched as "a woman of mean understanding, little information, and uncertain temper," the sequence suggests *information* is a quality of mind between intellectual capacity and receptiveness. It's not that Mrs. Bennet doesn't know what's going on, simply that (like Lady Denham in *Sanditon*, where the point is made directly) she is uneducated. Knowledge, training, experience, reflection, all expand the capacity of the mind. When Elizabeth Bennet finds herself bored by Sir William Lucas, it is because she already knows what he has to say: "He could tell her nothing new of the wonders of his presentation and knighthood, and his civilities were worn out like his information" (*PP*, 152). Civilities and information are what pass between people in casual polite conversation: *information* here refers to Sir William's informing Elizabeth.

In Jane Austen's time the phrase "a man of information" retained the idea of "formation," as in "the information of the soul." As the information of the soul is increasingly understood to occur in the process of reading—of the Protestant Bible, of the press by an informed citizenry, and of moral fiction—the two senses of the word begin to merge. First the process of reading, then whatever gets read, gets confounded with the improvement of the self and the community. By metonymy, the power to inform gets shifted to what does the informing. By the time Douglas McGrath harks back to the phrase, "a man of information" would appear to be a man well stuffed with hard facts, or data.

And what about a woman of information? The small-minded gossip Mrs. Bennet, who accepts as truth what is universally acknowledged, can be read as a satirical inversion or domestic counterpart of the man of information, that enlightened, cultivated, knowledgeable gentleman citizen who is Emma's and her culture's ideal. Mrs. Bennet is proud of being in the know about what's going on: "there is quite as much of *that* going on in the country as in town." Anne Elliot reads Italian and the navy list, but there is no "woman of information" named as such in any of Austen's works: Lady Catherine, who is ready to inform whoever will listen about what the weather will bring and the best way to arrange shelves, is not such a woman any more than Mrs. Bennet is. "Where people wish to attach, they should always be ignorant," the narrator of *Northanger Abbey* intones with heavy irony. "To come with a well-informed mind, is to come with an inability of administering to the vanity of others, which a sensible person would always wish to avoid. A woman especially, if she have the misfortune of knowing any thing, should conceal it as well as she can" (110–111). A man of information is tactful and sensitive to others, too. The private or domestic sphere is, as Ann Bermingham notes, dialogically and dialectically connected with the public sphere.[22] Austen's novels are about the education or information of young ladies, young women: with their characteristic obliquity and indirection, they suggest what the well-formed man must be.

When Fanny Price arrives as a child of ten at Mansfield Park, her girl cousins call her stupid because she lacks the "real information" they can boast of having—hard facts about "the principal rivers in Russia," "the chronological order of the kings of England," and "a great deal of the Heathen Mythology, and all the Metals, Semi-Metals, Planets, and distinguished philosophers" (18–19). The standard education of girls—disparaged, by the way, in the description of Mrs. Goddard's school in *Emma*—is scornfully detailed here. Fanny's cousin Edmund educates her by encouraging her natural "fondness for reading," which his sisters seem to lack. He makes "reading useful by talking to her of what she read, and heighten[ing] its attraction by judicious praise" (22). Julia and Maria, whose heads are stuffed in the course of their expensive "early information," or education, are spoiled rotten, have no morals, and fail at life, but Fanny the reader succeeds, winning not only Edmund's love but a student of her own, her sister Susan. Unlike Fanny, Susan is not interested in "information for information's sake" (418), that is, disinterested reading. But although "the early habit of reading was wanting" in Susan, she proves to be teachable. With her to guide, Fanny joins a circulating library. "She became a subscriber—amazed at being any thing *in propria persona*, amazed at her own doings in every way; to be a renter, a chuser of books! And to be having any one's improvement in view of her choice! But so it was. Susan had read nothing, and Fanny longed to give her a share in her own first pleasures, and inspire a taste for the biography and poetry which she delighted in herself" (398). Jane Austen's learned Latin wryly makes an educated masculine kind of fuss about Fanny's excitement; meanwhile the girlish exclamation points make another kind.

Back in the unheated East Room at Mansfield Park, Fanny's reading had included Crabbe's poems, and Dr. Johnson's The Idler, and Lord Macartney's "big book" about China. Both Fordyce and Mrs. Chapone, in their conduct books, warned against novels: they recommended that young ladies read accounts of distant lands so as to gain a sense of the wider world and of the superiority of England. (Prints of scenes in India and Barbados were wildly popular; Byron's travel poem, *Childe Harold's Pilgrimage*, was published two years before *Mansfield Park*.) Jane Austen herself read—in addition to poems and novels—sermons and Shakespeare and big books full of information—accounts of visits to China, the Hebrides, Iceland, India, Italy, and Spain. In a letter she reports on having found "Captain Pasley's *Essay on the Military Policy and Institutions of the British Empire*" (1810) "highly entertaining" (*Letters*, 198–199). But surely it goes without saying that most of what Fanny and Susan chose and borrowed and discussed were novels, the staples of the circulating library. (According to Anne Mellor, three quarters of the books in such libraries were novels.[23]) Is the fact that novels are not mentioned along with biography and poetry as the reading of the Price sisters the narrator's little joke?

The vexed exchange, in the movie, between Emma and Jane about Frank might be read as a joke also, whether or not it was intended as one. In the film as in the novel, Jane Fairfax cannot be frank about Frank, and Frank himself cannot be frank, because the lovers share a secret engagement. Secretive, attractive Jane is Emma's rival for the reader's attention as well as the attention of the inhabitants of Highbury: like Emma we want information about her love life. But the novel does not give it to us; *Emma* refuses to oblige. The narrator, who fastidiously averts her eyes even from the chaste scene in which Emma accepts Mr. Knightley, absolutely refuses to consider telling Jane's secret—the story of how and why she yielded to Frank, for money and also for love, in the first instance and the last. Although it teases us with lurid hints about Jane's adultery with Mr. Dixon, the novel doesn't begin to admit to concealing that truth. A lady, after all, doesn't tell what goes on in the bedroom, or in the sexual imagination or consciousness—which is where the untold story of Jane and Frank took place. A lady who is a novelist, like a young woman who wishes to attach, must conceal as well as she can any knowledge she has of such matters. Indeed any well-bred novelist had to, in Austen's time: Walter Scott, in *The Bride of Lammermoor*, is full of information about Scottish customs, but averts his eyes from the personal part of Ravenswood's letter to Lucy Ashton, "which, however interesting to the lovers themselves, would afford the reader neither interest nor information."[24] We never find out how a virtuous, respectable, admirable girl like Jane was seduced into a secret engagement to a rich but unreliable, not quite respectable or moral young man, and how it came about that an ambitious man like Frank ventured to risk everything for love of her. The narrator of *Emma* gets nowhere near this young virgin's sexual awareness, or sexual life, or for that matter her hankerings after Enscombe. She cannot do so because Jane Fairfax, a minor character, is a good and moral young lady, in this story, as *Emma* is a good and moral novel.

"Mystery; Finesse—how they pervert the understanding!" Mr. Knightley exclaims toward the novel's end. "My Emma, does not every thing serve to prove more and more the beauty of truth and sincerity in all our dealings with each other?" (446). But in fact what the novel serves to prove is that the mystery of human relations is endlessly charming. *Emma* stops short of making everything clear. To the extent that the heroine's own love story is compelling it is because she keeps little secrets from Mr. Knightley and from herself—

and because she's so keen on finding out about Jane, whom she suspects of sexual adventuring. The reader reads also to find out more about Jane—i.e., for information the novel refuses to give (but seductively points to). Jane Fairfax's bland reply in Douglas McGrath's film that all Frank's statements seemed accurate, from which we tend to understand she thinks "information" is a matter of facts, is best understood, I think, as a little joke about the limits of language—and of Jane Austen's novel. Emma's view—it is articulated by Harriet!—that a man of information is a man who's been improved into a gentleman by the process of reading women's novels about love is comical. The novel in what would become the great tradition deliberately evades information about the sexual life at the core of its plot, a plot that's compelling and powerful to the degree that that information is withheld. (Similarly, a coy "literary" film like McGrath's must be elaborately and egregiously chaste.) In Jane Austen's time as in ours, a story called, say, *Emma*, implicitly made a promise to be about relations between men and women. As the woman-centered novel "rose" from the hands of the likes of Eliza Haywood into bourgeois respectability and importance—as a Robert Martin's upwardly mobile girlfriend began to browbeat him to improve himself by reading gothic novels—it became increasingly elliptical about its unspeakable subject matter.

The change in the meaning of the word "information" from "a mental process" to "important stuff out there" is parallel to another, more recent change that privileges "information for information's sake" and encourages misplaced credulousness about the sources and the value of data. Jane Austen's careful deployment of the word, as well as the quality of her attention to it, suggests that we ourselves might do well to think a little more about it. Developing the idea current in her time that "a man of information," or an educated man, reads novels, Austen begins to suggest that novels are a source of intellectual enrichment precisely because they are non-instrumental, not useful like the Agricultural Reports or even novels like Lady Morgan's, and Maria Edgeworth's, and Walter Scott's, which were chockablock with anthropological details about different kinds of places and people. Even all these years after Melville on whaling and Philip Roth on the manufacture of gloves, "classic" novels about relationships, most of them chaste, still are looked at as sources of truths you cannot find in books of information.[25] Some readers of some kinds of books look there for explicit descriptions of what goes on in boardrooms and bedrooms—and kitchens, too—but most look for something more inchoate, maybe themselves. Leah Price has noted that "in late-twentieth-century America . . . the intellectual superiority of novel-readers over non-novel-readers appears to be more uncritically accepted than in any other time or place."[26] As the well-chosen adverb implies, this might or might not be a good sign.

FIGURE 17. Jeff Bezos—founder and CEO of Amazon.com—holding a Kindle. Photograph courtesy of Thomson Reuters.

Afterwords

Colorado Springs, 1999

When the cabdriver I flagged at the airport turned out to be a thirty-something blonde in an army cap who guessed in a cultivated voice that I had come to Colorado for the literary society meeting, I already felt I'd landed in a dust-and-mold-free version of Cranford. And the long-legged blonde I encounter on the street the next day, who's carrying a perilously high stack of books, might be my cabdriver's younger sister. It is October 1999, the second day of the 21st Annual General Meeting of the Jane Austen Society of North America, and we are waiting at a glaringly sunny corner for the traffic light to change. Like the cabdriver, this woman identifies me on sight, and a glance at the top of her stack of books makes it clear that she too is here for the meeting. I don't ask, but she explains. It's her first time at a JASNA convention, she tells me: she's only just started reading Jane Austen, started after she saw Emma Thompson—no, it was *Emma,* the movie, she corrects herself. (The theme of the conference in "the city nestled at the base of Pikes Peak" is "*Emma:* Austen at Her Peak.") That's why she bought all these books, she tells me—needs to catch up with all these people who know everything about Jane. She's a lawyer, a public prosecutor—"you know, rapists and murderers," she says lightly.

(When I murmur she must need a rest from that, she just stares.) She's just gotten off the phone with her husband, is what she really wants to tell me, and he thinks she's crazy for holing up in a hotel with a bunch of women on a gorgeous weekend like this. (Her pale eyes plead with me not to take his point of view.) She'd tried to explain to him, but didn't think she'd gotten through: the real truth is, and she tells me she knows I'll understand this, that there isn't a single woman at this event with whom she can't have a conversation. That's the reason she's here, for the talk. She doesn't need to explain to me that she doesn't have in mind anything like true confessions or embarrassing confidences, just talk about people, and what they are like. Gossip, sort of, about people we all know, like Emma Woodhouse and Jane Fairfax, and yes, maybe Emma Thompson too. Why they do what they do, how they feel about one another and themselves. How we feel about them. How they do or don't give their real feelings away, in the little things they say and do. How they negotiate by presenting tactful versions of their feelings.

Jane Austen's more learned admirers tend to admire her tone of "exquisite derision," as Mrs. Oliphant called it, about Jane West (1758–1852), who is described in the *Dictionary of National Biography* as the author of "novels of good moral tone," including one shamelessly entitled *A Gossip's Story*. "I think I *can* be stout against any thing written by Mrs. West," Austen wrote to her sister (*Letters*, 277–278). But a glance at the beginning of *A Gossip's Story* (1796) suggests that she might in fact have learned from "good Mrs. West." In chapter I, "The comforts of Retirement—Rural Elegance defined by example," the narrator introduces herself as a single lady (presumably without family cares) who lives in the country along with "many single ladies, like myself," and is "a very excellent gossip." She accounts for this excellence: she has, she explains, "a retentive memory, a quick imagination, strong curiosity, and keen perception. These faculties enable me not only to retain what I hear, but to connect the day-dreams of my own mind; to draw conclusions from small premises; in short, to tell what other people think, as well as what they do." Jane Austen's narrative persona was partly derived from her rival Mrs. West's; certainly she beat the older writer at her game by transcending it, by inventing, by her choice of words, the higher gossip.

And we have flown here to Colorado Springs to play Jane Austen's game: old Mrs. West's game never quite got off the ground. We are listening to papers and pretending together to celebrate Emma Woodhouse's wedding, and as the pleasant evening mellows some of us look fondly forward sentimentally to celebrating Elinor's and Marianne's, Catherine's and Elizabeth's and Anne's, down the road, at another convention. We are not exactly family, or dear old friends. Can this heterogeneous group of professors and scholars, writers of different kinds and assorted Jane Austen groupies, in fact be described as a literary society, like the Dickens and the Trollope people? Or are we more like the dreamy five-year-old whose best girlfriends also collect all the "Disney princesses" and never tire of hearing those heroines' stories, all of which end in white weddings? For Jane Austen's friends and nieces, who listened as she reread her stories behind a closed door—she worried, or pretended to, that her friend Martha Lloyd was able to repeat one of them word for word—the fun was similar, in sharing the same imaginary world.

Private Conversation

My son tells me he laughed out loud, rereading *Pride and Prejudice*. He was especially tickled by a piece of comedy I had never noticed. When Mr. Collins finally shuts the door on their carriage, and Elizabeth finds herself alone with Charlotte Lucas's younger sister Maria, driving home, the two young women have something like a conversation.

> "Good gracious!" cried Maria, after a few minutes silence, "it seems but a day or two since we first came!—and yet how many things have happened!"
>
> "A great many indeed," said her companion with a sigh.
>
> "We have dined nine times at Rosings, besides drinking tea there twice!—How much I shall have to tell!"
>
> Elizabeth privately added, "And how much I shall have to conceal." (*PP*, 217)

What's funny, of course, is Maria's having counted her visits to the great house, every one of which she plans to describe, in her father Sir William's style, to anyone who will listen. The conversation between her and Elizabeth is a classic instance of failed communication, of two people not being, as we say now, on the same page. Elizabeth is full of all that happened on her visit, all she won't be able to tell her confidante and dearest sister, all about Darcy's proposal, and Wickham and Darcy's sister. But Maria, to whom nothing has happened, thinks she has much to tell. We begin to understand Charlotte a little better: that she (like her sister) tolerates Lady Catherine begins to explain why she married Mr. Collins. The reader takes pleasure in the satire and the contrast of characters and sensibilities, also in Elizabeth's disdaining such conversation as Maria might provide (their shared four-hour journey is "performed without much conversation"). And she takes pleasure as well, surely, in being privy to Elizabeth's private conversation with herself about conversation, in the carriage, enjoying all the ironies of its being silent and solitary, and of herself, somewhere else, still being in on it.[1]

When Trilling wrote, notoriously now, that Emma has a moral life as a man has a moral life, he argued that the virtue of self-love is the element of her character that makes it possible for her to have a moral life. Emma's moral life, which we share, reading, is the sense that her life is first of all an engagement with moral issues, therefore important: the smallest of her choices, actions, and remarks matters. The philosopher Gilbert Ryle argued that Jane Austen was indebted to the British tradition of moral philosophy. Shrewdly noticing her characteristic uses of the word "mind" (as in Elizabeth Bennet's distinctive "liveliness of mind"), he suggested that for her "mind" is a secular version of soul. The moral life as Trilling and Ryle conceive it is not precisely the intellectual life. Nor is it what is sometimes called the inner life. It is related to those, yet different and distinctive, being not so private and intrinsically social, a function of relations to other people and to language, which is the inexhaustible subject of the great novelists, and at the heart of the process of reading novels, and being engaged in other people's minds.

Fly on the Wall

I am leafing through *Emma*, ostensibly to assess a new cheap edition for use in an upcoming course, but irrepressibly, like a person taking little breaks on a business trip to a beloved city, revisiting remembered spots and recalling past pleasures there, also looking for something new. At the back of my mind, too, is the medieval practice of letting your Virgil open to the page that will prophesy your future—the *sortes Virgilianae*—one of the things my Latin teacher told me that stuck. This *Emma* is a brand new volume, and it won't fall open for my purposes: I must injure the spine a little as I force an opening, as it turns out into a conversation between Mr. Woodhouse and his daughters.

Isabella, with her husband and children, is visiting for Christmas; the two Knightley brothers are talking to one another; and Emma has been success-fully steering the conversation of her closest relatives away from the shoals of fault-finding and imaginary fault-finding that threaten the mutually solicitous. She's much sharper than her father and her sister, both of them nervous hypo-chondriacs, and she has managed them pretty well so far. But she has just been threatened herself by their competitive earnest loving concern: Isabella has insisted the "very accomplished and superior" Jane Fairfax is the right com-panion for Emma, in response to Mr. Woodhouse's having praised the new arrival, Harriet Smith. Cool Emma successfully maintains her superior, comic point of view, from which we learn that other topics "of similar moment" are discussed and dropped "with similar harmony; but the evening did not close without a little return of agitation." The event that precipitates it is the arrival of Mr. Woodhouse's and Isabella's favorite health food:

> The gruel came and supplied a great deal to be said—much praise and many comments—undoubting decision of its wholesomeness for every constitution, and pretty severe Philippics upon the many houses where it was never met with tolerable;—but, unfortunately, among the fail-ures which the daughter had to instance, the most recent, and therefore most prominent, was in her own cook at South End, a young woman hired for the time, who never had been able to understand what she meant by a basin of nice smooth gruel, thin, but not too thin. Often as she had wished for and ordered it, she had never been able to get any thing tolerable. Here was a dangerous opening.
>
> "Ah!" said Mr. Woodhouse, shaking his head and fixing his eyes on her with tender concern.—The ejaculation in Emma's ear expressed, "Ah! There is no end of the sad consequences of your going to South End. It does not bear talking of." And for a little while she hoped he would not talk of it, and that a silent rumination might suffice to restore him to relish of his own smooth gruel. (*E*, 104–105)

But of course, talk of it he must, with the same thoughtless compulsion to say whatever occurs to him that drove Isabella to mention the bad cook at South End. Predictably, father and daughter argue over whether or not South End is salubrious and whether Isabella should have gone there, and which seaside resorts their different medical advisers recommend, until

Mr. John Knightley abruptly separates them by questioning the relevance, for his family, of Mr. Woodhouse's Mr. Perry's advice.

Reading for a moment, it was my pleasure to be a fly on the wall at Hartfield at this sticky family party, partly because I could see as clearly as Emma what was coming, but mostly because it rang true. While all happy families—and, indeed, other happy groups—may not be exactly alike, the people in them and of them often behave and speak in character, giving one the sense of watching a script inexorably played out in spite of the wills of the actors. Here Emma has this sense; we recognize her discomfiture, and enjoy how beautifully the tensions in the room are rendered. We see Jane Austen in action as the Gilbert White of the drawing room. Like Gilbert White, she observed keenly, and like him discreetly refrained from flat-footed conclusions and generalizations of the kind her critics have drawn—that Mr. Woodhouse is a petty and selfish old party, that Isabella inherits her anxiety like her brains from him, that intelligent, bored Emma sees as a novelist sees, that Jane Austen condemned the bourgeois family, or wrote ironically about it in bitterness and self-defense. People and the regimens they recommend for one another's health have changed over the years, but people at their most well-intentioned continue at cross purposes in spite of themselves, and *Emma* begins to account for how if not why better than any general explanation I know.

New York City, 2009

Most of the visitors to the Morgan Library's exhibition, "A Woman's Wit: Jane Austen's Life and Legacy," are women, mostly gray-haired. Some of them may remember, as I do, the Library's bicentennial Austen exhibition in 1975. I have visited this show several times; today I notice the tall, heavy, eccentric-looking young man who looks almost like an intruder in this context. I watch as he buttonholes the lady standing next to him, which startles her. "What was that fellow's name?" he asks in a loud, uneven voice. "You know, that French guy—the one who wrote about the death of the author?" He's a little out of control. She moves away, smiling and nodding, and from the safety of the other side of the room, I smile. The sound of the constantly running video is irritating me, and I am grateful for the impious diversion; also, the young man's question does seem apropos. Why so much interest in a dead author? Or is the interest in fact not in an author but rather in Jane Austen as what Roland Barthes might have called a text, that is, the author as "written" by the ongoing anonymous cultural discourse? But aren't the people here interested in Jane Austen, personally? What drives all these people—most wearing spectacles, several with walkers or light portable chairs to rest in—to file one behind the other and stand beside cases in a museum to read? How is this solitary activity, performed in a silent group, like and unlike reading a book, or a computer screen?

The museum's publicity boasts that the exhibit "achieves tangible intimacy with the author through the presentation of her manuscripts and personal letters," including "the darkly satiric *Lady Susan*, the only surviving complete manuscript of any of Austen's novels." The Morgan's Austen collection is incomparable, and there are real treasures on display. The rich banker enjoyed the best advice and acquired the best things: Jane Austen, so acutely aware of the power of money and what it destroyed and what it could buy, would have been impressed and (I hope) amused. The line drawing in the advertisement for the exhibit, of a pretty woman bent over a desk, is a detail of an illustration, by Isabel Bishop, for *Pride and Prejudice:* as usual, we are being asked to imagine Jane as Elizabeth. But there is stronger visual stuff here, including wonderfully bumptious caricatures by Gillray and Cruikshank. Items on display also include volume V of the 1782 edition of Frances Burney's *Cecilia*, propped open to the page that reads "the whole of this unfortunate business is the result of PRIDE AND PREJUDICE," and an advertisement for that same novel that mentions the "universally acknowledged" success of Burney's *Evelina,* and Nabokov's notes and drawings for his odd, brilliant lecture on *Mansfield Park*.[2] The suggestive scraps of paper with writing in Austen's own hand allow you to marvel at her careful record of small expenditures and her parsimonious use of paper, or to count, as I do, the commas in a sentence in a letter of April 1811 to Cassandra, which skewer the man who "came back in time to shew his usual, nothing meaning, harmless, heartless civility"—still forceful, those commas, after almost two hundred years.

The manuscript of *Lady Susan* is the Morgan's special pride: the pages, under Plexiglas, are tacked up on a wall like a twenty-first-century piece of visual art. It might be the priciest thing in Morgan's collection. The survival of the complete manuscript of this uncharacteristic work (and no other) is curious—one wants to find the fact (and its permanent residence in the palatial house of Morgan) meaningfully ironic. You might be moved to read it, here and now, as not uncharacteristic after all but ocular proof of D. W. Harding's belief that "regulated hatred" of the kind of people who most admire her novels was at the root of Jane Austen's genius. As I read it today, it strikes me as a well-timed reminder that the intimacy promised in the publicity for the exhibition will be less than cozy and comfortable. The figures in the caricatures on display make a similar suggestion. And of course you can get the idea directly by reading *Mansfield Park*, the ambitious problem novel written after *Pride and Prejudice*, which turns on its head not only that "light, & bright, & sparkling" story but also the whole notion that a novel is about an innocent young lady's "entry" into "the world," and explores, instead, the pains and awkwardness, the isolation and the suffering, attendant on family life at home.

Jane Austen was about thirty years old and still unpublished when she meticulously copied out *Lady Susan* on both sides of small sheets of unlined white paper that she carefully numbered in the upper righthand corner. Possibly she had composed all or most of it ten years before. The handwriting is clear, and the regularity of the widely and evenly spaced lines of script exemplary: in several instances new letters are begun close to the bottom of the paper, an indication of assurance and steady continuity. This is a manuscript fit for a publisher. But whatever the writer's intention might have been, it was not sent out, and remained unpublished until James Edward Austen-Leigh included it as an appendix in the second edition of his *Memoir* of his aunt, inevitably—if perhaps not deliberately—inviting biographical readings.

At first glance it reads like one of those ambiguous imitations or send-ups in which the aim is to scandalize by juxtaposing traditional genteel Jane with the unpleasantness she is imagined to have avoided: see, e.g., deliberately scandalizing titles like *Jane and the Unpleasantness at Scargrave Manor,* and *Pride and Prejudice and Zombies,* or for that matter *Jane Austen and the War of Ideas.* Lady Susan is the opposite of what you'd expect an Austen heroine to be, a beautiful, glamorous, devious thirty-six-year-old widow with a title and a daughter and a knack for seducing other women's men for the fun of it. Far from living decorously at home, quiet and confined, as the others do, she rampages from country house to country house, wrecking other people's families; she has contempt for little children and what she sarcastically calls "the sacred impulse of maternal affection," and writes confidentially that her daughter is "the greatest simpleton on earth." In letter I, she invites herself to Churchill, the home of her brother-in-law Charles Vernon; in letter II, addressed to her confidante Mrs. Alicia Johnson, in London, she writes,

"Were there another place in England open to me, I would prefer it. Charles Vernon is my aversion, and I am afraid of his wife." (It turns out Lady Susan opposed her brother-in-law's marriage, and persuaded her dying husband to sell his estate to a stranger instead of to Charles.) In spite of her fear, aversion, and disdain, she is obliged to depend on the comfortable and boring Vernons: Lady Susan has annoyed her current hostess, the wonderfully named Mrs. Manwaring, who has discovered she is Mr. Manwaring's mistress, and enraged Miss Manwaring the daughter as well by flirting with Sir James Martin, the man that young lady has her eye on. Lady Susan, who recounts all this with aplomb, tells Alicia that in fact she means to get Sir James to marry her own daughter, Frederica, "who was born to be the torment of my life," her mother writes, and accordingly is "violently against the match." Letters by onlookers continue the story: Lady Susan arrives at Churchill, where a horrified Mrs. Vernon watches in dismay as her younger brother, the rich and desirable Reginald de Courcy, falls victim to her overwhelming charms. Then Frederica arrives, and Sir James; the plot thickens and threatens to boil over until the pairs get sorted out in age-appropriate couples, Susan herself marrying the "under par" rattle, Sir James.

Is it a happy ending? Was marriage to this rich fool artful Susan's goal from the start? Did she play with Manwaring and torture her own daughter to cover up her plot? The letters—there are forty-one—don't resolve these questions; the Conclusion that follows, revealing that Frederica will marry Reginald, also fails to explain. "Whether Lady Susan was, or was not happy in her second choice—I do not see how it can ever be ascertained—for who would take her assurance of it, on either side of the question? The world must judge from probability. She had nothing against her, but her husband, and her conscience." The wry concluding epigram is an amusing distraction: the point is that Lady Susan is unknowable. Like William Walter Elliot, the unfathomable villain in *Persuasion,* she cannot be known because she is not embedded in a social context, therefore is unfit for personal relationships and a Jane Austen novel about the intersections of social and psychological lives.

A short fiction in letters about a woman who is the only good letter-writer in her story and indeed the only character who has a story—the others have nothing but Susan's on their minds—*Lady Susan* on several counts falls short of being a novel. It is a jeu d'esprit, a tour de force, not really Austen's "own way" of writing novels—an anomaly in her adult oeuvre. (That it drives one to French may be symptomatic.) It is interesting for dramatizing the relation of literary form to moral content. Letters, the medium of social life as well as for messages in her time, were always interesting to Jane Austen; she wrote them with self-conscious gusto (see, e.g., to her sister, "Sir Tho: Miller is dead. I treat you with a dead Baronet in almost every Letter" [*Letters*, 320–321].) She enjoyed rereading the exhaustingly epistolary *Sir Charles Grandison*. Short novels in letters are among her earliest works, and the reading and writing of letters are important acts in the novels. The moving and brilliant ending of *Persuasion*—the revised version of an earlier ending—involves the writing, delivery, and reading of a letter. It is possible that Austen made a fair copy of *Lady Susan* because she planned to revise it into a complete novel: "The Watsons," which she also left in manuscript, suggests that her habit, in revising, was to flesh things out.[3]

While the heroine's bad behavior is unusual in Austen's novels (but not her youthful stories), her high spirits, satirical wit, and the suave assurance with which she conceals her loneliness, poverty, and need are not. Neither is her contempt for the lesser people around her: the easy violence with which she dismisses Sir James for being "contemptibly weak" recalls another poor charming widow in her mid-thirties, the mother of Elinor and Marianne Dashwood, who feels "contempt" for her daughter-in-law Fanny, indeed "earnestly despises" her. (And good Mrs. Dashwood is right about Fanny.) The negative judgments that these different women coolly and matter-of-factly hand down, and even the moral vanity of both, are similar, and make you wonder whether they were not characteristic of Jane Austen herself. Her thrilling absolute judgments of characters she disapproves of give the reader the same kind of satisfaction: some people are a pleasure to know and loathe.

While most of the latest adaptations and fan fiction have continued to suggest, sometimes by insisting too much on them, that real evils are not acknowledged in Jane Austen's decorous novels about the courtship of virtuous virgins in pleasant country villages in a safe and clean England of long ago, scholars have long explored her personal familiarity with unpleasant things, and her best readers have noticed their importance between the lines of the novels, or at their fringes. Mary Favret, for example, argues that in *Persuasion* (as in our later real lives) war infuses the everyday.[4] A letter of 31 May 1811 to Cassandra is another good illustration: Austen interrupts two pieces of the usual commentary on the neighbors with a reflection about the news of a battle in a distant war, "How horrible it is to have so many people killed!" and immediately, as abruptly, "—And what a blessing that one cares for none of them!" (*Letters*, 191). Is she moved or callous, or is she both in turn? Are we to imagine her as a modern woman interrupted by the news, or as suddenly afflicted by a sorrow and anxiety usually kept well under-ground—perhaps the memory of her own dead, like her friend and Cassan-dra's fiancé, Tom Fowle? The letters make it clear: whatever the psychological provenance of the great novels, the woman who wrote them experienced and worked at managing feelings like contempt and disdain, and depression and sadness.

Contrary to the main current of popular opinion today, Jane Austen's nov-els are not first of all and most importantly about pretty girls in long dresses waiting for love and marriage; and they are not most importantly English and Heritage, small and decorous and mannerly and pleasant. Read with any degree of attention, they do not work well as escape reading: there are too many hardheaded observations and hard, recalcitrant details in them. Only the powerful force of the courtship plot makes it at all possible to see the morose, depressed, self-involved, and boring Edward Ferrars as an acceptable husband; no more need be said about Edmund Bertram. Real evils are repre-sented in all the novels—not only the unpleasantness of boredom, homeless-ness, and the governess trade and what *Sense and Sensibility* casually calls "the strange unsuitableness which often existed between husband and wife," but also ruined lives, dangerous illnesses, urban riots, the slave trade, and foreign wars. Winston Churchill said he read *Pride and Prejudice* for respite while suffering from a fever and directing World War II, but even the "calm lives" of the characters in that brilliant comic novel are shadowed by envy, spite, foolishness, fraud, and, yes, at a distance, war.[5]

Obsessed with sentimental nostalgia and the self-congratulatory pleasures of repetition, real profits, and ideal lovers and breasts, twenty-first-century Jane-o-mania has come a long way from the novels, and for the most part has even lost them. But even in its silliness the fascination with the novelist retains I think a tiny kernel of the old Janeite knowledge that Austen-land is a place where translating human worth and human relationships into cash is criticized, and the truth gets told and trusted, and good people look for real civility and love, a rootedness, relatedness, and belonging that is more enviable than wealth and manners. Jane-o-mania, in its wrongheadedness and banality, reveals our own inadequacies: stupidity and ignorance, arrogance and greed, the qualities Jane Austen mocked. But Kipling, in his post–World War I story "The Janeites" (1924), got Jane Austen right. So did Nicolas Freeling (following him) in his "Eurocrime" novel *The Janeites* (2002), a tale about a promiscuous Jesuit oncologist who gallantly stays true to what matters in a grim world where violent crime complicates international power politics. The reader takes pleasure in belonging to the in-group of Jane Austen's admirers and intimates, that doughty, gallant band of brothers (in the later novel, one of them is a woman) who will stick to their guns (such as they are) in defiance of the dark. Her best readers have felt the message on their pulses, that engagement in her comedies of love is an invigorating alternative and corrective to everyday war, tedious illness, numbed minds, and terminally boring death.[6]

I have been arguing the obvious, if forgotten, truth that Jane Austen is a serious writer, and also—following Trilling—that the current fuss around her, the discourse, the long conversation she has provoked, is to be taken and read seriously, if to different effect than it often is. I have also argued—and there seems to me to be no contradiction—that she is a comic writer who flatters and teases the reader into active complicity with her. *Lady Susan* is at first glance an atypical work: unapologetically satirical, it does not offer the solace of a delicious world to sink into, but instead an uncomfortable, embattled world. The heroine is of higher rank than is usual of Austen heroines: she is a middle-aged mischievous scheming and plotting woman, a mother, not a daughter, and not virtuous; and the novel is epistolary. Most importantly, Susan is a writer you cannot believe. Her charm, as she boasts, is her deceitful eloquence. Eloquence and honesty are Jane Austen's themes. In the anxious mind of novel-reading Catherine Morland, broken arches get jumbled together with broken promises. The arches represent the ruins of history and gothic novels, the promises represent the social forms and verbal exchanges—most dramatically made in marriages—that link people to one another. Like all Austen's novels, *Lady Susan* is about couples on the verge of marrying; it promises a plot that can bring people to the brink of disaster, and then bring them together—or in this case, maybe not. We can't tell—we can't know—because it all comes to the dead end of a lie—which is not the same thing as a fiction.

New York City, 2010

The memorial notice on the book page of the 21 April 2010 *New York Times* was striking: a name in big bold-face type in a black-bordered rectangle of white space, the familiar final accolade that Knopf, the distinguished publisher, gives its most distinguished authors. But the name, Nina Bourne, was not a famous author's, and the photograph above the notice—an old photograph of a young woman—was unusual. Arresting and vaguely familiar, it was evocative, perhaps a still from a film of the forties or a Cindy Sherman riff on one?—a picture of a pretty, slender young woman in an old-fashioned haircut and a once-stylish dress, posing for a moment against a schematic background of tall buildings, poised to take off and make her fortune in the big city, full of confidence, competence, energy, and hope, like a heroine in an old story. This presumably was, or had been, Nina Bourne. The copy beneath the photograph gave her name and dates and a line of explanation: "She shaped how books were published for 70 years." And below, in a different familiar type face: "The benevolence of her heart, the sweetness of her temper, and the extraordinary endowments of her mind obtained the regard of all who knew her and the warmest love of her intimate connections." A secret friend of Jane Austen—or a good student—would recognize the words as the inscription on her gravestone in Winchester Cathedral in England (which as many have noticed fails to identify her as a writer or a genius); interested others could find the text in a quick search on the Internet. The copy below it read, in bold-face type: "She was our Jane Austen, our beloved friend."

It turns out that Nina Bourne was a publishing legend, beloved by the people she worked with for so many years at Knopf. She made her mark to begin with as a publicist: all the obituaries mentioned that her "punchy" copy made Joseph Heller's *Catch-22* a best-seller. By all accounts she was a sharp, witty, well-connected, successful, and graceful literary lady, devoted to her work and still at work toward the end of her long life. She was a person of taste and high standards with a gift for light verse (some of it was published in the *New Yorker*) and a special enthusiasm for the novels of Jane Austen, whose tomb at Winchester she may have admired in the course of a rather recent Austen tour. Why, at her death, did her friends memorialize her with Jane Austen's obituary inscription, rather than making up an original one for her? Is a great writer's epitaph the most suitable one for a marketer of books? And in what sense could she, a publisher not a writer, fairly be called "our Jane Austen"? What do you have to do or be to be imagined, in our culture, as someone's Jane Austen—something like her?

To ask "Why Jane Austen?" is in effect to ask a larger question, about stories and why we tell stories—including stories about stories. The nineteenth century was the great age of the novel, that is, of psychologically inflected romantic fiction about recognizable or real-seeming domestic lives, a profitable, popular form of entertainment that would spawn, in the twentieth century, further novels and stories like them in the form of narrative films—and many of those adaptations of nineteenth-century novels. Various events in the history of the novel since Jane Austen have been credited with renewing interest in this author of only six "small" novels who died in relative obscurity in 1817: the so-called silver fork novels about the upper classes of the 1830s; her nephew's *Memoir*, published in 1870, and the subsequent publication by other family members of manuscripts and letters in their possession; the eagerness of publishers to reprint her books for profit, and of writers to imitate her works, and of readers to reread them, for profit but for the luster of the association as well; the work of R. W. Chapman, the classical scholar, who produced his magisterial edition in the 1920s; and F. R. Leavis's influential allegation that Austen's novels initiated the Great Tradition in English.

But in fact it is not one or the other or even several of those things but the whole history of English since Jane Austen—of Dickens and Thackeray and Trollope and Eliot and Edith Wharton and Henry James, and of the illustrated novels by Dickens and others that were popular before Hugh Thomson illustrated Jane Austen's novels, of the Regency Romances and Austen sequels (including the "Darcies") and the Jane Austen movies—that has demanded an explanatory story, and required the idea of Jane Austen as its source and origin. The old story that—single and singular—she was the virgin mother of the novel has been thoroughly debunked, but the ghost of the spinster spinner of love stories still hovers. The critical attack on the canon in the late 1960s, and feminist and queer and postcolonial criticism, and the new media and the sense of a new millennium have paradoxically given that myth new life; the study of the history of the book and the sense that the book is history have given it more force. The feeling that the twenty-first century marks the end of the hegemony of the novel makes a history of the novel seem necessary—a story about the form that first disseminated the stories we still more-or-less credit and consider normative about sex and class and gender, men and women and marriage, families and communities and nations . . . in effect, the story of civilization.

No longer credulous—indeed cynical—about truth-telling, savvy about fiction and interpretation, many of us see civilization now as a fiction, a story threatening to come to an end. Jane Austen is the focal point of nostalgia for that old story, a name for it. The nostalgia in question is not only for Heritage England, as people have noticed, but also for a world that seemed more comprehensible and coherent, and for the novel itself in its youth and vigor, the novel endowed (as it appears in retrospect) with an integrity, innocence, health, and prosperity, a hopefulness and seriousness of purpose, that has been or is being lost. And in the face of the Kindle and the Nook, the iPad and the graphic novel, not to mention the ongoing crisis in education and the widely lamented decline of serious reading, there is some anticipatory nostalgia as well for the once-thriving, once-glamorous, once-literary book business.

Introduction

1. Virginia Woolf, *A Room of One's Own* (1929; New York, 1981), 77.

2. Katie Trumpener, "The Virago Jane Austen," in Deidre Lynch, ed., *Janeites: Austen's Disciples and Devotees* (Princeton, 2000), 147.

3. Claire Harman, *Jane's Fame: How Jane Austen Conquered the World* (New York, 2010), 126; 124.

4. Francis Warre Cornish, *Jane Austen*, English Men of Letters series (London, 1913).

5. Woolf, "Jane Austen at Sixty," review of *Jane Austen's Works* in *The Nation and The Athenaeum* XXXIV (Dec. 1923), 433–434. See Claudia L. Johnson, "Austen Cults and Cultures," in *The Cambridge Companion to Jane Austen*, ed. Edward Copeland and Juliet McMaster (Cambridge, 1997), 211–216; Claudia L. Johnson, "'A Sweet Face as White as Death': Jane Austen and the Politics of Female Sensibility," *Novel* 22 (1989): 159–174. For elaborations on the image of the aunt, see Lord David Cecil, *A Portrait of Jane Austen* (London, 1978), and Fay Weldon, *Letters to Alice on First Reading Jane Austen* (New York, 1998).

6. Carolyn G. Heilbrun, *Writing a Woman's Life* (New York, 1988).

7. See Julia Prewitt Brown, "The Feminist Depreciation of Austen: A Polemical Reading," *Novel* 23 (1990): 303–313. Deborah Kaplan places the novelist and her novels in the context of women's culture in *Jane Austen Among Women* (Baltimore, 1992).

8. Claire Harman observes that "Jane" is the only famous writer people refer to by her first name.

9. On the profit motive, the locus classicus is Henry James's comment on the "publishers, editors, illustrators, producers of the pleasant twaddle of magazines; who found their 'dear,' our dear, everybody's dear, Jane so infinitely to their material purpose" (James, "The Lesson of Balzac" [1905; reprinted in *Jane Austen: The Critical Heritage*, ed. B. H. Southam (London, 1987), II, 228]).

10. Raymond Williams, *The Country and the City* (Oxford, 1973), 108–119.

11. R. W. Chapman's appendices to the novels list their incomes alongside the characters' names, which makes some readers laugh, today: we have more trouble than our forebears did facing the mirror she holds up to continuing social practices.

12. Juliet McMaster, "Jane Austen as a Cultural Phenomenon," in her *Jane Austen the Novelist* (Basingstoke, 1996), 14.

13. This is the first sentence of the essay by Lionel Trilling, "*Emma* and the Legend of Jane Austen," introduction to the Riverside edition of *Emma* (Boston, 1957); also published in *Encounter* (June 1957), and reprinted in *Beyond Culture: Essays on Literature and Learning* (New York, 1968), 28–49.

14. Frank Kermode, "Too Good and Too Silly," *London Review of Books*, 30 April 2009; Terry Castle, "Sister-Sister," *London Review of Books*, 3 Aug. 1995.

15. See Paula Byrne, *Jane Austen and the Theatre* (New York, 2002); Penny Gay, *Jane Austen and the Theatre* (Cambridge, 2002); Nora Nachumi, *Acting Like a Lady: British Women Novelists and the Eighteenth-Century Theater* (New York, 2008).

16. Trilling, "Legend," *Beyond Culture*, 31.

17. See, e.g., Mandy Hubbard, *Prada and Prejudice* (New York, 2009); and see Harman, *Jane's Fame*, chapter 7: "Jane Austen™."

18. Clifton Fadiman, "Lionel Trilling and the Party of the Imagination," *The New Yorker*, 22 April 1950, 115–118; reprinted in *Lionel Trilling and the Critics: Opposing Selves*, ed. John Rodden (New York, 1999), 143–146.

19. Coleridge quotes his essay in *The Friend*, no. 10: "Especially in this AGE OF PERSONALITY, this age of literary and political GOSSIPING, when the meanest insects are worshipped with a sort of Egyptian superstition, if only the brainless head be atoned for by the sting of personal malignity in the tail!" (*Biographia Literaria*, ed. J. Shawcross [Oxford: 1907; 1965], II, 27–28).

1. Why We Read Jane Austen

1. On the modal, see Nina Auerbach, "Jane Austen's Dangerous Charm: Feeling as One Ought About Fanny Price," in *Jane Austen: New Perspectives* (Women and Literature 3), ed. Janet Todd (New York, 1983), 208–223, and Zelda Boyd, "Jane Austen's

'Must': The Will and the Word," *Nineteenth-Century Fiction* 30.2 (1984): 127–143; see also Zelda Boyd, "The Language of Supposing: Modal Auxiliaries in *Sense and Sensibility*," in *Jane Austen: New Perspectives*, 142–154.

2. Daniel Mendelsohn, "But Enough About Me," *The New Yorker*, 25 Jan. 2010, 68–74.

3. Katherine Mansfield, "Friends and Foes," in *Novels and Novelists*, ed. John Middleton Murry (New York, 1930), 316; the famous phrase first appeared in a review, in 1920, of M. Austen-Leigh's *Personal Aspects of Jane Austen* and is quoted in *Jane Austen: The Critical Heritage*, II: *1870–1940*, ed. B. C. Southam (New York, 1987), 126.

4. See Ian Watt, *The Rise of the Novel: Studies in Defoe, Richardson, and Fielding* (Berkeley, 1965).

5. Matthew Arnold, *The Letters of Matthew Arnold to Arthur Hugh Clough*, ed. Howard Foster Lowry (London, 1932), 132, quoted in Sandra M. Gilbert and Susan Gubar, *The Madwoman in the Attic: The Woman Writer and the Nineteenth-Century Literary Imagination* (New Haven, 1979), 337; Virginia Woolf, *A Room of One's Own* (New York, 1929), 68. See also Woolf, "'Jane Eyre' and 'Wuthering Heights'" (1916), in *The Common Reader* (London, 1925); and "Charlotte Bronte on Jane Austen: 1848, 1850," in *Jane Austen: The Critical Heritage*, I: *1811–1870*, ed. B. C. Southam (London, 1968), 126.

6. Patricia Meyer Spacks, *Gossip* (Chicago, 1985).

7. Marilyn Butler, *Jane Austen and the War of Ideas* (London, 1975; rev. ed., 1987); see also Claudia Johnson, *Jane Austen: Women, Politics, and the Novel* (Chicago, 1988).

8. Gilbert Ryle, "Jane Austen and the Moralists" (1966), in *Collected Papers*, I: *Critical Essays* (New York, 1971).

9. Anna Laetitia Barbauld, "On Novel-Writing," in *The British Novelists* (1810). See also Claudia Johnson, "Barbauld's *The British Novelists* (1810/1820)," *Novel* 34 (2001): 163–179; and William McCarthy, *Anna Laetitia Barbauld: Voice of the Enlightenment* (Baltimore, 2008), 38 n. 1.

10. Mark Twain's letter of 13 Sept. 1898, first published in his *Letters* (1917), II, 667, ed. A. B. Paine, is reprinted in *Jane Austen: The Critical Heritage*, II, 232.

11. D. W. Harding, "Regulated Hatred: An Aspect of the Work of Jane Austen," *Scrutiny* 8 (1939–1940): 346–362; reprinted in Ian Watt, *Jane Austen: A Collection of Critical Essays* (New Jersey, 1963), 166–179.

12. Lionel Trilling, "On the Teaching of Modern Literature" (1961), *Beyond Culture* (New York, 1968), 10.

13. Edward Copeland quotes Moore in his introduction to the Cambridge edition of *Sense and Sensibility* (2006), xxvii.

14. See Kathryn Sutherland, *Jane Austen's Textual Lives: From Aeschylus to Bollywood* (Oxford, 2005), chapters 4 and 5, on print and punctuation.

15. See Patricia Meyer Spacks, "Women and Boredom: The Two Emmas," *Yale Journal of Criticism* 2 (1989): 191–205.

16. See, for example, Polly Shulman's comic, romantic young adult novel about teenage love and friendship, *Enthusiasm* (2006).

17. See Nora Nachumi, "As If! Translating Austen's Ironic Narrator to Film," in *Jane Austen in Hollywood*, ed. Linda Troost and Sayre Greenfield (Lexington, 1998), 130–139.

18. Boyle's short story is reprinted in the fortieth-anniversary fiction retrospective edition of *The Georgia Review* (40.1, spring 1980).

19. *JASNA News, the Newsletter of the Jane Austen Society of North America* 14.2 (summer 1998). See also, earlier, Andrew Wright, "Jane Austen Adapted," *Nineteenth-Century Fiction* 30.3 (1975): 421–453. Gerhard Joseph, writing about *Pride and Prejudice* in *Studies in English Literature* (2000), says that there were 68 "re-versions" of the novel between 1850 and 2000.

20. See Jennifer Frey, "The Patron Saint of Chick Lit," *Washington Post*, 24 Oct. 2004. For an example of chick lit check out, for instance, Rosemarie Santini's *Sex and Sensibility: Confessions of a Jane Austen Addict* (2005). (With an eye to course adoption, the academic publisher Routledge produced an anthology of critical essays, *Chick Lit: The New Woman's Fiction*, ed. Suzanne Ferris and Mallory Young, in 2005.) For a fresh variation on Darcy as well as one of his sisters-in-law, see *The Independence of Miss Mary Bennet* (2008), by the best-selling novelist Colleen McCullough. Much less original are, e.g., *Mr. Darcy Presents His Bride; Darcy and Elizabeth; Nights and Days at Pemberley; The True Darcy Spirit; Mr. Darcy's Diary; The Second Mrs. Darcy; The Last Man in the World: A Pride and Prejudice Variation*. Elizabeth Ashton, an English woman who published six "Darcies" in the course of the young century, went on to give us *Writing Jane Austen* (2010), a novel set in the present time about an American woman who is pressured by her publishers to complete a manuscript allegedly by Jane Austen: she tries and fails; the manuscript of course is uncovered as a fraud. In the questions for discussion at the back of the book, Ashton maintains that she herself would never do such a thing.

21. The Watkins book was also published as *Jane Austen: Town and Country Style*. On style see also, later, from a very different angle, D. A. Miller's *Jane Austen; or, The Secret of Style* (Princeton, 2003). For academic essays on the movies and more, see *Jane Austen in Hollywood*, ed. Troost and Greenfield (1998); *Jane Austen and Company*, ed. Suzanne R. Pucci and James Thompson (Albany, 2000); Sue Parrill, *Jane Austen on Film and Television: A Critical Survey of the Adaptations* (North Carolina, 2002); *Jane Austen on Screen*, ed. Gina Macdonald and Andrew F. Macdonald (Cambridge, 2003). See also the important collection of essays edited by Deidre Lynch, *Janeites: Austen's Disciples and Devotees* (Princeton, 2000), and a later collection, *Re-Drawing Austen:*

Picturesque Travels in Austenland, ed. Beatrice Battaglia and Diego Saglia (Naples, 2004).

22. Annabella Milbanke is quoted in W. Austen-Leigh, R. A. Austen-Leigh, and Deirdre Le Faye, *Jane Austen: A Family Record* (London, 1989), 175.

23. Pamela Regis, *A Natural History of the Romance Novel* (Philadelphia, 2003); Johnson, *Jane Austen: Women, Politics, and the Novel*, 73. Sigmund Freud, "Family Romances," *Works*, Standard Edition, trans. James Strachey (London, 1959), 9:241. Franco Moretti, *The Way of the World: The Bildungsroman in European Culture* (London, 1987), 222ff. William Gifford is quoted in Samuel Smiles, *A Publisher and His Friends: Memoir and Correspondence of the Late John Murray* (London, 1899). Scott's unsigned review of *Emma*, in the *Quarterly Review* dated Oct. 1815 (issued March 1816), xiv, 188–201, is reprinted in *Jane Austen: The Critical Heritage*, I, ed. Southam. Richard Jenkyns, *A Fine Brush on Ivory* (New York, 2004), 41.

24. Sutherland, *Jane Austen's Textual Lives*, 9.

25. The local Jane Austen Society joined in sponsoring a dramatic reading of Milne's play—"never before seen on a New York Stage!"—by the Mint Theater Company at the Lucille Lortel Theater on Christopher Street in New York City on 16 June 2003.

26. Edward Rothstein, *New York Times*, 10 Dec. 1995.

27. Martin Amis, "Jane's World," *The New Yorker*, 8 Jan. 1996, 31–35.

28. See Kingsley Amis, *What Became of Jane Austen? And Other Questions* (London, 1971), anticipating the deadliness of dinner with the Edmund Bertrams.

29. Recall that the subtitle of Kathryn Sutherland's book, which traces the story of Jane Austen's fate from Chapman's edition to the twenty-first century, is "From Aeschylus to Bollywood."

30. Constance Pilgrim, *Dear Jane: A Biographical Study of Jane Austen* (London, 1970).

31. Phyllis Grosskurth, *Byron: The Flawed Angel* (1997); Benita Eisler, *Byron: Child of Passion, Fool of Fame* (1999); Fiona MacCarthy, *Byron: Life and Legend* (2002). And, later, Edna O'Brien, *Byron in Love: A Short Daring Life* (New York, 2009).

32. Geoffrey Nunberg has helpfully done the numbers for me, on "Jane Austen" and "Lord Byron": 1890s, 26/84; 1900s, 52/54; 1910s, 34/127; 1920s, 76/148; 1930s, 119/162; 1940s, 85/141; 1950s, 135/156; 1960s, 89/134; 1970s, 175/161; 1980s, 241/320; 1990s, 350/82; 1995–2004, 504/87.

33. Scholarly articles include William Galperin, "Byron, Austen, and the 'Revolution' of Irony," *Criticism* 32 (1990): 1–80; Doucet Devin Fisher, "Byron and Austen: Romance and Reality," *Byron Journal* 21 (1993): 71–79; Rachel M. Brownstein, "Romanticism, a Romance: Jane Austen and Lord Byron, 1813–1815," *Persuasions* 16 (1994): 175–184; and Brownstein, "Endless Imitation: Austen's and Byron's Juvenilia," in *The Child Writer from Austen to Woolf*, ed. Christine Alexander and Juliet McMaster

(Cambridge, 2005), 122–137. Auden's poem was recalled by a "recreation" of Jane Austen by an Australian writer, Mary Corringham, who writes *as* rather than *to* a dead writer in *I, Jane Austen* (1971), in the same poetic form.

34. Linda Hutcheon, *A Theory of Adaptation* (New York, 2006), 31–32.

35. Jillian Heydt-Stevenson, *Austen's Unbecoming Conjunctions: Subversive Laughter, Embodied History* (New York, 2005), 207.

36. E. M. Forster, *Aspects of the Novel* (London, 1927; repr. 1958), 10.

37. Park Honan, *Jane Austen: Her Life* (New York, 1987), 143.

38. At the "Austen and Contemporary Literature and Culture" conference, Chawton House, June 2007, Mary Ann O'Farrell wittily called this "the conjugal imperative" in Austen titles. Among the early responses to Said's essay, reprinted in his *Culture and Imperialism* (New York, 1993), 80–97, are Susan Fraiman's "Jane Austen and Edward Said" (*Critical Inquiry* 21 [1995]: 805–821) and Brian Southam's "The Silence of the Bertrams" (*TLS*, 7 Feb. 1995, 13–14).

39. For her introductory essay to *Janeites* (p. 3), Deidre Lynch chose an epigraph from Trilling.

40. "Trilling's all-embracing 'we' had the effect both of companionable intimacy and of shared authority. It also implied a kind of humanist common sense, what every honest intellect will acknowledge in contemplating the exigencies of mortal existence. 'We' carried certainty and conviction, and an openness to the serious and the tragic that Trilling in his later work would identify as sincerity and authenticity" (Cynthia Ozick, "Novel or Nothing," *New Republic*, 28 May 2008).

41. Claudia L. Johnson, "Austen Cults and Cultures," in *The Cambridge Companion to Jane Austen*, ed. Edward Copeland and Juliet McMaster (Cambridge, 1997), 211–226; see also Johnson, "'A Sweet Face as White as Death': Jane Austen and the Politics of Female Sensibility," *Novel* 22 (1989): 159–174, and "The Divine Miss Jane: Jane Austen, Janeites, and the Discipline of Novel Studies," in *Janeites*, ed. Lynch, 25–44. Wayne Booth, in *The Rhetoric of Fiction* (Chicago, 1961), writes about the hearty "little band" of Janeites.

42. To Cassandra, 29 Jan. 1813 (*Letters*, 202). Compare Scott's *Marmion* vi, 38: "I do not rhyme to that dull elf / Who cannot image to himself."

43. Trilling, "*Emma* and the Legend of Jane Austen," in *Beyond Culture*, 34.

44. Philip Roth, *The Counterlife* (New York, 1986), 270.

45. See Alan Everitt, "Social Mobility in Early Modern England," *Past and Present* 33.1 (1966): 56–73; and "Kentish Family Portrait: An Aspect of the Rise of the Pseudo-Gentry," *Rural Change and Urban Growth, 1500–1800*, ed. C. W. Chalklin and M. A. Havinden (London, 1979), 169–199.

46. On this see, inter alia, Sutherland, *Jane Austen's Textual Lives*, and, e.g., Youme Park and Rajeswari Sunder Rajan, *The Postcolonial Jane Austen* (New York, 2000).

2. Looking for Jane

1. Deidre Shauna Lynch, "Introduction," in *Janeites: Austen's Disciples and Devotees* (Princeton, 2000), 9. Sutherland (and later Claire Harman) insists on Chapman's failure to credit his wife, Katherine Metcalfe, for her important work on his Austen edition.

2. For "England's Jane" see Kipling's poem "Jane's Marriage," reprinted in *Jane Austen: The Critical Heritage*, II, ed. Southam, 103. Sutherland does not notice the importance of the late-eighteenth-century construction of the national poet, which was spearheaded by the actor David Garrick and his friend Samuel Johnson. See, e.g., Pat Rogers, *The Samuel Johnson Encyclopedia* (Westport, CT, 1996), 155–156.

3. Virginia Woolf, "Jane Austen," *The Common Reader* (1925; New York, 1953), 139.

4. *Times*, 7 Dec. 1946.

5. Alison Light, *Forever England: Femininity, Literature, and Conservatism Between the Wars* (London, 1991). See also Jane Austen's letter to Cassandra, 8 Feb. 1807, about a discussion with a gardener: "at my own particular desire he procures us some Syringas. I could not do without a Syringa, for the sake of Cowper's Line" (*Letters*, 119).

6. Another version of this anecdote, which emphasizes the dyeing of the faded lock by English conservators in 1972, made it into the Jane Austen show at the Morgan Library in New York, 2009–2010. See *TLS*, 8 Jan. 2010.

7. *Intertextual note*: The heroine of Michael Thomas Ford's novel *Jane Bites Back* (2010), who has been bitten by the vampire Lord Byron and is doomed to eternal undeath, lives and works in a bookstore in upstate New York under the name "Jane Fairfax."

8. Claire Harman points out that a cousin of Mrs. Austen's, Cassandra Cooke, was a neighbor of the d'Arblays in Great Bookham, Surrey, and that her husband, Rev. Cooke, officiated at the baptism of the novelist's only child, Alexander, in 1794 (Harman, *Jane's Fame*, 15–16). It may be worth noting as well that the surname of the first wife of "Mad Jack" Byron, the poet's father, was D'Arcy. She was the mother of Augusta Leigh.

9. Mary Russell Mitford's letter of 3 April 1815 to Sir William Elford has been widely quoted: see, e.g., *Family Record* (1989), on "the plain, dumpy Mrs. Mitford, now the mother of one short fat little girl, who saw Jane at some time between 1792–95 . . . and jealously thought her 'the prettiest, silliest, most affected, husband-hunting butterfly she ever remembered'" (p. 81). See also George Holbert Tucker, *Jane Austen the Woman* (New York, 1994), 14, and Harman, *Jane's Fame*, 49.

10. Amanda Craig, "Walking the Dog," *Sunday Express*, 20 July 2003, 61. Emily Auerbach, in *Searching for Jane Austen* (Madison, 2004), 287, names a couple of Cambridge professors whose dogs are Willoughby and Darcy; she also notes J. K. Rowling's "discovery of a mean-spirited cat named Mrs. Norris," a feline character in her Harry Potter series. John Wiltshire, in *Recreating Jane Austen* (Cambridge,

2001), 9, observes that the English novelist David Lodge's imaginary American academic, Morris Zapp, has twins named Darcy and Elizabeth. (A character in Regina Maria Roche's *The Children of the Abbey* [1796] is named Sir Charles Bingley, which possibly influenced Jane Austen's choice of name for her character.) See also sirbingley.com.

11. S. Schoenbaum, *Shakespeare's Lives* (Oxford, 1991). In his introduction (p. viii), Schoenbaum attributes this to Desmond MacCarthy.

12. Simpson's assessment is in *Jane Austen: The Critical Heritage*, I, 243.

13. Helen Ashton, *Parson Austen's Daughter* (London, 1949), 108.

14. Lore Segal, "The Uses of Story: Jane Austen on Our Unwillingness to Be Parted from Our Money," *Antioch Review* 59 (2001): 252–258.

15. Harold Nicolson, *Byron: The Last Journey, April 1823–April 1824* (London, 1924), 274. I am grateful to Mrs. Margaret Wilson of Tonbridge, Kent, for alerting me to this curious, and mysterious, connection.

16. At least one of the boys grew up to be a door-banging man: of her eldest brother, James, who was visiting, Jane Austen wrote irritably in 1807, "I am sorry & angry that his Visits should not give one more pleasure; the company of so good & so clever a Man ought to be gratifying in itself;—but his Chat seems all forced, his Opinions on many points too much copied from his Wife's, & his time here is spent I think in walking about the House & banging the doors, or ringing the Bell for a glass of Water" (*Letters*, 121).

17. "At a conservative estimate, Jane Austen probably wrote about 3,000 letters during her lifetime, of which only 160 are known and published" (Deirdre Le Faye, "Letters," in *Jane Austen in Context*, ed. Janet Todd [Cambridge, 2005], 33).

18. In his introduction to *Sense and Sensibility* (Cambridge, 2006), Edward Copeland also opts for this interpretation, arguing further that "in deleting it she also forfeited the opportunity to score a point against Lady Middleton's elegant morality." He suggests that this change in the first edition, like two others, works to soften "a force of anger and mockery unlike anything to be found in her five other novels" (p. lxii). My own sense is that anger and mockery ripple through the entire corpus, but I agree that she was working hard here to keep these feelings under control.

19. Edward Dowden, "George Eliot," *Contemporary Review* 20 (Aug. 1872): 403–422 [quote from 403–404].

20. "General Preface" (1829), reprinted in *Waverley*, ed. Claire Lamont (Oxford: 1986), 356–357. Scott's anonymous review of *Emma* in the *Quarterly Review* is reprinted in *Jane Austen: The Critical Heritage*, ed. Southam, I, 58–69.

21. D. A. Miller, *Jane Austen and the Secret of Style* (Princeton, 2005), 39.

22. Kathryn Sutherland perceptively considers the origins and the stakes of versions of this story in *Jane Austen's Textual Lives: From Aeschylus to Bollywood* (Oxford, 2005), 89–104. For a shrewd and lively discussion of how a biographer's brief—or

point of view—colors the presentation of "the facts," see Hermione Lee, "Jane Austen Faints," in her *Body Parts: Essays in Life Writing* (London, 2005), 64–85.

23. Carol Shields, *Jane Austen* (New York, 2001), 43.

24. Mary Lloyd's daughter Caroline recalled her mother's description. See *Family Record* (1989), 121.

25. William Deresiewicz, *Jane Austen and the Romantic Poets* (New York, 2004); see also William Galperin, *The Historical Austen* (Philadelphia, 2003). And do see the entirely unrelated "Mr. Big," of *Sex and the City*.

26. Quoted in *Family Record* (1989), 184.

27. David Nokes, *Jane Austen: A Life* (New York, 1997), 182.

28. David Crane, *The Kindness of Sisters: Annabella Milbanke and the Destruction of the Byrons* (New York, 2002), 199.

29. See the map by Vladimir Nabokov, "Mansfield Park," *Lectures on Literature*, ed. Fredson Bowers (New York, 1980), 62.

30. Bharat Tandon, *Jane Austen and the Morality of Conversation* (London, 2003), 56.

31. See Daniel Defoe, *A Tour Through the Whole Island of Great Britain* (first published 1724–1726), ed. Pat Rogers (Harmondsworth, 1971), 99.

32. Malcolm Andrews, *The Search for the Picturesque: Landscape, Aesthetics, and Tourism in Britain, 1760–1800* (Stanford, 1989), 35. In England, in contrast, some suspicion of the local manufacturers lingered. General Tilney tries to impress Catherine with his patriotism and his taste by praising his own breakfast set, saying that "for his part, to his uncritical palate, the tea was as well flavoured from the clay of Staffordshire, as from that of Dresden or Sêve" (*NA*, 175).

33. Esther Moir, *The Discovery of Britain: The English Tourists, 1540–1840* (London, 1964), xv.

34. Moir, *Discovery of Britain*, 58.

35. Linda Colley comments on "the belief that stately homes are part of the nation's heritage" in *Britons: Forging the Nation, 1707–1837* (New Haven, 1992), 195.

36. Mark Girouard, *Life in the English Country House* (New Haven, 1978), 242.

37. Radcliffe is quoted in Moir, *Discovery of Britain*, 54.

38. Mrs. Austen's letters are quoted in *Family Record* (1989), 139–140.

39. Edward Said's "Jane Austen and Empire" derives from this perception.

3. Neighbors

1. J. M. S. Tompkins, *The Popular Novel in England, 1770–1800* (1932; repr. Lincoln, NE, 1967), 327–328.

2. Charlotte Smith, *The Young Philosopher*, in *The Works of Charlotte Smith*, 14 vols., ed. Stuart Curran (London, 2006–2007), 1:41.

3. Smith, *The Old Manor House*, in *Works*, 2:200.

4. Gary Kelly, review of *The Works of Charlotte Smith, Part I*, *Keats–Shelley Journal* 56 (2007): 208–210.

5. In her introduction to the World's Classics edition of *Emma* (Oxford, 2003), Adela Pinch argues elegantly that *Emma* is about nothing.

6. See her comment in a letter to her niece Anna, 9 Sept. 1814 (*Letters*, 275).

7. http://www.alternet.org/story/69243 (30 Nov. 2007). This is getting harder. As of September 2010, new "Jane-Austen" titles include Beth Pattilo's *Jane Austen Ruined My Life* (2009) and *Mr. Darcy Broke My Heart* (2010), Laurie Brown's *What Would Jane Austen Do?* (2010), Cora Harrison's *I Was Jane Austen's Best Friend* (2010), Sarah Waters's *Dancing with Mr. Darcy* (2010), and Alyssa Goodnight's forthcoming *Austen in Austin*. See also more and more on the Internet. On December 16, 2010, her 235th birthday, Jane Austen was honored by a Google Doodle.

8. *New York Times Book Review*, 30 Aug. 2009, 19.

9. Visiting an installation of Jane Austen–related books and things, I overheard a woman correcting a friend who had quoted Mr. Darcy: "Every Hottentot can dance," she insisted he had said. In fact Darcy says, as the first woman accurately recalled, "Every savage can dance"; the marginally more deplorable phrase is in the script of MGM's *Pride and Prejudice* (1940).

4. Authors

1. Burney, *Evelina*, ed. Edward A. Bloom (with Lillian D. Bloom) (Oxford, 1968, 1992), 761. Bloom quotes Burney's diary, Sept. 1778, from the manuscript in the Berg Collection at the New York Public Library.

2. Ellen Moers, *Literary Women* (New York, 1976). See also Anne K. Mellor, *Mary Shelley: Her Life, Her Fiction, Her Monsters* (New York, 1988).

3. William Hazlitt, "Lord Byron," *The Spirit of the Age*, in *The Complete Works of William Hazlitt in Twenty-one Volumes*, ed. P. P. Howe (New York, 1967), 11:69–68.

4. Letter by Lady Byron quoted in, e.g., "Lord Byron Vindicated," *Fraser's Magazine for Town and Country*, vol. 80 (1869), 609; see also *Quarterly Review*, vol. 127 (1869).

5. Iris Origo, *The Last Attachment* (1949; New York, 2000), 242.

6. See, most recently, Michael Thomas Ford, *Jane Bites Back* (2010), in which Byron's vampire kiss turns Austen into a vampire. (John Polidori, Byron's physician, was the author of the horror story "The Vampyre," published in 1819 and falsely attributed to Lord Byron; also see Amanda Grange, *Mr. Darcy, Vampyre* (2009), which retains the Byronic "y.")

7. *Byron's Letters and Journals*, ed. Leslie A. Marchand (Cambridge, MA, 1974), 3:248.

8. But a catalogue indicates that *Pride and Prejudice* and *Sense and Sensibility* were in Byron's library in 1813; see *The Letters of John Murray to Lord Byron*, ed. Andrew Nicholson (Liverpool, 2007), appendix C, 512.

9. *Byron's Letters and Journals*, 3:204.

10. Ibid., 234.

11. Ibid., 199.

12. See Caroline Franklin, *Byron's Heroines* (New York, 1992).

13. See my "Endless Imitation: Austen's and Byron's Juvenilia," in *The Child Writer from Austen to Woolf*, ed. Christine Alexander and Juliet McMaster (Cambridge, 2005), 122–137.

14. In *A Revolution Almost Beyond Expression: Jane Austen's Persuasion* (Delaware, 2007), Jocelyn Harris persuasively reads the last novel Austen completed as a book about 1814, Napoleon, and history.

15. For the complete poem see Jerome McGann, ed., *Byron: The Complete Poetical Works* (Oxford, 1980–1993), 1:268.

16. In the "General Introduction" to volume 1 of *The Works of Mary Wollstonecraft*, ed. Janet Todd and Marilyn Butler (New York, 1989), Butler writes: "*Letters written in Sweden* precedes *Childe Harold* by sixteen years; the 'plot' of the introverted traveler, nursing memories of a tragic and perhaps guilty passion, wandering off into desolate, dangerous places, is Wollstonecraft's before it is Byron's" (23).

17. Mary Wollstonecraft and William Godwin, *A Short Residence in Sweden and Memoirs of the Author of "The Rights of Woman,"* ed. Richard Holmes (London, 2007). All further references are to this edition.

18. Both are quoted in Holmes, "Introduction," in *A Short Residence in Sweden and Memoirs of the Author of "The Rights of Woman,"* 17.

19. Holmes, "Introduction," 16, quotes Hazlitt's "My First Acquaintance with Poets" from *The Liberal* 3 (1823).

20. Margaret Mead quotes from Ruth Benedict's sketch of the life of Wollstonecraft (1917) in Mead, ed., *Ruth Benedict: A Humanist in Anthropology* (1974; New York, 2005), 2.

21. The very latest scandal involving Claire Clairmont, Shelley, and Byron is the subject of "Byron's Lover Takes Revenge from the Grave," an article in *The Observer*, 28 March 2010. See Daisy Hay, *Young Romantics* (New York, 2010). For further connections between life and art in and around "The Aspern Papers," see *The Notebooks of Henry James*, ed. F. O. Matthiessen and Kenneth B. Murdock (New York, 1947), 71–72, and Marion Kingston Stocking, "Miss Tina and Miss Plin: The Papers Behind 'The Aspern Papers,'" in *The Evidence of the Imagination: Studies of Interactions Between Life and Art in English Romantic Literature*, ed. Donald H. Reiman, Michael C. Jaye, and Betty T. Bennett (New York, 1978), 372–384.

22. See Eve Kosofsky Sedgwick, *Between Men: English Literature and Male Homosocial Desire* (New York, 1985).

23. Julian Barnes, *Nothing to Be Frightened Of* (New York, 2008), 33–34.

24. Margaret Doody, who examined the manuscript, notes this in her and Douglas Murray's edition of *Catharine and Other Writings* (Oxford, 1993). See Austen's fiction manuscripts online, http://www.janeausten.ac.uk/index/html.

25. April Alliston, introduction to Sophia Lee, *The Recess* (Lexington, KY, 2000), ix.

26. Forster's 1924 review containing this comment is reprinted in *Abinger Harvest* (London, 1936).

27. Mary Waldron, *Jane Austen and the Fiction of Her Time* (Cambridge, 1999), 16.

28. Bharat Tandon, *Jane Austen and the Morality of Conversation* (London, 2003), 56.

29. Claire Harman follows Claire Tomalin, in *Jane Austen: A Life* (New York, 1997), 246–247, in attributing the language to John Murray himself; see Harman, *Jane's Fame: How Jane Austen Conquered the World* (New York, 2010), 51, on Murray's finding "the correct, fulsome form of words."

30. Gifford is quoted in Samuel Smiles, *A Publisher and His Friends: Memoir and Correspondence of the Late John Murray* (London, 1891), 1:282.

5. Why We Reread Jane Austen

1. Stuart M. Tave, *Some Words of Jane Austen* (Chicago, 1973), 30.

2. "On a Book Entitled *Lolita*" (1955), reprinted in *Nabokov's Congeries*, ed. Page Stegner (New York, 1968), 235.

3. Jane Austen disparaged the expression as "thorough novel slang," but a recent writer gleefully borrows it from "an English traveler," Austen's contemporary, to describe the Palais Royale in 1803 as "a vortex of dissipation." Graham Robb, *Parisians* (New York, 2010), 22–23.

4. Most contemporary readers agree that Jane Austen must have meant the double entendre, but see John Wiltshire's Introduction to *Mansfield Park* (2005) in *The Cambridge Edition of the Works of Jane Austen*.

5. See Sutherland's chapter "Speaking Commas," in *Jane Austen's Textual Lives: From Aeschylus to Bollywood* (Oxford, 2005). Sutherland relies on a distinction made by the linguist Geoffrey Nunberg.

6. I paraphrase Virginia Woolf's well-known allegation; in *A Fine Brush on Ivory: An Appreciation of Jane Austen* (Oxford 2004; 2007), 121, Richard Jenkyns—correctly, I think—maintains that Woolf is wrong here.

7. The Compact Edition of the Oxford English Dictionary (Oxford, 1971), II, 3493, cites Robert Burton, *The Anatomy of Melancholy* (1621), I, I, ii. x, 40: "Understanding is a power of the soule, by which we perceive, know, remember, and Iudge."

8. "A Vindication of the Rights of Woman," in *Works of Mary Wollstonecraft*, ed. Janet Todd and Marilyn Butler (New York, 1989), 5:166.

9. Daniel Cottom, *The Civilized Imagination: A Study of Ann Radcliffe, Jane Austen, and Sir Walter Scott* (Cambridge, 1985), 112.

10. Barbara M. Benedict, "Sensibility by the Numbers: Austen's Work as Regency Popular Fiction," in *Janeites: Austen's Disciples and Devotees*, ed. Deidre Lynch (Princeton, 2000), 72.

11. Henry James, "English Writers: Anthony Trollope," in James, *Literary Criticism* (New York, 1984), 1339.

12. Emma Tennant, *Emma in Love* (New York, 1997), 85.

13. Angela Thirkell, *The Brandons* (London, 1939), 13.

14. Marilyn Butler, *Jane Austen and the War of Ideas* (London, 1975; rev. ed., 1987), 251.

15. Mark Schorer, "The Humiliation of Emma Woodhouse" (1959), in Ian Watt, ed., *Jane Austen: A Collection of Critical Essays* (New Jersey, 1963), 98–111.

16. A recent writer interprets in McGrath's way a letter in which Jane Austen describes an acquaintance of her brother Henry, a Comte d'Entraigues, as "a Man of great Information and Taste." Susannah Fullerton comments that "Jane Austen spoke more truly than she knew. . . . He was in fact a political intriguer and professional secret agent working, sometimes simultaneously, for the French royalists, for Russia, for Prussia and, possibly, against the English as well. He was playing a dangerous game. In July 1812, a little over a year after Jane Austen met them, the Comte and Comtesse were brutally murdered in their house at 27 The Terrace, Barnes, Surrey" (Fullerton, *Jane Austen and Crime* [Sydney, Australia, 2004], 14). In Frank Churchill, perhaps, "a man of information" was on his way to becoming a man of secret knowledge, as well.

17. Johnson, according to Boswell's *Life*, quoted by Trevor Ross, "The Emergence of 'Literature': Making and Reading the English Canon in the Eighteenth Century," *ELH* 63.2 (1996): 397–422.

18. Arthur Young, *A Tour in Ireland, with General Observations on the Present State of That Kingdom: Made in the Years 1776, 1777, and 1778*, quoted in Katie Trumpener, *Bardic Nationalism: The Romantic Novel and the British Empire* (Princeton, 1997), 38.

19. Charles Hoole, *A New Discovery of an Old Art of Teaching Schoole* (1660), quoted in D. S. Palmer, *The Rise of English Studies* (London, 1965), 10.

20. See Benedict Anderson, *Imagined Communities* (London, 1983).

21. Swift, *Gulliver's Travels*, ed. Herbert Davis (London, 1959), IV, 4, 240.

22. See the essay by Ann Bermingham, "Elegant Females and Gentleman Connoisseurs: The Commerce in Culture and Self-Image in Eighteenth-Century England," in *The Culture of Consumption (1600–1800): Image, Object, Text*, ed. Ann Bermingham and John Brewer (New York, 1995), 489–513.

23. Anne Mellor, citing Richard Altick, describes the readers and the contents of circulating libraries in *Mothers of the Nation: Women's Political Writing in England, 1780–1830* (Bloomington, 2000), 3–4; 88.

24. Walter Scott, *The Bride of Lammermoor* (1819), chapter 27; Oxford World's Classics (2009), 288.

25. But see Mary McCarthy, "The Fact in Fiction" (1960), in *On the Contrary: Articles of Belief, 1946–1961* (New York, 1966), 249–270.

26. Leah Price, *The Anthology and the Rise of the Novel* (Cambridge, 2000), 5.

Afterwords

1. In connection with the subject of conversation in and around Jane Austen, see Marylea Meyersohn, "The Duets of *Pride and Prejudice*," in *Approaches to Teaching Austen's Pride and Prejudice*, ed. Marcia McClintock Folsom (New York, 1993), 148–151. See also Sheila Kaye-Smith and G. B. Stern, *Speaking of Jane Austen* (New York, 1944) and *More About Jane Austen* (New York, 1949); Antonia S. Byatt and Ignes Sodre, *Imagining Characters: Conversations About Women Writers* (New York, 1997); and Bharat Tandon, *Jane Austen and the Morality of Conversation* (London, 2003). Jocelyn Harris is, as one of her publishers puts it, "particularly intrigued by the conversations" of Austen with other writers: see her *Jane Austen's Art of Memory* (Cambridge, 1989) and *A Revolution Almost Beyond Expression: Jane Austen's Persuasion* (Delaware, 2007).

2. See the chapter on *Mansfield Park* in his *Lectures on Literature*, ed. Fredson Bowers (New York, 1980), 8–63.

3. See the elaborate, quirky, wrongheaded but suggestive argument that Austen revised *Lady Susan* into *Mansfield Park*: Q. D. Leavis, "Jane Austen: A Critical Theory of Jane Austen's Writings," in *A Selection from Scrutiny*, ed. F. R. Leavis (Cambridge, 1968), II, 1–80.

4. Mary A. Favret, "Everyday War," *ELH* 72 (2005): 605–633.

5. See Winston Churchill, *The Second World War*, 5: *Closing the Ring* (London, 1952), 377.

6. In the first decade of the twenty-first century, as the Janeite imagination grew ever more lugubrious, envisioning close encounters with vampires, zombies, and more, seekers of eternal rest through Jane had to be discouraged—on horticultural grounds—from leaving human ashes in the garden of the Jane Austen's House Museum. See Emily Andrews, "Jane Austen Museum Forced to Ban Fans from Scattering Human Ashes in Her Garden," *Daily Mail*, November 30, 2008, http://www.dailymail.co.uk/news/article-1090696/Jane-Austen-museum-forced-ban-fans-scattering-human-ashes-garden.html#; and, for an American interpretation, "There'll Always Be an England," *The New Yorker*, January 3, 2011, 71.

Jane Austen is referred to as "JA" in this index. Page numbers in italics refer to images. Abbreviations to identify people and locations in Jane Austen's work are as follows: *Emma* (E); *Lady Susan* (LS); *Mansfield Park* (MP); *Northanger Abbey* (NA); *Persuasion* (P); *Pride and Prejudice* (PP); *Sanditon* (S); *Sense and Sensibility* (SS)